ARC
D0398912

AMERICAN RIVER COLLEGE

Beyond Widowhood

Beyond Widowhood

From Bereavement to Emergence and Hope

Robert C. DiGiulio

THE FREE PRESS
A Division of Macmillan, Inc.
NEW YORK

Collier Macmillan Publishers
LONDON

The Free Press
A Division of Macmillan, Inc.
866 Third Avenue, New York, N.Y. 10022

Collier Macmillan Canada, Inc.

Printed in the United States of America

printing number
2 3 4 5 6 7 8 9 10

Library of Congress Cataloging-in-Publication Data

DiGiulio, Robert C.
Beyond widowhood.

Bibliography: p.
Includes index.
1. Widowhood—United States—Psychological aspects.
2. Bereavement—United States—Psychological aspects.
3. Consolation. 4. Self-actualization (Psychology)
I. Title.
HQ1058.5.U5D54 1989 155.9'37 88-30985
ISBN 0-02-907882-2

The author is grateful to the following for permission to reprint:

From "At least, my dear" by Edna St. Vincent Millay. From *Collected Poems,* Harper & Row. Copyright © 1940, 1968 by Edna St. Vincent Millay and Norma Millay Ellis. Reprinted by permission.

From "The Vision of Sir Launfal," in *The Poetical Works of James Russell Lowell,* Houghton Mifflin Company, 1924.

From "Fireflies" by Rabindranath Tagore, in *A Tagore Reader* edited by A. Chakravarty. Reprinted with permission of Macmillan Publishing Company from *Fireflies* by Rabindranath Tagore. Copyright 1928 by Macmillan Publishing Company, renewed 1955 by Rathindranath Tagore. Reprinted with permission of Macmillan Accounts & Administration Ltd., Houndmills, Basingstoke, Hampshire, RG21 2XS.

From "Man and Superman" by Bernard Shaw, in *Nine Plays,* Dodd Mead, 1946. Reprinted with permission of The Society of Authors on behalf of the Bernard Shaw Estate, 84 Drayton Gardens, London SW10 9SB.

To widowed people
and to those who help them

Contents

Preface

This book had its beginning in 1979, when I wrote and submitted a manuscript for a proposed book called *When You Are a Single Parent*. Since I was thoroughly married with three children, I decided to approach the subject from the point of view of a child raised in a single parent home, having experienced the death of my father years before. The book was published in early 1980, almost simultaneously with my second book, *Effective Parenting*.

Effective Parenting came out in May; within five weeks I received a call from my publisher telling me that big promotional plans were being arranged for the book and that I would be contacted by the publicity people with an itinerary at the end of June. I asked her how the book was doing. She told me that sales were fantastic; never had a new book of theirs taken off like that; and because of the advance demand the book had gone into its second printing. After hanging up the phone, I danced around the kitchen, doing ring around the rosey with my oldest daughter, Christine. I sang "ten thousand copies!" over and over again till we stopped. Tired and sitting on the floor, she asked, "Ten thousand copies of *what,* Dad?"

That night I called bookstores at random, asking if they had "that new book *Effective Parenting.*" I called a Waldenbooks in San Francisco, another in San Antonio, and a B. Dalton's Booksellers in Boston. They all had my book. *My* book!

Less than a month after this flurry of publishing, I lost my wife, my oldest daughter, and my in-laws when their car was demolished by a speeding truck. On that same June day I received my itinerary for promoting *Effective Parenting*. The promotional tour was to start with the "secondary markets" of Hartford, Connecticut, Springfield, Massachusetts, and Albany, New York; with radio, television, and bookstore appearances. I asked my sister to call them back and ask if it could all be postponed. I was too numb to care at the time. But, before my world fell in—leaving me, ironically, an authentic single parent of my two surviving daughters, one five years and the other twenty-three months old—I had already begun a third book, having written a few rough chapters on parenting through divorce and widowhood as a sequel to my first book.

After the first months of numbness and almost obsessive anger, I drifted back to my typewriter to continue that third book, now asking questions I had never even considered before: First came, "What happened?" then, "Why me? Why them?" and finally, "What now?"

Once past the "six-month space-cadet basic training" (as one widow called the initial numbness period), I avidly sought answers to my "Why them?" and "Why me?" questions. My search began in solitude, as I read "grief books" that friends had given me.

I moved ahead, then fell backward. Since my promotional tour had been canceled (about two hours after I came back from the hospital), I had been keeping a "bereavement journal" at the suggestion of Susan Hirsch, who had been handling the marketing of my book. For a few moments each day—usually at night when my loneliness was almost tangible—I sat and wrote a summary of my day and how my daughters were faring. My journal was filled with anger and self-pity.

Almost reflexively and in desperation, I turned to other widowed men and women as an alternative to obsessing over my own loss, and as a way of getting some answers that no one had yet provided. I sought out and began attending support groups in Vermont, New Hampshire, and Connecticut as an observer, asking questions.

At least I was not alone.

Or was I? Despite the comfort I felt in hearing that other widowed men and women shared my experience of the cycle of pain interrupted by brief periods of calm, for the first time in my life I experienced depression; embedded in that depression was a thought of suicide. I scared myself into the lives of others.

A crackly-voiced woman representing a widowed persons' support group called and asked me to speak at their next meeting. They could pay me ten dollars for expenses, she said, and I could talk about whatever I wished for as long as I wanted, provided that I reserved time at the end for their questions. *Their* questions?

What about *my* questions? Like many others experiencing depression, so much still seemed so irrelevant; life seemed pointless at times. But I had to prepare for that lecture, and as I sat and reflected on what I'd say, I realized that the best way was to base my talk around my two most pressing questions.

First, what did it mean to be widowed? What was a widower or a widow? They seemed such silly, empty words—negative labels.

Second, why had this happened to me, to us? What did we all have in common? Had we perhaps stepped on a crack at precisely the same moment one day in November 1966, marking us as destined for widowhood? Or were we all uniformly being punished for the moment or moments when—while we were married—we may have wished we had never gotten married? Was it just simple bad luck, being in the wrong place at the wrong time? If only I could find every other widow, talk with every other widowed man and woman, maybe I could find out if they had stepped on that crack or said "till death do us part" just a little too loudly when they got married. There must be millions of men and women out there who were waking up thinking the same words. "Oh . . . yes," experiencing the same kind of abysmal sadness each day, and who dreamed at night that they walked together with their husbands or wives by a road, worked together in a garden, argued over money or kids, or touched eyes over a candlelit dinner. I simply had to talk to enough people, read every book about widowhood, and the one common secret I knew we all shared would become clear to me—to all of us.

The two "what" and "who" questions became crystallized, for as I spoke—and the more questions I asked myself—the more I realized that we were grappling with a question even bigger than "why us": Were we going to go on as widows and widowers for the rest of our lives, or could we somehow grow; become something not incomplete, better? Free ourselves from a past no matter how warm it was, move out of the comfort of memory to find something new about our lives; to make something new in our lives?

At the end of that first lecture, which I ended by describing a firm resolve to make my life good for my two surviving toddler daughters and myself, a tall, attractive woman came toward me, took my hand, and said, "That was *real*. Thanks." She wiped her eyes with a piece of coffee-stained napkin and looked straight at me. "Real," she repeated. And she walked away. I sat holding my hand under the table.

Her warmth and the receptiveness of other widowed men and women encouraged me to probe further into the experience of widowhood. Who was widowed? How did they react? As Rabbi Harold Kushner expressed it in the excellent book *When Bad Things Happen to Good People,* I reasoned that I—like millions of other people—had been good; we had lived honest though imperfect human lives. So why were we suffering? My questions multiplied: When does the hurt end? Does it ever get better? Why am I having headaches? Where shall I go? What do I need to do, to be? Although I knew her life was over, I needed to know why I was still so attached to my wife. That feeling was eloquently described by playwright Robert Anderson in *I Never Sang for my Father:* "Death ends a life, but it does not end a relationship, which struggles on in the survivor's mind toward some final resolution, some clear meaning, which it perhaps never finds." If I couldn't find a final resolution, at least I sought some insight into this cruel turn of fate.

Turning my energy toward finding the "one common secret" of widowhood, I enrolled at the University of Connecticut, attracted by its doctoral program in family studies (and a sister and brother-in-law nearby to help me care for my daughters) and an excellent library that would give me access to a wealth of research literature on the subject of widowhood. Beginning the Widowhood Project in 1982, I met and spoke with hundreds of widowed men and women whose thoughts and feelings became data for both my journal and that project, focused on identity and adaptation in widowhood.

Thus, the analysis in this book is grounded in three sources. For the Widowhood Project, open-ended structured interviews were conducted with a cross-sectional sample of eighty-three widowed women, whose responses were subjected to statistical analysis. Code numbers were assigned to each interviewed widow, whose only identification consisted of age. Coded data was then sorted into one of three groups: young (18 to 39 years); middle-aged (40 to 54 years); and older (55 and older). The widows ranged in age from 22 to 74, with an average age of 48 years. The average age of widows at the time of spouse's death was 44 years of age, with a range of 19 to 74 years, and the average at marriage was 23 years, with a range of 16 to 55 years. Widows had been married for periods of time ranging from less than one year up to 46 years; the average number of years married was 21. The period of widowhood also showed a wide range: At the time of interview, widows had been widowed from less than one year to 27 years; the average duration of widowhood was 5 years. Widows were mostly Caucasian, middle-class, Protestant, and most were employed outside the home.

In addition to quantitative data collected from structured interviews, qualitative data was gathered from hundreds of conversations with widowed men and women on every conceivable topic ranging from kids to cars and from death to remarriage. The third source is my personal experiences as I moved through widowhood. Most of the quotations in this book are from my informal conversations with widowed men and women.

Essentially, this book is a culmination of my search to uncover how others coped with widowhood, how they were addressing those critical questions. For there *are* answers to widowhood, and they emerge most powerfully neither from facts and figures nor from isolating ourselves in a laboratory. The answers are found in other widows—the answers *are* other widows. The answers to how we can live our individual lives with a semblance of happiness arise from a clear understanding that we men and women are parts of others. Our losses are theirs; our pain is unique yet not unknown to others. Our longings are personal, yet not so singular that others cannot understand them. There is nothing a widowed person can feel that has not been felt by another, yet those feelings are unique. When we relentlessly inquire of ourselves, the answers to our and others' widowhood become clearer. As James Baldwin emphasized in his introduction to *Nobody Knows My Name,* "The questions which one asks begin, at last, to illuminate the world, and become one's key to the experience of others."

As my interviews progressed I realized that the one common secret we widowed shared was a special kind of deep hurting that had no name. That hurt was there—nameless—no matter how wonderful, how lousy, how short or how long our marriages had been or appeared to have been. For some, the special hurting had persisted for years; for others, only weeks or days. But I also learned that there was far more to widowhood than merely one truth, for I found hundreds. But for all the truths I found, there seemed to be one essential characteristic of a successful moving beyond that deep nameless hurting that affected the widowed: The key was the realization that to resume living a full life depended solely on the decision of the widowed to do so. Whether to live a full life no matter how difficult life had been in the past, or to live a full life perhaps for the very first time, what was involved was *permission* to be happy again.

My goals are to help those who are widowed and others gain insight into both the pain and the process of survival in widowhood. Widowed people adapt to their losses and grow in many different ways and at many different rates. But the widowhood experience is not unique (although for almost a year I felt it was), since almost every adult human being who has ever loved has experienced—or will experience—the loss of a loved one.

When I first thought of writing about widowhood my perspective was that of a professional author and educator. While retaining that perspective, I write now also as a husband and a father who came back from a funeral with two girls crying for their mother, their sister, their grandparents . . . a younger one who tried to "nurse" at my chest, crying and annoyed as she sought out a breast instead of this strange bottle I prepared for her . . . and an older child who alternated between telling me that she was going to get a shovel and "dig up Mommy" and her sister Christine, who had to come back to help her finish the Play-Doh model house they were building.

As both author-educator and widowed father, my goal was to write an informative and readable book, one providing helpful perspectives on widowhood and loss and, most important, stimulating growth *beyond* widowhood instead of promoting adjustment to it. I believe that an emphasis on merely adjusting to widowhood may lead to a resignation of oneself to "fate." This type of "adjusting" can be a harmful, misleading focus, for when the time is right (determined for each of us by our own interior clocks), widowhood needs to be wrapped up and put away. No, I don't mean we need to forget our past lives or repress our present feelings, but we need to reach a point at which widowhood stops interfering with our lives *today*. Some widowed people compared the widowhood role to a pair of shoes: For a time they serve a very useful purpose, but once worn out we need to discard them. Under no circumstances should we continue to wear them (or adjust to them), nor can we leave them around to be stumbled over now and again. For the essence of the growth through widowhood is to move beyond widowhood—beyond the need to be merely an "adjusted widow."

This book is intended to educate, and to illuminate. It is not intended as a substitute for medical or psychological treatment or advice of physicians, psychologists, or other physical and mental health professionals. This book is no "song" or tribute to widowhood, but it is my clear statement that within the experience of losing one's spouse is the beginning of hope. For most widowed, it gets better. Ultimately, as I look back over the eight years following my widowhood, I realize that my life is different, yes, but it is *good*. My life is good, and I can say without a trace of guilt or discomfort that in so many ways it is better than it ever was.

If you are widowed, this book is my hand extended to you in sympathy and comfort, especially in those early days when you are positive you have been left totally alone. And while I cannot presume to know the depth of what you have lost, perhaps I can encourage you to recognize what you have *not* lost—what may be a source of comfort, even of happiness. My first such recognition came when my five-year-old Aimee told me when we got back home from the funeral: "You still got me!"

Some important people gave some helpful feedback as my doctoral research advisory committee: Gene Thomas, Abby Dreyer, Nancy Sheehan, and the late Marie F. Peters of the University of Connecticut. I was quite fortunate to have Dr. Gene Thomas as my major advisor; his perspicacity was especially instrumental in my focus on the research aspects of adult development and widowhood. My thanks also to research assistants Emily Jacobs and Peggy Toole for their tireless, painstaking, and compassionate help with the collection and coding of data. I am indebted to Gene Fucci and Don MacLeod at the Kiewit Computation Center of Dartmouth College for helping me unravel the mysteries of mainframe computing. Psychologists John Philpin and Neil Marinello generously served as judges, alternate coders of data, and scorers for part of the data analysis. Paul K. Robbins—as always—nudged me when I needed it and played Yahtzee with me when I couldn't sleep.

Personally, I wish to thank Joe Healy, former executive director of THEOS (They Help Each Other Spiritually), the most extensive network of spiritual support for the widowed in the United States. Joe's caring and warmth have touched the lives of thousands of widowed both directly and indirectly. He is a friend who touched my life directly, and I am grateful our paths have crossed. Another special person is Sister Connie Charette, past leader of the Bridgeport, Connecticut, THEOS chapter. Because of her inspirational and contagious energy and interest, the widowed members of her group attended, talked, socialized, laughed, cried, and grew stronger together.

Along the way I met leaders of dozens of support groups in the United States and Canada. While they are unnamed here, they are absolutely real to the thousands of widowed with whom they live and work. They seek no headlines or glory greater than seeing a widow move from devastation to a rebirth. I thank them for allowing me an opportunity to witness, share, and feel at home with widowed men and women they help. In the process of doing research for this book, I was fortunate to speak with Stephen Alexander, program specialist at the Widowed Persons Service, who was very helpful in providing information about the WPS, and Doris Sharkey of THEOS, who suggested additional resources.

It was a stroke of good fortune on my part to have Laura Wolff as my editor. Her suggestions were consistently right on target; her ability to guide me in visualizing my book as a whole, finished product was invaluable. Helena Z. Lopata's kind comments and constructive suggestions on my manuscript were gratefully received. I appreciate the generosity of Nancy Sharlet, J. Jeffrey Grill, Pauline Grippen, and Al Cannistraro, who took time from their busy schedules to read portions of my manuscript and offer constructive feedback. Phyllis R. Silverman has illuminated how women grow through grief, and is one of few researchers to address the differential plight of widowers. I thank her for her comments.

Perhaps most of all I am indebted to the hundreds of widowed men and women I met over eight years of professional research and personal growth through widowhood. There was simply no substitute for hearing—firsthand—each story of devastation, recovery, and growth through widowhood and beyond. Many gave of their time to freely share their stories, and while I have fully protected individual identification by scrambling all names, personal descriptions, places and situations, I remain deeply appreciative of each man and woman who helped me realize that each unique story is a part of a larger story that all widowed people share.

If you are not widowed, this book may help you support, encourage, wake up, shake up, and hold the hands of those who have lost loved ones. And I hope it can help you encourage those widowed who are suffering prolonged grief or otherwise not recovering well to get competent professional help.

I hope to give you a glimpse of the hurt, the process, and the recovery. I *can* only give you a glimpse, because a walk through widowhood—especially in the early months—is a solitary expedition. But it is an expedition that can be hopeful, inspired by the momentous challenge to move beyond widowhood toward the realization that "my life is good."

CHAPTER 1

Images and Reality of America's Widowed

It is striking that this inevitable and universal phase of life would be so patently neglected as an area of serious study.

—RICHARD WILLIAMS

Over fifty years ago, Thomas Eliot observed:

> About death, as about other life-crises, there has been a spontaneous unwillingness to face reality, and a corresponding accumulation of rituals, stereotyped attitudes and practices, euphemisms, jokes, and so on, as a buffer between the individual and stark reality . . . we do not know from actual personal evidence what practices, new or old, are comforting or under what circumstances cause conflict.[1]

This observation was echoed by others who claimed that bereavement was unexplored,[2] neglected,[3] or the subject of only intermittent inquiry[4] since the beginning of the twentieth century.

However, since Eliot's 1930 comments, two events have caused some light to be shed on the subject of bereavement. The first was World War II. Testimony of wartime atrocity and suffering was brought home by returning soldiers and other witnesses. Those who would never return also touched the lives of many who found themselves bereaved survivors. By the end of 1944, awareness of the human destruction wrought by the War—no longer confined to newspaper accounts or newsreels—was acute.

The question of national survival was all but settled; in its place was the question of individual survival.

Erich Lindemann shed light on the experience of bereavement with his landmark 1944 study of the survivors of the disastrous Cocoanut Grove fire, where almost five hundred men and women died when flames (and panic) swept through a Boston nightclub in 1942. Noting similarities between those who lost loved ones and his non-bereaved patients who suffered from ulcerative colitis, Lindemann set a foundation for subsequent study of the physical and psychological effects of human bereavement.[5]

While this work spurred attention to human survival after loss, bereavement resulting specifically from the death of a spouse still awaited illumination. Until recently, few scholars or clinicians (with the exception of gerontologists and some social workers) studied widowhood. Most of that research addressed widowhood from one of two perspectives: widowhood in the context of aging, or widowhood brought about by deaths of men in war.[6] Other kinds of widowhood, such as that experienced by widowers, young and middle-aged widows, widows as single adults, or widows who raise children, have fallen outside the scope of avid scholarly attention.

Such limited focus is particularly disturbing in view of the fact that widowhood is often considered the most stressful life event,[7] with serious health consequences[8] and the threat of death soon after one's spouse dies,[9] especially early death for widowed men.[10] Widowhood has also been associated with social isolation and loneliness,[11] economic problems,[12] and psychological difficulties including depression[13] and increased susceptibility to suicide.[14]

Despite the urgency suggested by the available literature on widowhood, the death of a spouse and widowhood have been relatively neglected because of what English anthropologist Geoffrey Gorer so aptly terms the "pornography of death"[15] that exists in our culture. The view of death as pornographic—repulsive and repellant—results from fear, which produces "a strange silence about death."[16]

Both the process of civilization and the advent of technology have covered up the bare facts of life, and have reduced our awareness of human vulnerability to illness, injury, and death.[17] Our lives are filled with many activities and objects that help us remain aloof—viewing at a safe distance the pain of others, emotionally untouched by the universal human experience of death as the end of life. Consequently, when we are forced to confront death, it is perceived as an alien, little-known, and thus fearful event. Fear generates anxiety.

In *A Streetcar Named Desire,* Tennessee Williams noted that "funerals are pretty compared to death." During and after the funeral we make believe death isn't real, never happened, or if it did, it's over and done with. The subject is brought before the public only in sensational, historical moments when a celebrity dies or through the fictitious—often caricatured—media representations of widows and widowers.

Since we fear death, we distort and caricature it, separating it from life. In his inimitable fashion, Kurt Vonnegut described an ideal solution toward resolution of all problems encountered when one's spouse dies: In *Cat's Cradle,* the fanciful world of "Bokonon" comprises members of a "duprass" (a close and highly intimate marriage), who always die within one week of each other, mostly because their identities are so closely interwoven.[18] In Vonnegut's Bokonon there is no need to pose questions of personal survival, since there are no survivors.

Of all media, television has been a most formidable offender in perpetuating stereotypes of what life is like after one's spouse dies. In fact, nothing illustrates our highly dichotomous and contradictory views of the plight of American widowed so vividly as their portrayal on television. In a content analysis and review of over one thousand television shows appearing on the four major networks (CBS, NBC, ABC, and the extinct DuMont network) in the first thirty-five years of network television, I found that of nearly two hundred shows that focused on a familial or a parent-child(ren) relationship, leading roles were held by a widowed woman in almost 20 percent of all the family network shows evaluated, despite the fact that widowed women comprise only 6 percent of the U.S. population. More surprising, of all the family network shows evaluated in that same thirty-five year period, widowed men played starring or significant roles in 27 percent of all network shows despite the fact that widowed men comprise only about 1 percent of the United States population! Widowed men held leading roles in such television blockbusters as "The Beverly Hillbillies," "The Andy Griffith Show," "Dif-f'rent Strokes," "My Three Sons," "The Real McCoys," "The Brady Bunch," and "Bonanza." (In fact, for five consecutive years—from 1962 to 1967—each number-one-rated show was one built around a widowed man!) Even "All in the Family" evolved into a widowed format in 1980 when Archie was stripped of Edith, leaving him a widower with no immediate object for his derision.

Some of the most successful network television shows from that period were precisely those featuring a widowed man or woman: possibly the most popular television show of all time, "I Love Lucy," was reborn in 1962 as "The Lucy Show," with a widowed Lucille Ball with two children. Instead of her previous pratfalls and a scowling Desi Arnaz, the plot of her latter show revolved around her attempts to snag a husband.

Ten years later, Redd Foxx portrayed Fred Sanford ("Sanford and Son") as a widower who had lost his wife Elizabeth. Sanford kept his son Lamont in line by proclaiming, "I'm coming, Elizabeth, I'm coming!" whenever Lamont threatened to leave the junk business.

Except for "The Lucy Show," network shows featuring a widowed woman have proved less popular with viewers than those highlighting a handsome, usually wealthy, widowed man. Shows featuring widowed women, such as "The Doris Day Show," "The Eve Arden Show," "Anna and the King," "Good Times," "Harper Valley P.T.A.," "Julia," and the venerable DuMont network's "The O'Neills" have hardly drawn the high ratings that "widowers" Lorne Greene, Buddy Ebsen, Andy Griffith, and Fred MacMurray attracted.

Although television has clearly not ignored the widowed, it has significantly misrepresented them. Television's widowed were depicted as overwhelmingly Anglo-Saxon and decidedly wealthy; most possessed either high-status occupations or they had *no* obvious means, need, or reason to earn a living. Their greatest need, it seemed, was a babysitter-nanny like Andy Griffith's "Aunt Bee," who kept Opie (and Andy) in line, or a housekeeper to give a "woman's touch" to Ben Cartwright's male-infested Ponderosa. Television's widowed men had no emotional needs whatsoever. When not depicting widowed men fictionally as handsome bon vivants, television gives us the other extreme of a depressing docudrama depicting the death of an elderly woman in the tenements.

There is one notable exception: actress Betty White (a widowed woman in real life), portrays widowed Rose on NBC's "The Golden Girls," one of very few network shows to portray a widowed woman with authenticity and sensitivity. One episode showed Rose setting a table for her birthday party. She set the cake and candles before her deceased husband's empty chair and spoke gently to the empty chair—a poignant and touching tableau.

Unfortunately, "The Golden Girls" may not be a harbinger of television shows accurately presenting realistic widows. In fact, television's treatment of widowhood may be worsening: The 1987–1988 television season scheduled four new comedies, all with a single male head of household. Of those four new shows, three focused on the plight of a widowed man: The best was NBC's "A Year in the Life," which presented Richard Kiley as a realistic widowed father of grown children. It was soon canceled. ABC's "Full House" was "about a widower dad trying to raise three daughters—the pestered pop enlists the aid of his brother-in-law." And in ABC's "I Married Dora," a widowed man "trying to raise a son and daughter is so desperate for help around the house that he marries his Salvadoran maid so she won't be deported."[19] (The fourth new show—although not about widowhood—was hardly more comforting to those who are uneasy about satirical disparagement of human relationships: NBC's "My Two Dads" had two men attempting to raise a daughter who is the natural child of one of the two dads, but neither is certain which one is the natural father.) Of course, widowhood and (in this case) paternity are but two victims of television trivialization; many substantive human issues suffer when television scriptwriters turn their serious or comedic attentions to "real life."

The media misrepresentation of, as well as the dearth of research on, and services for, widowed people becomes all the more striking in light of the size of America's widowed population. If widowhood were a disease, it would receive exacting, immediate, and thorough attention from epidemiologists throughout the country: Over thirteen million U.S. adults are widowed.[20] Hardly a fringe group, the number of unremarried widowed women and men equals the combined population of our three largest cities.

And although divorce has lately and barely surpassed death as the most frequent cause of marital dissolution, the total number of widowed represents an increase of almost one million widowed since 1972; in fact, the population of widowed in all age groups is growing *faster* than the total population.[21]

The discrepancy between numbers of widowed men and widowed women is large and is getting larger. Fifty years ago widowed women outnumbered widowed men by a three-to-one ratio; now that has grown to a five-to-one ratio. In 1980 there were 11,240,000 widowed women and 2,104,000 widowed men in all age groups in the United States. Unless mortality rates change drastically, the ratio will become even more disproportionate over the next twenty-five years, with widowed women outnumbering widowed men by almost ten-to-one. As contemporary men and women delay their first marriages into their late twenties and early thirties, they are effectively shortening the number of years they will spend married. While women and men are tending to live longer, women—widowed or not—are tending to live disproportionately longer. The differences in living patterns are also pronounced: Almost 60 percent of all women who live alone are widows, yet only 17 percent of men who live alone are widowers. Living alone is particularly characteristic of older persons, especially elderly women: Although 85 percent of all women have been married by age thirty, more than half of all women live alone by age sixty-five.[22]

Widowhood is not solely a gerontological phenomenon: Although elderly people comprise the greatest number of widowed, younger and middle-aged widowed—including many still involved in child rearing—represent a surprisingly substantial portion: 1,560,000 men and women fifty-four years of age or younger are widowed, and slightly over 250,000 are thirty-nine years of age or younger. Over 1,000,000 children younger than eighteen years of age are living with a widowed single parent, and nine out of ten of those children and adolescents live with a widowed mother.

Many widowed people obviously have many of the same burdens as their married peers (such as child rearing, schooling, and financial pressures), yet there are marked differences between the economic and social worlds of the married and the widowed. Widows and widowers must face not only personal grief and issues of adaptation to the death of their spouses but also the sudden devalued status of not being married. Those with children have the additional job of helping their youngsters work through the grief of losing a parent. Socially, the young widowed are at a particular disadvantage, because widowhood is an "off-time" occurrence for them, a glitch in the young adult stage of the life cycle.[23]

Financially, widowed women probably occupy the lowest rung in American society, despite a popular assumption that they enjoy the largesse of insurance policies or other generally lucrative legacies. Widowed women are more frequently left with bills than windfalls: legal fees, religious donations, funeral and burial or cremation expenses, and even florists' fees (I know of one who was billed $300. for a floral spray). And there are other bills, too. The ones that hurt in other ways, ones that stare at you by day and awaken you at night. Like that pink one from the ambulance service for its necessary-but-futile dash to the hospital "that night," or that painfully explicit itemized one from the emergency room. Offsetting these bills can be difficult: Social Security provides a $255 lump-sum death benefit at a time when simple funerals can approach or exceed $5,000.

Other financial benefits available exclusively to widowed men and women are exceedingly difficult to locate; I could find only one: Florida allows widowed women (but not widowed men) a five-hundred dollar reduction of their property taxes. Describing the financial condition of American widowed women, researchers Peterson and Briley found that "these women have the lowest income of any segment of our population, and the minority women among them have an even lower standard of living."[24] While monthly survivor's benefits are available for some of those covered under Social Security, the stereotype of "the Merry Widow" benefiting from a fat insurance policy just isn't the case for the majority of America's millions of widowed men and women.

Social Security aside, life insurance has traditionally been the recommended, and perceived-to-be-important, source of lump-sum income for the widowed. However, the facts belie the assumption that death benefits paid to survivors constitute a significant source of financial support. Death benefits—money paid to another as a result of the death of an insured person—make up a very small share of life insurance income and payments: While life insurance companies in the United States had $234 billion in income in 1985, they paid back $95.7 billion (41 percent of income) to policyholders, of which only $18.5 billion (8 percent) was in the form of death benefits paid to survivors. Canadian life insurance companies had an income of $9.4 billion in 1984, yet they paid back $6.5 billion (69 percent of income) in benefits to policyholders, of which $1.4 billion (15 percent) were death benefits paid to survivors. Taken as a percentage of income, Canadian life insurers paid surviving beneficiaries almost double the death benefits paid surviving beneficiaries in the United States.[25]

As recently as 1974, only 6 percent of all life insurance policies had a face value of more than $50,000; in 1984 the percentage of policies with a value of over $50,000 had grown to 14 percent. But even then the average life insurance policy was worth only $14,270. On all types of life insurance policies, $16.7 billion was paid to three million beneficiaries (usually surviving spouses) in 1984; this amounts to an average payment of $5,437 to each beneficiary.

Furthermore, it must be kept in mind that most middle-aged and older widowed women who were fortunate enough to have been named a beneficiary of an insurance policy were those for whom those policies were purchased years ago when the rapid inflation of the 1970s could not have been foreseen: A policy purchased in 1948 with a then-generous face value of $2,000 would have comfortably helped a widow in 1958 support herself through her first year; in 1978 that policy might only have covered the cost of a funeral; in 1988 it would have bought no more than one fancy casket. Consequently, those policies purchased many years ago (usually in the hands of older widows) have even smaller death benefits than the averages cited above. Finally—and in response to those who believe that double indemnity clauses for accidental death make widows very wealthy—it must be remembered that accidents caused only 4 percent of all deaths in 1984. Of those who died accidental deaths and had life insurance policies in effect at the time of their deaths, double indemnity on the average policy for that small number of widows would have yielded an average payoff of less than eleven thousand dollars per beneficiary in 1984.[26] Although adequate financial resources during widowhood will improve the quality of life, insurance—and financial support—meet only part of the needs of widowed people.

The United States still lacks widely available support services aimed specifically at alleviating the economic and social difficulties of widowed women and men. Social welfare and other general nonprofit volunteer services do exist, but they serve the widowed through another context such as age, poverty, or illness. Why does a widow who is not poor have to seek help at a welfare office? Why should a widow in perfect health attend a hospital support group run by medical personnel? Why should a widow who is not in good health be forced to choose between flowers for her husband's funeral and quality medical care for herself? Where do we turn to find out about available support services? Are there in fact *any* services outside of church-run support groups in or near large cities? Where, for example, can atheist widows go for support? How many mental health or social service providers have been trained in working with the bereaved?

Who is helping widowed men and women? We know that adult children are a source of support for elderly widowed parents, yet we also know that the kind and amount of support they give is variable at best. In a recent investigation, widowed people were asked to rate sources of professional support that were most helpful to them after their spouses died. Of all potential and actual forms of support available to them, whom do you think the widowed perceive as being most helpful? Physicians? Social workers? Nurses? Clergy? No. Funeral directors ranked first by a wide margin as being "a great help" to 76 percent of widowed men and widowed women![27]

Widowhood cuts through the broadest cross-section of American society. Regardless of age, race, or financial advantage, the death of a spouse is an inevitable consequence of an intact marriage. And an inescapable consequence of that death is the return to the old role of single adult and the assumption of a new role as well: that of widow. As a transitional role, widowhood serves a vital purpose. But in a society that holds marriage to be the standard it is difficult for some to move into a role that many may have worked hard to avoid—as reflected in their having chosen marriage—that of being single, of being *alone*. Nevertheless, growing through widowhood requires an eventual confrontation with the painful process of bereavement; growing beyond widowhood means leaving behind both bereavement and the role of widow. Healthy growth beyond widowhood calls for each widow to emerge, moving gradually yet inexorably toward personhood again. Or toward personhood for the very first time. Survival demands no more; living a full and happy life again demands no less.

CHAPTER
2

Experiencing Bereavement
Despair and Relief

The most I ever did for you was to outlive you. But that is much.

—EDNA ST. VINCENT MILLAY
from *At least, my dear*

Thursday, June 26

Tennis lesson in Woodstock at 9:00 A.M.; almost canceled it because of forecast 95-degree heat. At 8:30 A.M. Chrissie came downstairs; I met her on the bottom step. She encouraged me to play, telling me she'd probably take the girls swimming at Stoughton Pond.

"Do you want breakfast?" she asked.

"No thanks. I had some coffee," I replied as I stood to kiss her. She pulled away, teasing in mock shame.

"No! I have 'draa-gon mouth'!" she laughed, imitating the television mouthwash commercial.

I called "Bye everybody!" to my mother-in-law, Olga, and my daughter Christine, who were snuggled on the sofa bed in the other room; everyone else was still asleep upstairs, unwilling, I guess, to face the heat.

Chrissie smiled at me as I walked out the door; she was

on the porch as I got into my white VW Rabbit. Tennis racquet on back seat? Check. As I turned to find my racquet, Chrissie called out a time-tested phrase of couples married for many years: "What would you like for supper?" (Which meant "What should I buy so that each of us will refuse to cook supper so we have to go out to eat?")

"Someplace air-conditioned!" I answered.

She winked and smiled. Someone called "Maaaa!" from inside the house.

I started the car, I waved to her, and I never saw her again.

After tennis I went directly to the office of the superintendent of schools to find out how much money my school could spend on books. I was alone in the office when the phone rang:

"Hello, this is the Vermont State Police calling from the Bethel Barracks. I need to locate a Robert—uh—DiGiulio."

He pronounced it with a hard g.

"DiGiulio. This is he speaking."

Police? Me? I froze.

"Mister DiGiulio. . . ."

"What's wrong, officer?" I interrupted.

My voice shook. He took a deep breath and again identified himself.

Something was wrong; I interrupted him again, needing some instant reassurance.

"My wife. Is my wife okay? What happened? My baby? Tell me!"

"Mister DiGiulio, I need to talk with you in person and. . . ."

He wouldn't reassure me. Something was *very wrong. Tears came to my eyes; I wiped them off and wiped off my glasses. My chest hurt.*

"Please, officer! Please tell me: Are they all right? Did something happen to my wife? My baby?"

"Look, Mister DiGiulio. . . ."

"Please *stop calling me Mister DiGiulio, for God's sake!"*

He was even-voiced, patient and still formal.

"Mister DiGiulio, where are you now?"

"At the school superintendent's office on Route Four in Bridgewater."

I couldn't find a chair; I sat on the floor. I pulled the phone off the desk; it crashed to the floor. He told me to stay put and he'd send a cruiser to pick me up.

"Officer, please. I can't wait here . . . I can't!"

"Sir, our cruiser is on its way to you. Stay there."

I hung up and desperately tried to call two friends; I kept mixing the digits of their phone numbers. No luck. I called my home. No answer. Nothing. I was panicking; I packed my briefcase and flew toward the door. The phone rang. I flew back to it. (please God, let it be the police saying it was a mistake!)

"Good afternoon. I'd like to speak with the director of special education. This is the State Education Department. . . ."

"What—?"

"This is the State Education Department. . . ."

It made no sense. How could they? Who? I dropped the phone and ran out the door. Incredible heat crashed against me. There—my car is there. Threw briefcase through open window into back seat. Got in. Lit cigarette. Got out of the car and ran out onto U.S. Route 4. Desperate. Nothing. No police cars coming.

Ran back to my car. Two lit cigarettes in ashtray. I began to bargain with God. Pulled out onto Route 4. A car almost hit me. I drove toward Bethel, burning my eyes through the windshield for a police cruiser heading toward me.

(Hold it. It could be anything! *Chrissie isn't dead! How stupid! She's been injured and they decided not to tell her parents. After all, I'm her husband, and they always tell the husband, not the parents.)*

Cars seemed to go by me like blurs. I crushed one of the cigarettes.

(Or what really happened was that the house burned down, and they can't reach Chrissie because she's at Stoughton Pond! The telephone will sound *to a caller like it's ringing, even though it's been . . . disconnected . . . or melted . . . by the heat?)*

It's 1:15 P.M. *No police car coming. Can't think. Something's wrong.*

I knew she wasn't alive.

The police cruiser! The car was coming toward me; I flashed my lights and blew the horn, waved my arm out the window. He slowed to view this unknown maniac; I screamed my name at him. He nodded and motioned me to pull over. I drove my Rabbit onto someone's lawn, watching him desperately in my rearview mirror. Tore out of the car and dashed back across Route 4. He told me to get into his police cruiser. I got in.

"No! Please don't tell me. No! Please don't—no!"

Like a child creating noise to block out painful words, I held my hands to my ears and spewed out refusals. He began to speak, but I watched his mouth, matching the pitch of my crying to the moving of his lips. He tried to talk above my noise.

"Mister DiGiulio, it is my duty to tell you . . ."

"Nooo!" I grabbed his right arm. He resisted; I almost pulled it out of its socket. I apologized, then did it again.

"I'm sorry. Look . . . please don't say anything. Just give me a few seconds. A cigarette. Do you have any?"

He gave me neither time nor cigarettes. I looked at his eyes as he shifted his gaze from the windshield to me. He swallowed.

"Mister DiGiulio, there was an accident this morning in Weathersfield. . . ."

"No! Please don't tell me. My wife, my baby . . ."

"It is my duty *to tell you . . ."*

"Well, I don't care. I don't want to know!"

". . . and your wife . . ."

"Stop! I don't want to hear this!"

". . . and your seven-year-old daughter were killed this morning in Weathersfield."

I tried to get away, out of the cruiser. Couldn't see anything but groped for the handle. He put his arm across to restrain me. He told me he was sorry. I sat and cried.

We drove away; he said nothing more. The radio crackled. I apologized profusely for my behavior. He nodded.

"My baby. And my Aimee. Where are they?"

I was prepared to hear anything now; I hoped I had someone left to be with.

"The baby was in the car. She's in Springfield Hospital. We're going there right now."

I felt a wave of nausea.

"Is she in intensive care? What about Aimee?"

"The baby is alive. But that's all I know."

"But Aimee! *I have* three daughters! *Where's Aimee?!"*

"Mister DiGiulio . . ."

"Dammit, call me Bob," I demanded, irritated and sick.

"Bob, I don't know where she is. I'll radio ahead, but we only found two children at the accident."

My head was throbbing. Aimee had been thrown, I knew, into the woods somewhere. He spoke mumbo jumbo into his radio; a crackling woman's voice responded. I couldn't decipher a single word.

"Your daughter—the baby—is not badly injured. She's not in intensive care. We'll be there soon."

Our police cruiser was met by another. They led me by hand from one police car to another. Like a trained bear, I followed. I asked the new officer about Aimee as we drove away.

"She's fine," he answered. I searched his face for signs of lying.

"She's at a neighbor's house," he continued, "and she wasn't in your wife's car. She was with a neighbor."

I nodded dumbly. I recognized the neighbor's name he recited.

I saw barricades ahead. The highway was closed. He turned left to detour. Before I could get the words out, he nodded yes, that's where it happened.

Past the barricades I could see nothing but more road.

I ran out of cigarettes; he gave me a pack of Kents from his sun visor. He said his name was Bill. I asked about his family and where he came from. How hard it must be to be a state police trooper.

I remembered my in-laws.

"Bill, my mother-in-law and father-in-law are up to see us from New York City . . ."

I put my head in my hands.

". . . and I don't know how to tell them. My wife—their daughter—and Christine is . . ."

He looked stricken. He placed his hand on my left kneecap.

"Bob," he spoke in a kind but uncertain voice, "your in-laws were in the car."

And it became a crummy movie. This can't be real. I stared out the window. I knew the answer before I asked the question.

"Are they alive?"

He looked at me quickly, then straight ahead. He shook his head, slowly.

"No, they didn't make it. Sorry."

The hospital. Bill brought me in. I'm desperate to see my daughters. Katie. Aimee. People in white give me water and pills. I sit down; I stand up. There's my friend. Was it a big truck that hit them? Are these people all lying to me? They take me upstairs. In a room. Katie. Katie! She is in a clear plastic crib; part of her head is shaved. A spot of blood.

I pick her up. I will never let her out of my arms again! *Someone keeps telling me that Aimee is alive, too and will soon be here. I ask when. Right away, a few more minutes. I can't stand up when I try. Katie's face is pressed against my neck. She looks at me and softly says "Dada." She has purple welts. They make a V from shoulder to abdomen to shoulder. Her cheek is bandaged, as is her right arm. She is alive. All right. I won't let go of her; I sit on a cot with her against my chest. It's my fault because I let go of them. I won't let go again. I swear that they will have to kill me too to make me let go again.*

The door opens and Aimee walks in. I am relieved again. Anne and Neil brought her to me.

"Hi, Dad! What are we doing here?"

She is puzzled as she walks around the cot and kisses me. Her eyes grow large as she sees Katie in my arms.

"What happened to Katie?"

I can hardly speak—I whisper, "She's okay."

"Where's everybody? Where's Mommy? Where's Christine?"

All I can do is swallow. I lay Katie down on the cot and have Aimee put her head against my shoulder.

"Aimee, Mommy and Christine . . ."

I can't continue. She tilts her head, puzzled.

"Mommy and Christine . . . they died. They—"

She sat up and stared at me.

"For real, Daddy? Please don't joke."

"For real. Oh, I wish *it was a joke."*

She cried—a strange, long, loud wail.

"No, Daddy, don't joke! *Mommy said she wasn't going to die for a long, long time!"*

She put her thumb in her mouth and lay back on the cot. She sat up suddenly.

"When are we going home? I hate this place! Will Grandma be my new mother now?"

On the back of the hospital room door is a poster of a warm rural scene and poetry—poetry I remember from Catholic school many years ago. Part of an excerpt I had to memorize, by our fourth-grade "grade poet," James Russell Lowell:

> *And what is so rare as a day in June?*
> *Then, if ever, come perfect days;*
> *Then Heaven tries earth if it be in tune,*
> *And over it softly her warm ear lays. . . .*

While the particular circumstances of my initial confrontation with the death of loved ones were not typical, I was soon to find—as they recalled and shared their experiences facing a spouse's death—that many of my feelings and reactions had also been experienced by other men and women.

In retrospect, what was most powerful about my immediate experience was an overwhelming amount of fear. There was a fear that if this wrenching pain were to continue my life itself would be threatened. There was actual physical pain: I vividly remember a constant and pulverizing headache, throbbing pain that did not respond to medication. Accompanying the physical discomfort—and almost in spite of the actual pain—was a lingering question as to the reality of the intense grief I was experiencing: Did this really happen? It was either totally make-believe—a fantasy—or it would culminate with my understanding that it was real. If it was make-believe, fine; I could get through it. The fantasy that a spouse's death is unreal does carry many men and women through the earliest moments and hours of pain. But if it *wasn't* make-believe, what would happen? How could I get through tomorrow, and the next day, and the day after that? How could I live? What would I do?

The "answers" to these questions soon evolved out of the necessity of daily living. To go on with life, there were things I simply *had* to do. Despite the clear feeling that I wanted to do absolutely nothing, even the barest living of life—basic survival—compels us to act: Eating means one must lift a fork; one's hand must grasp food. Sleeping demands basic warmth: A blanket must be gotten, a shirt unbuttoned, shoes removed. After my wife's death I quit my job, for I simply could not carry out what the job required, even upon appeals from my supervisor who was willing to modify my duties. Because after my wife's death I became aware that what was required for the job was not important because it was not needed for *my* survival. After three months, however, I went back to working solely because I needed money to buy food for myself and my children. But during the first three months of my grief I did not work because I simply did not want to—it was totally irrelevant to me.

Along with fear I felt intense anger. I sought revenge; I asked about the truck that hit my wife's car. Perhaps what restrained me from acting out violent thoughts was the balancing thought that this wasn't really happening to me, thus there was a good chance I'd be retaliating with no justification. I was intensely angry at my wife as well, and the anger was couched in many disguises, some of them irrational: I asked why she drove carefully, calculating how—had she been going only about five miles per hour faster—the truck would have missed her car as it swerved out of control. Or why when she stopped at the store for sodas she was not quicker (or slower) in reaching the checkout line, because a few seconds either way would have put her car safely out of the path of the truck.

In my distress I questioned why she had chosen that day to go swimming with her parents and our children, and why her parents had not come a week earlier as had been planned initially. Some of my anger was more rational: I was furious that she often declined to wear her seat belt—especially frustrating because I installed extra and strong seat belts in her car. Seat belts that often remained in the crease of the front seat. (Later I learned that the impact was so severe and direct that in this case seat belts were ineffectual, with one exception: our tethered infant seat clearly saved baby Katie's life.)

But the main reason for my anger was personal: *She left me.* My first conscious thoughts—as I sat at my kitchen table—were of anger and deep resentment at being deserted. As a priest held my hand and prayed, I thought what monumental nerve she had deserting me, leaving after promising to be with me always.

Having lost other loved ones in addition to a wife made being left alone especially devastating: My daughter's death was impossible to comprehend and more difficult to sort out, for I had no one to cry with over her. No one I knew had lost a child; worse, no one else had lost *this* little child. A friend suggested I contact Compassionate Friends, a support group for those whose children have died. But the thought of going to a support group by myself—amid couples—was not something I could bring myself to do, nor did I wish to talk to anyone about her. I suppressed thoughts of her for months. Looking at her picture and remembering how little time we had together are still—years later—poignant. But it is a feeling that is now soft-edged, because the memory of her spirit and energy eventually warms me from my sadness.

One of the first widowed men I met after becoming widowed myself was Andy, a forty-three-year-old bakery deliveryman. Widowed eleven months earlier, Andy was a reluctant attendee at a church-sponsored support group in New York City. Andy and I shared a brief discussion at the end of the meeting, and he invited me to his home for an interview. Andy's pain was prototypical of the often-unexpressed suffering of many widowed men.

A can of Spaghetti-Os sat atop a kitchen counter piled with dishes, and two cats ate out of crusty plates on the floor. Clothes were heaped atop one chair; a television sat on the other. Andy turned off the Mets game as he talked.

"I can't get her out of my mind. I get these headaches now," he said pointing to his temple as if in an aspirin commercial, "and they're constant." I asked if he'd seen a doctor recently. "Yeah, I'm going Monday after work. My blood pressure's up, and they're going to put me on pills. DeeDee—that's what I call my wife—was always bugging me to lose weight and see a doctor. I'm going to do it for her.

"What's today—the third? It was eleven months ago to the day that she passed away. She was a good-looking woman." He pulled out his wallet and showed me a wedding snapshot.

"Eleven months ago. They called me at work and told me she'd . . ." Andy fought back tears, took a breath, and continued. ". . . she'd been hit by a drunken asshole. He stopped, and I got us each a glass of water. When he continued he told me she'd been Christmas shopping downtown and her car was hit head-on as she crossed an intersection.

Since the funeral he had come directly home from work, had dropped out of his bowling league, and had spent almost all his free time with his brother and sister-in-law.

"All I can think of is when I can see DeeDee again. I still can't believe she's gone. It's like she's going to walk in"—he gestured toward the front door—"with her arms filled with packages, like she always did. Jesus, she loved to shop! I used to tell her how she spent more money than the both of us made! But I was good to her. I never held back on my paycheck or anything all the years we were married. I made sure there was money for Donny [their son] to go to private school; they never wanted for anything.

"Every night I dream . . . each night it's a little different. Last night I dreamed she was in the hospital—alive—but her room was this tiny room far away. It had this tiny white door at the end of this long, long hospital hallway, and the doctors kept telling me I couldn't see her right now. I kept trying to go there but at the nurse's desk they all kept pulling me back, telling me I could go in later, but not now. Ever see these soap operas on TV? DeeDee got me hooked on them. The funny thing is that these soap operas have somebody die, and then they bring them back a few shows later. Maybe that's what I'm hoping for with DeeDee. That she really isn't gone and she's gonna come back." He smiled and shook his head: "Am I gonna give that woman hell for leaving me!

"Or some other nights I dream that she's left me for another guy, which is ridiculous because she never even looked at another guy. I talk to her and say 'Why'd you do it?' In my dream she's cold and very hard, which is *nothing* like DeeDee. I keep asking her, 'Why'd you do it? Why'd you leave me?' " He laughed and asked if I'd join him for a couple of beers. He opened a refrigerator well stocked with beer.

I asked him who he had to help him. "I don't need any help, I need my wife. But thank God I got Donny. He's an honors student at NYU, and I also got my brother and his wife. Sometimes when I get sick of this place I go over there."

His heavy face was tearstained. "You know how bad I wish I could have her back?" he asked, holding out his arm. "I'd cut this right off if I could see DeeDee again. Even for one hour!"

Like a number of men I would soon meet, Andy was still completely focused on his wife and fundamentally lost without her. His dreams that she was still alive were examples of denial; the doctors (whom he perhaps felt failed him by not performing a miracle) were keeping his wife away. Socially, Andy was isolated except for his son and his brother's family, and psychologically he was still incapable of moving ahead.

And as happened during so many of my meetings with widowed men and women, Andy cried during our meeting. Crying is the most characteristic observable behavior of widowed men and women in early bereavement. In fact, it is a universal reaction, having been identified in seventy-three out of seventy-four societies studied outside of Western civilization.[1] While men and women cry equally in almost half of sixty societies for which crying frequency was rated, in all the other societies where frequency was unequal, adult women cried more than men.

Accompanying crying in almost all societies is a strong sense of fear among newly bereaved men and women. In addition to fear of loss of self or of the unknown life without the spouse, we may be experiencing a fundamental human awareness, encoded in our unconscious minds early in the history of our species, that the death of any member of one's social group heightens the probability of impending death for each other member.

Similar to 80 percent of the widowed women I interviewed who reported sometimes experiencing overpowering feelings of fear, Andy's strong reaction to the loss of his wife was reflective of his fear. I remember him shrugging his shoulders, repeating, "I don't know. I just don't know." He was concerned about his health, and he was afraid to confront the truth that his wife would in fact never come back to life. Andy's inability to accept his wife's death at this early point in bereavement highlighted his attachment to and dependence on her. His attachment is easily understood ("I love her"), but his dependence is not. First, it was a clear threat to his illusion of strength and autonomy: He had been raised to perceive dependence as acceptable for the infirm, the elderly, children, and perhaps women, but not for men. Second, while he had words to describe his connection to his wife ("love," "devotion"), Andy had no words to describe his feelings of need, of dependence. His wife's death revealed a personal emptiness for which he literally had no words.

By contrast, Erin, a thirty-nine-year-old business executive who was widowed one year before our meeting, already appeared further on her way to being able to separate from her former marriage. A tall, intense, and attractive woman, Erin invited me to sit at her dining room table—a table strewn with papers, ledgers, and pencils. She cleared a space for me amid her "homework," as she called it. Her home reflected the financial success typical of upper-middle-class Nassau County. Erin explained that although she missed Thomas, her family and friends had "filled in nicely." "I'm lucky," she claimed, "having my father nearby. He did all the 'husband-things' for me—mowing the grass, fixing the car. I didn't want to do a thing for months after Thomas died, but Dad took over the business and saved it from going under." Her forty-year-old husband had died suddenly of a not-totally-unexpected heart attack due in part to a congenital heart condition. Erin felt this made Thomas's death "more bearable, I guess, than being hit totally out of the blue like some women I know." Although she never expected Thomas to die so early in his life, the doctors had told both of them that another heart attack was possible with no warning.

Erin pointed to the papers on the table. "I'm still a little disorganized," she said with a smile. "But it's amazing how distracting this can be. I mean in a good way. You never know when something like this will happen. We—I mean, I knew Tom wasn't in perfect shape, but you still don't think that at age forty he'd just go like that." Erin snapped her fingers: "Bingo. He was gone. Thank God he didn't suffer. I don't think he did—the doctor said he died peacefully. I still don't know if he [the doctor] was just trying to make me feel better, though."

I asked Erin what she thought it meant to be a widow. She reacted with distaste: "Widow? I'm too young to be a widow; you know what I mean? I wish I had the luxury to sit back and cry all day! But that won't pay the bills, and it won't bring Tom back." She shook her head. "No it won't." When asked if she would consider remarriage, Erin gave an answer that was a common reply of a number of widowed: "If the right man came along. But I definitely won't get married just for the sake of being married. I'm not desperate, and I have plenty to keep me busy." She looked at me and then away as she added, "But if I ever do it *won't* be to a man with a heart condition!"

Though statistically speaking Andy is far more likely to remarry than Erin, he is not prepared even to consider it as a possibility, while she is already open to it. Andy and Erin are only two people in the universe of widowed people, but in some important ways they are illustrative of the differences between men's and women's typical reactions to the death of their spouses. While one cannot predict the course of an individual's recovery based solely on gender, there are clear indications that as a group men do not weather widowhood in as healthy or successful a manner as women.

Widowhood—more than any other life event including personal illness, imprisonment, or divorce—requires the greatest life readjustment,[2] irrespective of gender or specific circumstances of loss. Only recently, however, have the symptoms of psychological and physiological trauma of surviving the death of a spouse been connected to those of other highly stressful life events like war, rape, serious accidents, and personal illness. Although stress disorders among returning soldiers have been recognized for centuries (called shell shock in the 1900s, "nostalgia" during the 1800s), it was in 1980 that the term *posttraumatic stress disorder* (or PTSD) was identified and recognized by the American Psychiatric Association. Applied typically to characterize the psychological problems that affect combat veterans, PTSD includes numerous symptoms that also affect widowed men and women, especially within the first year of widowhood: a reexperiencing of the traumatic event through flashbacks, dreams, or sudden feelings; a feeling of numbness toward persons and events; and other disturbances including loss of sleep, loss of appetite, difficulty concentrating, sadness or numbness, and a loss of interest in formerly engrossing pursuits. A recent conference on the subject of PTSD noted similarities among the effects of war, sexual abuse, rape, the witnessing of a violent crime, and personal accidents or illnesses. Conference organizer Dr. Matthew J. Friedman, chief of psychiatry at the Veterans Administration Hospital in Vermont, claimed that "different kinds of trauma had much more in common" than had previously been supposed.[3] As such, PTSD has become one important model in the understanding and treatment of victims of different sources of trauma.

Medical researcher and cardiologist Michael Brodsky stated that "an emotional broken heart can really kill you," as he discussed how stress can cause palpitations, rapid heartbeat, and even heart failure. His study (reported in the *Journal of the American Medical Association*) was based on subjects who suffered from irregular heartbeats and fainting yet had no evidence of heart disease or defect. But they did have one major condition in common: They had all experienced recent severe emotional trauma.[4]

The body's immune response appears to become disrupted following the loss of a spouse,[5] and researchers have found a measurable effect of bereavement on human endocrine function.[6] When experimenters artificially induce sadness in subjects they also find physiological changes.[7] Bereavement—especially when it occurs as a result of a significant loss—places the bereaved at a very high risk due to constant and more intensified stress.

In a study undertaken at the Mount Sinai School of Medicine's Department of Psychiatry, a team of researchers examined men whose wives were in advanced stages of breast cancer. Measuring the men's lymphocyte stimulation responses (reflective of their immune system functioning) before and after the deaths of their wives, the researchers found a highly significant suppression of mens' immune systems as early as one month after the wives' deaths.[8] They also found an intermediate level of suppression between four and fourteen months after the death of the spouse. While short-term suppression of lymphocyte activity is normally noted after periods of short-term stress such as that incurred by sleep deprivation or space flight, the effects on lymphocyte stimulation of surviving the death of the spouse persisted at least two months following the death. While firm conclusions are not yet warranted, this is perhaps the clearest evidence to date connecting the effects of surviving the death of a spouse with direct physiological debilitation.

Men seem particularly susceptible to the stressful effects of grief accompanying the loss of a wife. In 1858, researcher William Farr was the first European to point out the connections between men, marriage, and mortality, when he noted that "marriage is a healthy estate. The single individual is more likely to be wrecked on his voyage than the lives joined together in matrimony." Farr then analyzed national data on French mortality rates, which had become available for the first time, concluding that:

> Young widowers under the age of 30, and even under the age of 40, experience a very heavy rate of mortality; and after 60, the widowers die more rapidly, not only than husbands, but more rapidly than older bachelors.[9]

Indeed, one hundred years after Farr's observations, the facts on men and widowhood remain ominous, and more recent information only verifies Farr's findings. Only over the past twenty years have medical and social researchers begun to look at the condition of American widowed men, and some initial reports of what they've seen are rather startling: A Johns Hopkins University study of more than four thousand widowed persons revealed that widowed men have a death rate 26 percent higher than their married peers and a 61 percent higher rate was noted for widowed men in the older (fifty-five to sixty-four years) age group.[10] Widowed men die ten times as often from strokes and six times as often from heart disease. (The implications for younger minority-group widowed men are even more foreboding: The death rate for nonwhite widowed men between the ages of twenty-five and thirty-four is almost two and one-half times that for nonwhite widowed women in the same age group.) Within the first six months following the death of a wife, the death rate for men increases by about 40 percent. Suicide is four times more common among widowed men than widowed women, and white widowed men have the highest suicide rate of all groups. Numerous studies have agreed on the disproportionately higher suicide rate among widowed men—in some cases a suicide rate three or four times higher than that of married men.[11]

A recent twelve-year survey of widowed men and women revealed that men are much more likely to die (not solely from suicide) within several years after their spouses die than married men the same age. According to Moyses Szklo, a researcher at the Johns Hopkins School of Hygiene and Public Health and one of the survey's leaders: "Missing a spouse affects a man's quality of life in so many, many ways . . . even if he joins a club or some other social activity, something is always going to be missing—someone to pay attention to him, to go out with him."[12]

Although the incidence of mental illness is higher for the widowed as a group than among their married counterparts,[13] and although in Western culture women have higher rates of depression and mental illness than men, among widowed women and men that ratio is reversed: Widowed men exhibit higher rates of mental illness and depression than do widowed women.[14]

Certainly loneliness and depression in the early months of bereavement are common to both widowed men and widowed women, and a widowed person can experience extremes of either or both conditions. But they may be more intensely experienced by men because of the withdrawal of highly focused emotional support men receive from their wives.

This dependence, which serves men "well" in marriage but poorly in widowhood, is well addressed by Jean Baker Miller, who suggested that men have become overly dependent on wives to provide the affiliation (or "connection") they require as human beings.[15]

I learned that although both women and men relied on their partners for emotional support, for women that reliance had not been as exclusively limited to their partners as it was for men. Women's support networks prior to and immediately following the death of their spouses proved to be richer: Women seemed to be able to derive emotional support from friends and family as well as from spouse before becoming widowed, and that emotional support system was still present during and after the spouses' death. Men's networks of friendship were not as extensive or as continuous as women's, and they were different, focused on "doing the same thing" (drinking, gaming, competing) instead of engaging in a shared experience. *What* the men were doing was more important than the fact that they were doing it together; in many cases the "what" was more important than whom they were with. When I met bereaved men, they were likely to discuss sports or politics with me (as they would with almost any other man) instead of discussing women, other men, widowhood, friends, relatives, life, death, or their wives. (More men asked me my opinion, for example, of how I thought the New York

Yankees would do than of how well I was doing, and more men told me how they thought the Yankees were doing than told me how well they were.)

Both men and women gain highly focused attention and emotional support from close relationships like marriage, which has implications for how long grief will last and how intensely it will be experienced. Recognizing the importance of the lost relationship in recovery from bereavement, University of Texas professor Larry A. Bugen identified two dimensions that are "prime predictors of the intensity and duration of bereavement": closeness of relationship and the mourner's perception of the preventability of the death.[16] Bugen stated that the closer the relationship (a "central" relationship), the more intense the grief reaction. Conversely, if the relationship is "peripheral," or less close, the grief will be relatively mild. For example, the death of a husband is more central than the death of a coworker, and the grief process is far more intense when one's spouse dies than when a casual acquaintance such as a neighbor passes away.

In my investigation, those widowed who had had close marital relationships ("We did everything together"; "We couldn't have been closer!") described clearly intense grief reactions. Regardless of cause of death, close marriages produce intense grief when death occurs. Some were very aware of the connection between the closeness of their relationships and the amount of pain they felt when they ended: One widow—who happened to be the oldest woman I interviewed—said, "I wish I had despised my husband just a little—that would have made things easier after he died. I would've done it all over again," she added, because "knowing such a wonderful man was worth it." When the widowed men or women viewed the marriage relationship as not especially close ("We hardly saw each other"; "We had our own lives"), they did not manifest as intense grief.

In addition to the intensity of grief, the survivor's perceptions of the preventability or unpreventability of the death affected how long the grief process lasted. If the death was seen by the survivor as having been preventable, the grief would persist for a longer period of time than if it was seen to have been unpreventable. Testing Bugen's hypotheses in my investigation, I found that widowed women whose husbands died suddenly (usually through accidents) adapted better than did widows whose spouses died in more "preventable" ways (like suicide or alcohol-related deaths). Those whose husbands died of an illness described a more lingering and recurring grief. In addition, while accidental deaths tended to produce initially stronger grief reactions than did anticipated deaths, on a long-term basis those whose spouses died in unpreventable, "act of God" ways showed higher levels of adaptation and well-being. Ultimately, the important factor is how the survivor interprets or perceives the death and not merely the objective circumstances of the loss. For example, some widows whose husbands died in auto accidents regarded their spouses' deaths as having been preventable ("If only he had fixed the brakes. . . . If only I had driven him to work that morning!"), which promoted a lingering of grief. Other widows whose spouses died under similar accidental circumstances believed those circumstances to have been unpreventable, attributing them to fate or simple bad luck.

Widows became aware of the existence of stronger feelings of grief at certain times during their first year of bereavement, and toward the anniversary of the death of the spouse. Numerous widowed women admitted feeling a certain apprehension as the anniversary date approached, typically making sure they were going to spend that day fully occupied. These days of heightened grief occur within the first year (and past the first year) as well: Eighty percent of the widows I interviewed reported such heightened episodes of grief consisting of rather intense feelings of sadness and loneliness. Of those who reported heightened grief, 83 percent experienced feelings of mild-to-severe sadness, while 12 percent had "positive" reactions on those days. ("Positive" reactions were largely warm memories and happy reflections instead of feelings of sadness.)

When did these episodes occur? By a wide margin, Christmas was the most frequently mentioned time of intense grief. Even after the first year of bereavement, more than half the widowed women I interviewed still experienced heightened grief at or around Christmas. The distribution was relatively equal with respect to young, middle-aged, and older widowed women, although older (fifty-five years and higher) women cited Christmas more frequently than did their younger counterparts.

Other days, such as annual times of celebration, were difficult as well: approximately 28 percent cited the anniversary of their wedding, and 22 percent mentioned their late husband's birthday as difficult days. The "one-year marker point"—the first anniversary of the death of the spouse—was stressful to more young and middle-aged widows than to older widows. Surprisingly to me, only 20 percent cited that particular day as especially difficult. Finally, Sunday was named as a difficult day more frequently than were other days of the week (my sample was largely Christian), but it was not named nearly as frequently as was Christmas, the wedding anniversary, or the deceased husband's birthday.

How women dealt with—or reacted to—those days and times of heightened grief was critical to how well they coped with or adapted to widowhood. While women as a group coped well (compared to men), there were marked variations in their styles of coping. Those women who coped well (those who scored relatively high on adaptation and well-being indices) tended to be occupied with other matters, such as regimented housework (if they were home), or similar "mindless busywork" done to get one's mind "off things." On the other hand, the activities of widows who were not coping well were generally centered around their loss; they tended to engage in prolonged crying, purposeful seclusion, visits to the cemetery, and religious activities.

There was a third group of widowed women who coped well by purposefully seeking out constructive activities (rather than "mindless busywork" or activities focused on the deceased) on those days. These activities, which ranged from helping the elderly at a local hospital to getting a new hairstyle, usually involved contact with other people. As may have been expected, men's coping patterns largely revolved around immersing themselves in their occupations; one man declared that since his wife died he had "buried" himself in his work. Escape and avoidance seemed to characterize most of the widowed men's coping styles. Other men hesitantly admitted not getting enough exercise; eating, smoking, and drinking too much; and not getting outside very much, choosing, typically, to watch television or sleep.

In the vignette I presented earlier, Andy—like other men I would interview—showed few effective coping behaviors, and no purposeful engagement in constructive activities (besides work). But few men were as expressive as Andy; many were less inclined toward talking about their feelings. Although Erin was highly involved in her business, this did not preclude her from spending time with her family and close friends. Her adaptive coping behaviors effectively limited her opportunity to engage in self-pity.

Erin's adaptation exemplified a larger dimension of broader personal growth which many widowed women experienced. I was surprised to find that almost half of the women characterized the period beginning with the death of their spouses as one of predominantly positive change in their lives. Although none of the women said that widowhood was a joyful or a "positive experience" unto itself, many did describe an "identity rebirth" after their husbands died. As may be expected, this growth was synonymous with "independence" and "more assertive" behavior, including a discovery that they were far less incompetent than they thought they were while married. (It would not be accurate, however, to blame marriage as harmful to women's growth: Widows who perceived that life had improved after the death of their spouses described the change as intertwined with a maturity that comes not only because of loss of a close relationship but through aging. When the marriage relationship ended, objective reflection revealed to some widows how they may have been involved in "highly draining," spouse-dependent marriages, spending an inordinate amount of physical and emotional energy they could now devote elsewhere.)

While widowhood was an "opening" experience for some women (who were amazed to discover, for example, that operating a power lawnmower was within their range of capability), widowhood was not a time of personal discovery for widowed men in the same way. I venture to say it was a "closing" experience for many men. While both men and women learned that being a "superwidow"—doing the job of two—was difficult (especially when children were involved), men were more likely to pay someone else to perform tasks (such as child care) formerly performed by their spouses rather than try to do both jobs. Taking care of household tasks—from mowing lawns to arranging for child care—is part of the basic "survival" enterprise essential to healthy bereavement: To continue to live, and to carry on one's life, can be literally a matter of life or death. We can gain some insight into why and how some widows survive—and even thrive—while others are devastated by the experience, by examining similarities between widowed "survivors" and survivors of mass disasters.

Like the survivor of a mass disaster, widowed men and women may experience "survivor guilt," in which a person feels guilty that he or she is still alive while another has died. Survivor guilt implies that the survivor was spared because of the death of another; his or her survival was therefore "paid for" by the death of an other person. For widowed people, the guilt may be strongly felt because the survivor and the deceased were typically closer than survivors of mass disasters. Survivor guilt can be especially powerful, and for survivors of disasters, guilt is followed by the experience of "psychic numbness." This numbness serves to protect the survivor by blocking out both the death event and the strong guilt that accompanies it. The initial numbness experienced by newly widowed men and women is similar to the psychic numbness in that it also protects the surviving spouse from absorbing the reality and implications of the death of a loved one.

Writer Robert J. Lifton examined the experiences of survivors of Hiroshima, Nazi death camps, and the Vietnam War.[17] He found that witnessing death leads either to new growth for those who survive or to shrinking and constriction brought about by a long numbing. Some survivors, Lifton points out, accomplish positive growth only by "hitting bottom," a sensation many widowed persons experience within the first year of widowhood.

While there are parallels between survivorship and widowhood, there are at least two differences: First, seeing the death of one's spouse is emotionally a solitary experience. Due to the exclusivity of marriage, the loss of a spouse leaves only one widow or widower from that death. While others can offer sympathy, the surviving spouse can comfortably turn to no one who is in the same position, having lost that particular person as spouse. Survivors of mass disasters can see others who have lost loved ones, perhaps even those who have lost more than they. Second, while the sense of numbing may be similar to the reaction to a mass disaster, the loneliness of widowhood is more intense, because the widow lacks the opportunity to engage in mutually constructive activity that would (at least physically) begin to ameliorate the disaster. For example, the survivors of the massive 1986 Mexico City earthquake could draw some comfort from the realization that—whatever the reason for this disaster—they still had one another, still alive and still capable of working together to reconstruct what had been destroyed. Even if one's spouse was killed, the survivor could see—if not draw solace from the fact—that there were others who lost spouses and loved ones; they too were—just as surely yet as inexplicably as the survivor—spared.

Mexico City widows were witness to other Mexico City widows; the sense of aloneness is moderated when others share the senselessness of unexpected death. Aloneness—felt by itself and by oneself—is the most frightening emotion a widowed man or woman can experience.

In my solitary movement through grief I gradually became aware that my life was changing; without my wife, daily occurrences took on different meanings, ranging from visits from friends and relatives (Why does everyone leave so quickly now?) to conversations (Nobody mentions her name). and even choices of food for dinner (more fast food)—all these took on a different texture and meaning. At times there were humorous touches: mail personally addressed to Chris DiGiulio from Ed McMahon promising her a chance to be the envy of her neighbors by winning a Publishers' Clearing House Sweepstakes, or mailings offering her low-cost term life insurance with "no physical exam required." But other mail—from real people—was difficult, including the "how-are-you?-please-write" letters from her more distant friends who hadn't been in touch for a year or so; worst perhaps were the phone calls from those friends or college acquaintances who had not yet heard.

So much had to be changed: I sat at my wife's place at the table, slept on her side of the bed, and moved my clothes to her closet. I also went about trying to tie up loose ends, her "unfinished business" that needed taking care of, ranging from crewel work to painting the dining room—two jobs of many she'd been in the process of completing when she died. I grieved the sadness she would have grieved had she been here; I mourned both her inability to get satisfaction from completing those tasks she had begun, and her no longer being present to enjoy simply being with the people she loved and who loved her.

I began to grieve not only for her and for my loss of her as my wife but for the loss of my life—the way it had been. Clinging to those things that did not change (mostly objects and photos), I characterized those things that had (mostly relationships and perceptions) as uniformly bad changes, unwanted evidence that all this was really not a dream.

Although I was under great stress (which displayed itself in constant headaches and an inability to sleep) during the first two or three months after her death, along with the strong grief was a strange sense of peace that grew partly from the realization that although someone I had loved was gone, she was at the very least now at peace. Although she was not alive, since I soon realized there was absolutely nothing I could do to reverse that, I was comforted by the knowledge that she was not suffering or in pain. This realization was important, and it imparted a sense of peace.

The sense of peace also came from analyzing my marriage in a more objective way than was possible while the marriage relationship still existed. I gradually began to realize how much energy I had invested in different parts of the relationship. For example, I had felt totally responsible for her happiness; my "script" was to provide her protection from sadness. Now that she was no longer alive some of my patterns of behavior were obsolete, at times even ludicrous. Like a man who spent a life at the seashore listening (and accustomed to) the sound of the waves only to be suddenly transported to the desert, my environment was now silent, with a peacefulness that was at once calming and alien.

Until I began my investigation, I had no words for what I've just described. As I talked with and interviewed widows of different ages and circumstances, I was surprised to identify widowhood as part of a larger, most intriguing, and unexpected theme. In addition to feeling the sense of peace I had experienced, there were persons who had marriages that were difficult, marked by incompatibility, prolonged illness, alcoholism, or varying degrees of conflict. The death of their spouses brought them a much stronger sense of peace than I had experienced, because it marked the end of an onerous situation. In those relationships, death brought a sense of relief to the survivor. Relief actually conveyed more information about the experience of marriage than of widowhood, especially since a number of widowed women experienced a real liberation and release from an onerous situation; a release they would not have sought—and did not seek prior to widowhood—through divorce. Despite the fact that divorce is an available option to all married Americans, and despite the greater acceptability of divorce as an alternative to marital incompatibility, there are millions of men and women who stay in unhappy and unfulfilling marital relationships. In light of this, it should not have been surprising to hear almost one-half of all widowed women frankly admitting that although they were saddened by their husbands' deaths, they were *relieved* that an unhappy part of their lives had ended. Even those widows who had characterized their marriages as "happy" often described relief, predominantly relief from "doing what someone else wants," "cooking food I don't like," "taking care of a sick man," "doing all the dirty work," or "raising the kids with no help from him."

Of all widowed women interviewed, almost 40 percent experienced relief following the deaths of their husbands, and a majority of women characterized changes in their lives following the death of the spouse as positive, or at least as a mixture of positive and negative changes. Feelings and expressions of relief were common among elderly widows who had nursed ill husbands for a number of years, and relief was clearly expressed by those few widows who experienced spousal assault or verbal abuse while married. Relief was especially common—almost uniformly present—among widows of alcohol-abusing husbands.

Olga, a forty-seven-year-old grocery cashier whose husband died three years earlier, was one such widow. "I'm free. I hate to say it, but for the first time in my life I can go *where* I want, buy *what* I want, and not have to answer to anyone." Olga described her marriage to Steve as "rocky," made very difficult by his constant drinking.

"I tried everything: getting him to go to AA, pleading with him, asking his brother to talk to him, nothing worked. Steve loved to drink."

She nodded toward a huge framed family photograph on the piano. "He was good to the kids . . . never hit them or anything. But he never did much with them. Or with me. I covered up for him a million times when he came home too sick to eat supper. And you know what?" she asked, looking directly at me. "I became just like him. I never drank, but I thought like him, I never dressed up, I never went anywhere . . . he was very suspicious, too. Or I should say he *became* very suspicious. Drinking *changed* him. When we got married he didn't drink very much, but it only got worse and worse, little by little." She shook her head. "I should've put my foot down twenty-five years ago!

"He wasn't what you'd call a socialite or somebody with a lot of friends. Steve had his drinking buddies and that was it. Drinking and football, just like in the comic strips. After he died, I felt like . . . like a slob. Other women were dressed up, going to work, independent, and I was part of this house. Like the wallpaper," she said, pointing to the wall. "Sitting here and crying like an idiot," she added.

"I bought myself new clothes, threw out half of the junk in this house, and I know you can't tell but I lost twenty-two pounds. Things like that Steve used to do now I do, and some of them I never thought I could do! I hate to say this but I don't think I'll ever get married again. You can never say never, but for now there are too many things to do, and I like not having a husband boss over me, telling me 'don't do this . . . how much did that cost . . . why did you get that?' I went right from being a daughter to being a wife, with no time in between to figure out what *I* wanted out of life. It may sound cold, but since the funeral I've become a different person . . . I miss Steve, but I miss who he was twenty years ago which was gone long before he died. No, you can't go back and I don't *want* to go back, being what I was when we were married. Steve would never recognize me if he came back today. And I don't just mean physically."

Young, middle-aged, and older widowed women seemed equally likely to have experienced a degree of relief following the loss of their spouses. Sometimes mixed with a strong sense of guilt at being relieved, many widows sought to explain and qualify their admissions of relief. Most of the explanations revolved around alcohol, with the widow believing that when their husbands drank, they were "different" men from the men they loved: "When Bob drank he was a stranger to me . . . he was a totally different man."

Several widows cited the relief they felt when they no longer had to tend to an ill husband. Chronic and terminal illnesses were cited as debilitating factors by a number of widowed; when asked about her thoughts on remarriage, one widow stated up front: "I don't care if he's rich, poor or ugly. As long as he's *healthy*, I'd marry him. I *never* want to take care of a husband again, being a nursemaid for ten years!" This was spoken by Jenny:

"Do you know what it's like to have a hospital bed in your living room for seven years?" Jenny was an attractive forty-nine-year-old teacher widowed 18 months. She pointed into the living room of her downtown Rochester apartment. The living room looked different from the rest of the rooms—almost museumlike with photos, paintings, heavy wooden furniture. "Right there," she pointed "was Paul's bed for seven years. I took care of him every day. I fed him, changed him, washed him, walked him around, rubbed his legs.

"After he di . . . was gone, I saw a counselor for three months. I felt so *guilty* because I was finally free from all that. And I couldn't handle it. He was a good man, but after he got sick there was nothing for me to do but come home from school and tend to him. Paul wanted me to quit teaching at school and stay with him all day. But I couldn't." She began to cry softly.

"I couldn't. Deep down inside I knew *I* would die along with him if I had to be here all day. So I hired nurses to be here between eight and four. He hated every one of them, and made me feel guilty about it." She corrected herself: "No, I made *myself* feel guilty. The counselor helped me to understand that he was sick, and not in his right mind. And, I am the type . . . I *was* the type . . . to think everything was my fault. But no more. Whenever I feel guilty, I think of all the wonderful things I did for Paul, especially taking care of him all night long and every day I didn't work for seven years!"

A small number of widows reported that they had experienced verbal abuse during their marriages, and Wanda, widowed 9 months, expressed relief from physical abuse.

Wanda's tiny attic apartment was in the Southend section of Boston. As I stepped over toys scattered on the living room floor, two children were in a playpen, one crying as he held up his arms, the other intently biting the playpen railing. The television was blasting. As I entered her apartment, twenty-five-year-old Wanda was speaking into the telephone, wrapped up in the long coiled wire as she opened the door. She pointed to the sofa, and walked away from me still talking into the phone.

She took the crying child into another room and returned, sitting across from me in a dirty armchair. She tried to light a cigarette with a disposable lighter; her hand shook. Talking through her cigarette Wanda asked me to excuse the appearance of her apartment; she'd had a "tough morning." After describing in detail all that had gone wrong that morning, Wanda told me her husband Glen had been hit by a car and died soon after in a California hospital. Her eyes looked tired as she spoke; her face was elderly.

"He was a shifty bastard, always trying to pull the wool over somebody's eyes. Like always some deal going. I wouldn't be surprised if he was run over on purpose, all the enemies he had. The police said it was an accident, but I wouldn't be surprised, you know? I don't miss him one bit."

She got up and picked up the quiet infant.

"Not one bit," she repeated. Tears came to her eyes and she hugged the baby tightly. "The son-of-a-bitch used to beat me, like, he was always cheating on me, you know?" She wiped her eyes with a tissue, and became animated with my next question. "How is my life different now? Like it's a *thousand* times better without him. He used to do shit . . . I mean, drugs. But even when he didn't he was no good. You may think, like, this sounds crude, but I'm glad he's gone."

As for her future, Wanda had already signed up for a high school equivalency program, and said that her friend Beanie would baby-sit while she went back to school. "I knew Beanie since third grade . . . like we been friends now seventeen years. And if it wasn't for her I'd do this." She drew her hands quickly across her wrists as if to slash them with a razor.

While Wanda did not feel that she had grown since Glen's death nor that there were any outstanding positive aspects of her life, she did have hope, which was expressed in terms of her relationship with her children, with Beanie, with the probability that she'd soon have her high school diploma, be able to "get off welfare," and get a job. Certainly Wanda was not typical of widowed women interviewed, but the sense of relief felt by women whose husbands were not abusive was often just as profound.

There was also a deep, intangible sense of relief among women who characterized their marriages as "happy"—those women who were spared dealing with gripping illness, alcoholism, or abuse. For many, irrespective of marital happiness, widowhood seemed to be the first opportunity for self-expression and self-discovery.

These women were relieved not in the sense of celebrating their husbands' passing, but of, "Now I can go on with my life" or "I'm going to enjoy life now. Joe never liked to dance and go out. Damm it, I'm going out!" "Get married again? I'd have to be crazy. I'm having too much fun!" Characteristic comments were, "I never knew I could . . ." or "I never knew I had it in me!"

Forty-three percent of all widowed women interviewed expressed a degree of relief; of that group, so did 40 percent of all young widows (thirty-nine years of age and younger):

> I became stronger after he died. I relied on him much more than I should have. I'm a much stronger person now.

> I no longer had to deal with his alcoholism. I have more control over the finances; I'm more financially stable now, but money's harder. . . . I grew up 100 percent—I had to rely on myself.

> Life is much better now. I'm more at ease. My marriage was "the pits." He had affairs. . . . I'm so glad the bastard is gone. He used to hit me and the kid, and he ran around behind my back. Good riddance. What would I say to him if he was here now? I'd say "Thanks for screwing up my life."

> Once he found out about his cancer he became very selfish and very bitter. He got a transfer from Ohio where we were, to Pennsylvania to be nearer to his family, but things became worse. We did manage to talk some things out . . . but that was a very difficult time. I'm glad for him and for me that it's over.

> [My husband] was a transvestite. I had to keep this to myself. I was worried that [my sons] would find out about their father, but now I can talk to them and be honest with them. You see, I felt like a lesbian with him . . . he insisted that we make love while he wore a negligee. He would threaten to hit me if I didn't take pictures of him when he dressed up like a woman. We both saw a psychiatrist in New Jersey and it helped me understand him a little better . . . but it really didn't change things.

Middle-aged widowed women continued the predominant theme of relief; of all middle-aged widows interviewed, almost 50 percent expressed feelings of relief:

> I'm more independent now, especially from his children by his first marriage. They created a big problem in our marriage.

> Periodically, he would get involved in an affair. Three times while we were married. I wanted him back each time, but it wasn't meant to be. I was seeing [my boyfriend] when [my husband] had his last affair, but after [my husband] died [my boyfriend] died six months later. A year later, my son died. That was God's punishment to the both of us.

> His personality dominated mine. We had very different ideas about raising children which didn't make life easy at all.

> If two people should never've been married it was us. We were opposites. But I've learned to enjoy today. If my husband came back I'd say, "I can make it on my own." I'm not a homebody anymore, and I actually enjoy being alone. . . . He went on drinking binges which were bad. We were very possessive of each other which was no good, either.

> I honestly don't miss him the way he was. It's a relief not to have to drive him to the hospital three times a week. I don't *ever* want to live with illness again. No, there wasn't a "big adjustment" for me after his death. Just peace.

The predominant relief theme of older (fifty-five years of age and older) women was that of relief from caring for a spouse, especially one who was chronically ill. Although as a group widowed women expressed relief from a spouse who drank excessively, relatively few older widowed women mentioned it. Whether this reflects a hesitancy on the part of older widows to admit their spouses abused alcohol or whether it is an indication that alcohol abuse was less prevalent is unclear. Older widows were also less likely than middle-aged and younger widows to express relief from infidelity and violence. Statements of relief were expressed by 37 percent of older widowed women:

> I became much more tolerant of others and aware of others' opinions. He was so intolerant. I'm more empathetic and more independent since he died.

> Do you know what it's like to have a cot set up in your bedroom for three years and watch your husband die a little bit every day? For three years that cot was there. I couldn't have nobody over, with him there. Not that I'm ashamed of what I did. But I don't ever want to live with a sick person again.
>
> Mostly I have personal freedom now. I no longer had to care for him. And even before that it was a very lonely marriage. I've always had to make my own life.
>
> Life is easier for me; I'm more outgoing now. I became like a nurse all of a sudden. I gave him better care than the nurses. I was at the hospital and cared for him *every day* he was in that hospital.
>
> I'm able to be more independent. We were two very different people. . . . I raised the kids all by myself even when he was alive. Life isn't perfect now but it's a hell of a lot simpler!

Again, it is important to emphasize that these women were not necessarily relieved at their husbands' deaths per se, but their husbands' departures from their lives—no matter how untimely or sad—provided relief. Perhaps the spirit of relief was captured by Thomas Mann who alluded to this intangible: "What we call mourning for our dead is perhaps not so much grief at not being able to call them back as it is grief at not being able to want to do so."[18] Relief arises among widows who perceived at least part of their marriage identity to have been constricting, perhaps not as fulfilling as earlier in the marriage or never as fulfilling as they had hoped. Understandably, relief is strongest among those widows who said they had highly unfulfilling marriages.

Relief can also be situation-specific, keyed to a particular, difficult aspect of a marriage. Numerous widowed women, for example, expressed relief upon being freed from the chore of taking care of a chronically ill husband. Reflecting on relief can help the widow understand herself better, especially in her contemplation of future relationships. Some widows proclaimed boldly that they'd never marry a man who drank; others were wary of a remarriage to a chronically ill person.

It is important to note, however, that some widows with happy marriages also expressed relief. Other studies show women's marital satisfaction decreasing markedly over time, thus even those with "happy" marriages are likely to be less happy as years pass. Wives are aware of—and report—more stress in their marriages than do men. Almost twice as many men than women report "nothing wrong" with their marriages, and their satisfaction does not decrease over the life of the marriage.[19] These findings may reflect women's higher initial expectations about marriage, or perhaps greater objectivity or more rigorous scrutiny. The relief she experiences when her marriage ends may provide the widow with new insight into herself, as well as into the flaws and burdens of her marriage. However, relief by itself does not enable a widow to move beyond widowhood. Her identity must be rebuilt or reformulated.[20]

This was not the case with most widowed men. When they talked about their widowhood experiences, men seldom made overt statements of relief. The closest they came to expressions of relief were phrases of consolation: Death brought deliverance from pain for those wives who had suffered terminal illness. "At least she's not suffering anymore" was typical. Some men told me they were happy their wives "don't have to see me like this." But there were few statements of relief similar to those expressed above by widowed women. Widowhood provided little new freedom, self-discovery, opportunity, or relief for men.

Of those relatively few men who easily discussed their widowhood, most did not see the loss of the marriage relationship as being as significant a loss as the loss of the person ("You can always get remarried") to whom they had grown attached, who knew them, and who represented a permissive forum for a range of emotions and persuasions denied them outside of marriage. For many men I met, wives were the only really close relationships they had had in life, with the possible exception of their mothers. Some were so utterly dependent on their wives that they could not comprehend life being bearable without them. A few widowed men were not attached to either the person or to the marriage relationship, and they appeared to experience widowhood more like a "painless divorce," with less turbulence than widowed men whose dependency was marked.

Men's relative inability (or disinclination) to articulate a positive side to widowhood is consistent with the generally adverse outcomes men experience as widowers. Widows generally fare better:

Evidence from my investigation, and from other studies indicate that despite the pain of bereavement, most women survive without psychological damage.[21] Widowhood is one of life's salient turning points for both men and women, yet what is an ominous situation for many men is for some women a second chance, or—in the words of more than a few widows—"a new lease on life."

CHAPTER 3

Identity Loss and Reformulation

In human society, at all its levels, persons confirm one another . . . in their personal qualities and capacities, and a society may be termed human in the measure to which its members confirm one another.

—MARTIN BUBER, *"Distance and Relation"*

One of the first widowed women I interviewed described her life since her husband's death. She told me that the hardest part was not living on less money or explaining his death to their children, nor was it his burial or enduring the pity of others. "It's what he meant to me that I miss so dearly. Even when he was sick, just having him as a part of my life and knowing he was *there* made my life important." She told me how, despite her taking care of him throughout his chronic illness, she gave little thought to his dying. Living without him was literally unthinkable.

As she and I and millions of widowed men and women came to learn, despite our hopes for endless love, married life ends. Despite the common conception of adulthood as a plateau of stability, it is in fact a period of continuous change. Human life is replete with transitions beginning at birth and extending through late adulthood. The loss of a toy, entering school, a first date, rejection by a friend, starting a job, getting married or divorced, confronting an "empty nest," and retirement all challenge the illusion that life is stable and unchanging. No event, however, is as powerful as the loss of a spouse. Even for those whose spouses' deaths are not unexpected, widowhood is so profound that it always seems to come too abruptly: "I knew my marriage wouldn't last forever, but I never expected it to end this way. Or so soon." The death of a spouse has such a powerful impact precisely because of its effect on the surviving spouse's sense of personal identity.

The development of that identity begins early in life as the infant perceives his own physiological needs (for food, warmth and safety) and how adequately they are satisfied by the adult(s) on whom he depends for survival. These perceptions provide the basis for the child's initial assessment of who he is and how others value him.

Identity begins as self-esteem: a feeling that one is wanted, and thus, valued. The infant's self-esteem is tenuous, dependent on the sum of messages from the object of primary attachment—usually the parent. These "messages" the infant receives, regarding how wanted he or she is, will naturally be affected by physiological factors (a colicky infant may irritate the parent, who then behaves in a rejecting manner), socioeconomic factors (parents with limited resources and social skills may provide inadequate stimulation or nutrition), and psychological factors (a parent who truly wants an infant will be more likely to show affection and acceptance).

As the child grows, society begins to play a substantial part in the child's developing identity. Through childhood, the child gains experience by engaging in activities alone, as part of a pair, and as part of a group. Messages received at home can now be verified in light of the new ones the child receives from newly significant adults: teachers. They provide assessments of intellectual ("You're a fine student"), physical ("She's the fastest runner in the class"), and social ability ("He's popular").

Early in adolescence, the peer group becomes a more important source of verification than parents, teachers, or other adults. This is a critical time for identity development as adolescents "try on" new roles, sometimes based in imagination, strive to gain peer acceptance, and form new kinds of close friendships. To an adolescent, having a "best friend" implies a deeper closeness and greater sharing of confidences than it did during childhood. Early adolescent cross-sex friendships and romantic relationships ("puppy love") are ways in which adolescents clarify their identities in revealing images of the self to others. We "use" peers to learn about ourselves. What they reflect back to us provides an ongoing validation of what we see ourselves to be:

> To a considerable extent adolescent love is an attempt to arrive at a definition of one's identity by projecting one's diffuse ego image on another and by seeing it thus reflected and gradually clarified.[1]

For an adult, three elements are required for the formation of a stable identity: A sense of "inner sameness and continuity," whereby individuals experience that who we are today is who we were yesterday, last week, and last year. Second, we need to perceive that others whose opinions we value acknowledge our "inner sameness." Social reflection also affirms that we actually are who we perceive ourselves to be. Third, our self-perceptions must be validated in specific life experiences.[2] For example, I may think of myself as being a nurse, and that may have been reinforced by my attending nursing school where others reflected back to me my budding identity as a nurse. That identity is then validated as I gain experience actually working as a nurse.

Even for those individuals who initially forge a relatively strong identity, it is not fixed for the rest of life.[3] For

> identity . . . requires a threefold continuity; a continuity of significant others; a continuity with one's past self; a continuity with one's anticipated future self.[4]

Love, which was so important in the establishing of identity during adolescence, is even more important in identity maintenance. Intimacy with another person provides the "threefold continuity" for identity to be renewed. In the joining of individual identities, intimacy creates a new identity. Without obliterating each individual's identity, this new identity (usually symbolized by marriage) ideally provides a "reciprocal mirroring," a mutual confirmation of each partner's personal identity. By being a part of the valued "we," or marriage identity, each partner's stake in the marital identity is also enriched and enhanced. In the consistent reflection of ourselves, marriage supports and stabilizes personal identity and is the means of ongoing personal "identity renewal."[5]

However, an intimate relationship (such as marriage) can also pose a risk to oneself if one has not yet developed a clear sense of identity. Many women who are now middle-aged and older typically went from "being a daughter to being a wife." Because this was the norm, it did not serve to disrupt: Few women had clear occupational goals that were thwarted or postponed by marriage. Contemporary women are perhaps more cautious, aware that entering a committed relationship can

> swallow up the individual, making her (more often than him) lose sight of her own interests, opinions, and desires . . . losing a sense of one's self may also lead to being exploited, or even abandoned, by the person one loves.[6]

While contemporary teenage girls and young women have access to a variety of occupational roles, today's older and middle-aged widows had access to fewer career paths and were not often encouraged to develop independent identities when they were young. Thus, because "wife" and "mother" were two of very few acceptable roles available to women, the marriage identity made up a large part of their personal identity. Helena Lopata discusses the identity facet of "mother" saying: "It is interesting to note that 95 percent of all the widows still believe motherhood is among the top four roles for a woman to perform."[7]

Jean Baker Miller pinpoints how men's and women's identities take a different turn, also based on the close connection of women with children. Because women have always been responsible for child care and have been socialized to become skilled at, and to value, endeavors of human support, nurturance, and affiliation, they incorporate caring as an important part of their identity; whereas "men are not encouraged to believe that such activities [child care] are an inner and thoroughgoing requirement of a sense of self."[8] Furthermore, the highly dependent nature of children—and especially infants—is more threatening to men influenced by the cultural emphasis on an ideal of an individuated and unencumbered "Marlboro man"—an American myth.

As the originator of the "identity crisis," Erik Erikson has had a profound effect on the mapping of human identity. He emphasized individual identity formation as the gateway to adulthood and the linchpin of healthy development. Consistent with the thinking of many nineteenth- and twentieth-century theorists, Erikson regarded separation from others—the achieving of individuation—as part of the agenda of normal development. This reflected early-twentieth-century American and European valuations of accomplishment and achievement.

Recently, psychological researchers and others who have studied female development have challenged the applicability of Erikson's theory, at least to women. They note that women's identity development is not focused toward complete separation from others as an ideal outcome. Saying that she wanted to "restore in part the missing text of women's development,"[9] Carol Gilligan claimed that

> the elusive mystery of women's development lies in its recognition of the importance of attachment in the human life cycle. While developmental theorists have emphasized the importance of autonomy, separation and individuation, women have known the importance of others. However, instead of valuing this quality, they feel criticized for weakness.[10]

Affiliation is integral to a woman's identity formation, remaining important throughout her life. Her identity is solidified not in separation from or competition with others or by exceeding others' achievements, but by being attuned and responsive to, and emotionally part of, other human beings. For those women who value being married, the marriage identity augments and enriches personal identity. Yet marriage is not unconditionally beneficial to a married woman's identity. The relationship may be unfulfilling, or it may be so one-sided that her realization of who she is becomes secondary, subordinate to the needs of the other person or to "the relationship."

The ideals of individuation and freedom from affiliation that society has prescribed for men's identities do not serve as ideals for women—and they do not really work for men either. Perhaps sociologist Nancy Chodorow correctly identified the missing dimension in male identity when she wrote:

> [A boy represses] whatever he takes to be feminine inside himself, and, more importantly, by denigrating and devaluing whatever he considers to be feminine in the outside world.[11]

Male identity, despite its appearance of being something quite substantial, may often be largely empty, based on "not being" instead of "being." If it is independence, then independence from what or whom? If it is separateness, then separateness from what or whom? Separateness contradicts basic truths about human needs for closeness throughout the life cycle, including the deep need for interpersonal attachment and acceptance by others. Both men and women have these needs. Both sexes' personal identities require ongoing confirmation by another or others. Although men may still be more likely to perceive themselves as having a distinct sense of personal identity separate from their married one, the marriage identity is at least as psychologically important a complement to their personal identities as it is for women. Autonomy and achievement have made some men powerful and a few very rich, but neither has ever fulfilled men's inherent human need for affiliation. This makes men dependent on women, contributes to their shorter lives, and helps explain why married men live longer than unmarried men and why widowed men who do not remarry have higher suicide and mortality rates than those who do.[12]

Because of a popular perception that men must achieve, compete, and separate from others in order to acquire and maintain identity, men's needs for affiliation and for a richer identity definition have been neither socially sanctioned nor encouraged, existing only "under the surface of social appearance."[13] Consequently, although men intuitively know that marriage meets their needs, the perception is less clear on a cognitive (thinking) level. Indeed, it is striking how men fail to discern the importance of their close marital relationship even after the loss of their spouses, whereas widowed women seem to know all along how important this relationship is to them. There are indications this may be changing. Themes of men fleeing closeness with women have characterized American culture and literature for much of our nation's history. From *Walter Mitty* to *Huckleberry Finn,* and from *The Great Gatsby* to *Arrowsmith,* men escaped to the company of other men, not for sharing or affiliation but for play, work, combat, or serious research. In 1920, *Life with Father* author Clarence Day wrote that "The real friendships among men are so rare that when they occur they are famous." Today, however, those friendships may be becoming less rare. Recent attention to men's midlife crisis reflects men's need to develop more fully parts of their identities that had been set aside. During their late forties and early fifties, men frequently cite "wanting to be with family" as their main reason for changes in their occupational orientation. For example, actor Clint Eastwood recently declined to run again for mayor of Carmel, California, saying that he simply wanted to spend more time with his son and daughter. After winning his first game as the newly appointed manager of the Texas Rangers baseball team, former star Eddie Stanky resigned: "After the excitement calmed down I started getting lonesome and homesick." He stayed up all night, called his wife "around 5 after 6 and I told her I was coming home."[14]

For many men, on reaching middle age, much of the urgency to prove themselves has passed, and they shift their priorities. Daniel Levinson described this period of time as

> the fullest and most creative season in the life cycle [of men]. They are less tyrannized by the ambitions, passions and illusions of youth. They can be more deeply attached to others and yet more separate, more centered on the self.[15]

As evident from the phrase "attached . . . yet more separate," although this can be a "creative" time for men, it is also a time of turmoil, because getting close to others one formerly viewed as adversaries (other men and increasingly, women) is stressful—a transition that can bring about dissatisfaction and depression for some men.[16] (It is poignant that—after almost fifty years of life—some men continue to define themselves as "separate." That is a lot of distance created over the years.)

Perhaps the most significant impetus to change the traditional definition of masculinity may have come from the women's movement, which in the course of working for social equity for women has highlighted issues pertaining to men as well. Living in a society that permits women greater choices of and access to a variety of occupational and social roles, men become less bound by rigid definitions surrounding their roles as well. Thus, as women are less persistently defined as the ones who value affiliation in relationships, maleness becomes less synonymous with being an unaffiliated and unaffiliative individual.

When a man or woman experiences the death of a spouse, the perception of personal identity becomes disoriented, and at least part of it is perceived to be "lost" along with the spouse. At first, this disorientation is a numbing similar to shell shock experienced by soldiers during combat. Sigmund Freud called shell shock a regression to the "stage of unlearned function,"[17] but the first direct acknowledgment of this type of identity loss grew out of Erik Erikson's work with World War II veterans. He described these veterans in terms all too familiar to those who have worked with widowed men and women whose spouses have died unexpectedly:

> The boundaries of their egos have lost their shock-absorbing delineation: anxiety and anger are provoked by everything too sudden or too intense, whether it be a sensory impression or a self-reproach, an impulse or a memory.
>
> In some cases . . . ego impairment seems to have its origin in violent events . . . above all, the men "do not know any more who they are": there is a distinct loss of ego identity. The sense of sameness and of continuity and the belief in one's social role are gone.[18]

As numbness recedes, the perception of identity loss becomes less global.[19] It is more subtle, expressed by the question, "Who am I now that my spouse is dead?" The widow's present sense of identity is damaged, because her most significant love object (who helped her maintain her identity) is gone. Her past becomes clouded as well, because her deceased spouse was her most crucial witness to experiences, joys, feelings, losses, and successes. Third, her anticipated future self—the woman she planned to become—has also changed dramatically. The death of her spouse tolls the end of the relationship and signifies the widow's loss of the most powerful influence on continued identity renewal, because "an identity is a fragile thing when it stands by itself."[20]

When her husband dies, a widow loses her marriage identity, the verifying "vehicle" that provided a reflecting back of who she is. Lynn Caine—the author of *Widow*—suggested that because of the loss of this reflection women lose more in widowhood than men. Caine felt women tend to tie up more of their identity in the status of marriage, and she implied that women value the marriage identity more than men value theirs. British social worker Lily Pincus echoed those sentiments:

> A little girl is brought up with the idea that the greatest achievement for her will be to marry, be a beautiful bride, and become a wife and mother. Getting married, therefore,

> is an occasion for rejoicing and is seen as the achievement of a new status and new identity . . . while this situation offers many compensations and is freely and joyfully chosen by the majority of women in our society, it may also weaken their sense of autonomy.[21]

But when her spouse dies, a widow does not lose the network of friends and family members who can continue to provide at least part of the identity reflection formerly provided by her spouse, although they cannot provide the intensely personal reflection a close spouse can provide. The "secret ingredient" of identity reformulation is a widow's ability to establish new relationships, not as a substitute for her past marriage identity, but as a satisfying present endeavor that will permit her to see—and leave—her past in the past. Moreover, it will give her an "updated," revised reflection of who she is. Having evolved a new definition of her self, she will be able to grow beyond widowhood.

Each widowed woman is challenged to develop her new identity, one that is necessarily different from her past identity. This must be done no matter how fulfilling or unfulfilling her marriage may have been, and no matter how enriching it was to her sense of herself. This is a painful part of growing through widowhood, because it demands living in the present. Although her past marriage will always remain a part of herself, it must not overwhelm her present, nor should it prevent her from embarking on new relationships.

Although both men and women experience loss when a spouse dies, the nature of that loss tends to differ between the sexes. At first, however, both men and women experience the "shell shock" type of identity loss: an immediate perception of numbness that affects especially those whose spouses have died unexpected deaths. But after this reaction, different patterns appear. Women, because they are more likely to have incorporated the marital relationship into their sense of themselves, feel that they have therefore lost not only a spouse but a part of themselves.

The severity and pain of this feeling is reflected in the defense against it. Newly bereaved women I interviewed were likely to say they still felt their husband's presence:

> When I was cooking I would turn to talk to him. I was sure he was there, but I'd start to talk to him and only then it would hit me: He's gone.

One month after the death of her spouse, Yoko Ono Lennon wrote a letter describing her perception of the marriage identity she shared:

> John and I believed that we were one mind taking two bodies at this time "for convenience," "*and* it's more fun," as he put it. Lately, we were calling ourselves "the group" . . . "I like both of you," he used to tease me.[22]

Although for most widowed women the "presence" of the spouse and of the marriage fades within the first twelve to eighteen months, for a few it continues:

> Even though it's been almost six years, I still wait for my husband to come home from work. I can see him opening the door, telling me he's home as he drops his briefcase. It's still as clear as can be to me.
>
> I know he's not here, but I still feel him within me. We are still married. He's not here for others to see because he's inside my heart. Right here.

No men I interviewed or spoke with described their deceased wives as being "within themselves." Their remembrances were usually tied to the past; men would be likely to show me a wedding picture from their wallets or tell me about their past lives with their wives. Although men were capable of being as profoundly grief stricken as women, they did not consider their present and future selves as being affected or damaged by the death of a wife.

One of the most striking differences between the widowed women and widowed men I interviewed was that women asked the "Who am I?" question, while men did not. This reflects the difference in how men and women view their marriage identity. Married men rarely describe themselves as "the husband of" their spouse, and when their spouse dies men see their personal identity as remaining intact. When asked to describe themselves, women will describe themselves as a part of a family and relationship, while men describe personal occupation and offer other factual information about their activities.

Men's loss of the marital relationship has a dramatic effect on their personal fulfillment, happiness, health, physical well-being, and longevity. Yet because they believe their personal identity ("who I am") is clearly separated from their marriage, men rarely recognize damage to their personal identity when their spouses die. But they still feel empty, lost, and lonely. In losing their marital identity, men—like women—feel they have lost an important part of their lives, yet for men what they have lost *has no name*. It is only notable in its absence.

Consequently, men's generally less-than-satisfactory adaptation in widowhood is partly predictable, given the rigid role taking that characterizes their social and marital relationships. Marriage as the only stable, affiliative enterprise available to men, enriches a man's identity and is extremely beneficial for his health. Yet when the person who has been the focus of all his affiliative needs (his wife) dies, he is left with the loss of that part of his identity. Ivan Podobnikar, director of the National Institute of Widows and Widowers in Columbus, Ohio, claims that men have a more difficult time in adjusting to widowhood because in part of the "infantilization" they experience in marriage. He believes that the "photos of Israel's Menachem Begin looking depressed and physically wasted since the loss of his wife" in 1982 exemplify "a generation of men who are heavily dependent on their wives for physical, emotional and other kinds of support. What's worse . . . they're unwilling to call for help."[23]

Widowed men's grief seems more despairing than widows' grief; it also appears to be more unremitting. Men did not report feeling relief following their wives' death, whereas 40 percent of the widowed women with whom I spoke did express relief. Two explanations may account for this difference, each related to the roles men and women performed while they were married.

One involves caregiving. Men were as concerned about their ill spouses as women were about theirs, yet men did not actively nurse or tend to their spouses as women did. Instead, men saw their most effective support grounded in securing the best medical or nursing care they could. Many women who expressed relief following the death of an ill spouse were those who spent much time and energy caring for their spouses before they died. Hence, the death of a spouse meant the end of caregiving which was—for some women—quite exhausting. The caregiving of women by men was out of character: Men are not expected to care for the ill or weak in our society; they thus feel powerless to help when confronted with the need to do so. To give such care would also be an admission that their spouse had a serious or terminal illness, a fact few men could or would confront. Given this denial, men were more likely than women to characterize the death of a seriously ill spouse as something unexpected or sudden.

Another explanation involves "codependence," in which a marriage partner becomes drawn into the unhealthy behavior of the spouse. A husband's gambling or his drug or alcohol dependence and his wife's ongoing attempts to deal with his needs and behavior can turn into her becoming codependent, especially if her wish to help her spouse prevents his experiencing the full consequences of addiction. For example, alcohol codependence begins long before death. It begins with a wife's efforts to seek help for her spouse (getting him to AA meetings or to talk to a counselor), then "covering up for" her husband's addiction and its results, and finally seeking to protect herself and their children from his behavior. No matter how beloved or benevolent an addicted spouse may have been, after his death a widow is released from both his dependence on alcohol and his dependence on her. Whether brought about through freedom from caregiving or by an end to codependence, relief serves as an important "balancing" device, helping the widow attain a sense of emotional equilibrium.

As they discussed their marriage relationships, men spoke of their spouses as unique individuals, yet marriage appeared to remain external to a deeper, emotional self. While men may feel satisfied by their marriage relationship, this is not acknowledged on a cognitive level, perhaps because boys are not strongly reinforced to value—and *admit* valuing—a marriage relationship. If they have a "happy" or "great" marriage, it's because they married that specific person. They did not use words like *fulfilled* (which women did), perhaps reflecting their lack of investment of the self in the relationship. Because they focus on their spouse instead of on the relationship they shared, "contribution" for men is object related, centered on contributing to the other person's welfare, contributing money for necessities and time and labor toward a specific task or objective.

A few widows who had felt unfulfilled in marriage blamed themselves for not having been supportive enough or for not having given enough while married. Even those widows who were aware of their unfulfilling marriages while married may have been hesitant to end their marriages. A woman may stay in an unsatisfying marriage for many reasons, including low self-esteem, lack of money, fear of being alone, unawareness of alternatives, consideration of childrens' needs, or because of religious restrictions. When a woman derives satisfaction solely from being married instead of from a fulfilling marriage relationship, her personal identity is maintained but not enriched by the marriage identity.

There is increasing evidence that how well men and women cope with identity-threatening stresses—especially the severe stress brought on by the death of the spouse and the resulting bereavement—may depend on the variety of roles that make up our "selves." Adults whose identities are multifaceted—who define themselves in terms of their activities and commitments in several spheres—seem to have better protection from the impact of highly stressful life events like widowhood or divorce. They are less likely to succumb to depression and illness than are people whose sense of themselves is more limited. For example, a widow who sees herself as a financial counselor, mother, sister, aunt, daughter, and volunteer tutor will enjoy greater protection from the harmful effects of stress and marital identity loss than will a widowed woman who sees herself as having, for example, only two major roles: widow and mother.

The number of roles a widow occupies is not the only important factor in stress reduction. The distinctions, or "spaces," between those roles may be just as critical in protecting against the ill effects of stress. For example, researcher Patricia Linville[24] cites a woman going through a divorce who sees herself only as a wife and lawyer. If those two roles are closely related in her memory (maybe her husband is also a lawyer, and they have had many interactions in the practice of law), her protection from stress will be lessened because there is little separation between her role as a lawyer and her role as a wife.

On the other hand, if her predivorce identity encompasses many roles that are more distinct from each other (such as lawyer, wife, friend, and political organizer), she will enjoy greater protection from the effects of the stress of divorce because there will be two remaining roles that are unaffected by the divorce (political organizer and friend). These intact roles will serve as a buffer against the effects of stress. The importance of having several—but not an exhaustive number of—roles explains why the widowed women I interviewed who were "busier" seemed to be adapting well, unlike those who had few things to do in their lives. However, an overload of roles, as in the attempt to be a "superwoman," can create more stress than it will offset.

In addition to the number of roles and the spaces between those roles, the access widows have to different types of roles has an effect on their adaptation. Access to social roles like friend, lover, or spouse depends largely on existing social ties, personality, and appearance. Access to paid employment and the status attendant on various occupational positions depends primarily on work experience and education (and somewhat, of course, on personal connections).

While education has a bearing on which nonfamilial roles a woman can occupy, there is no one-to-one correlation between education and adaptation (widows with Ph.D.s are not necessarily the best-adapted). However, women with at least one degree from a two- or four-year college adapt well in widowhood, and generally better than widows with no more than a high school education. Highly educated women also are more likely to engage in more and varied social activities and often have greater career choices and more financially and professionally rewarding opportunities open to them.[25]

Those "multiple choices" and that flexibility are important. When roles are stripped away during times of crisis and great personal stress, the survivor who has not developed alternate roles is at a disadvantage.

Fortunately there is reason to believe that contemporary widowed women are more flexible than their predecessors in the lives they can envision and shape for themselves. Again as a result of the women's movement, contemporary women (and younger women in particular) suffer fewer role restrictions than did their forebears. Although women's wider choices in occupation and opportunity outside the home do not—by themselves—provide a buffer or shortcut through grief, they do provide access to alternative roles that are especially important when the role of wife is replaced with that of widow.

Hence, the importance of role alternatives for women besides "wife" or "widow" cannot be overstated, because the role of the American widow is a myth. Helena Lopata noted that the security provided by clearly defined roles for widows presently exists nowhere in the United States except within "ethnic enclaves of new immigrants."[26] Widows outside ethnic enclaves who may wish to remain widows (and some do) will adhere to a role that is poorly defined and of low status—a role not valued by most Americans. By contrast, when their spouses die, middle-aged and elderly Italian women join a clearly defined social group of widows. In their uniform black, they sit together at the front of the church, deriving a certain security and prestige from a role that has no counterpart in mainstream American society.

For widowhood is a role fully defined by the absence of something—by "nothingness." Researchers Schlaffer and Bernard described the common feelings of social isolation and desolation among German widows. They highlighted both loss of status and loss of identity as key components of the experience of widows.[27] Not surprisingly, the loss of one's spouse has been described as the single most stressful life event, more stressful than serious personal illness, separation, or divorce; being sentenced to prison; or living through the death of a parent or child. The death of a spouse, even in "loosely connected" couples, also requires the greatest life readjustment of any stressful event, and this holds true across all age groups and cultural backgrounds.[28]

While women's roles have become more flexible and varied, the women's movement has had unfortunately little additional impact on the definition of widowhood. In fact, the very achievements of the women's movement may make certain aspects of the widow's life more difficult—or at least more complicated. As in other areas of life, like dating and marriage, the greater freedom women now enjoy has served to blur the limited but distinctive patterns an American widow could comfortably assume in the past. Ritual is gone, as is the "wait five years" rule under which a widow did not remarry or even entertain men within five respectful years of a husband's death. Few women would welcome a return to those rituals. Although they provided security, they failed to include both a "rite of passage" (guided route) and "rights of passage" (permitted behavior) for widowed women to grow through widowhood *and beyond,* just as they failed to promote women's growth in other spheres.

Essentially, widowhood is a powerful role that makes one powerless. Widowed women lose status among their peers. Many complain of feeling "like a fifth wheel" in the company of other married people. Widowed men who are left with dependent children lose some of the power enjoyed by other men, for they have inherited a stereotypical "woman's role," an unpaid position less valued by the "real world" outside the home. Given a choice between child care and occupation outside the home, few men choose child care. And both widowed men and widowed women are powerless when they assume a negative identity ("I'm a widow") that elicits pity from others.

Whether marriage has provided a woman with her entire identity, a key component of it, or an excuse for never fully developing it, widowhood challenges her to construct her new personal identity. Women today have more freedom than previous generations to choose occupation and life-style, yet freedom alone provides no protection from the disequilibrium of widowhood. Action and activity are vital. No matter how many options are available to a widow, if she cannot (or will not) avail herself of them, they are worthless. A widow must allow herself to engage actively in new relationships rooted in the present, which will provide opportunities to see herself in a different, though at least equally illuminating, light than in the past. This is the foundation for moving through and beyond widowhood.

CHAPTER
4

Growing Through Widowhood
Encounter and Respondence

Those who cannot endure the bad will not live to see the good.

—YIDDISH PROVERB

Seen in its broadest perspective, bereavement is an adaptive process that is both a reaction (to the death of a spouse) and an action (a movement toward wholeness of being). Both the reaction to death and the movement toward wholeness are normal and healthy responses to the serious life crisis faced by widowed men and women. Bereavement is the period specifically devoted to the full expression of grief—a normal and healthy reaction to the loss of someone (and something) very important. The expression and dissipation of grief set the stage for the return to wholeness.

Soon after the death of their spouses, widowed people confront the contradiction posed by bereavement. On the one hand, life is apparently unchanged, consisting of many of the same routines, occupations, surroundings, and people as before. Yet it has changed dramatically, because the deceased spouse, and all that he or she represented, is gone. Early in bereavement numerous widows say, "I don't know *what* to believe anymore." The sameness of life can have a mocking quality, for it only looks the same as before. It feels very different. This contradiction early in bereavement is ultimately very confusing.

But there is hope. As one moves through bereavement, the disharmonious perception of sameness versus change lessens, because routines of day-to-day living gradually bring a new equilibrium. And as widowed men and women grow through bereavement, they realize that although life changed drastically at the death of the spouse and is still altered, it is today—right now—stable. This first recognition of equilibrium is an enormously important landmark. Providing the first sense of stability in what had been viewed as a tumultuous, confusing, and frightening world, it roots the widowed person more securely in the present. Living in a changed social environment that reflects a changed person back to the widowed individual provides the first reflection many receive of a new identity.

The feelings and experiences of widowed people as they proceed through bereavement are predictable. The most intense grief is usually experienced shortly after the death of one's spouse. While all of bereavement is marked by mourning, only early bereavement will bring intense numbness, denial, and anger. These are not normally experienced so powerfully later in bereavement. These predictable phenomena form fairly distinct stages in the transition through bereavement, although there is some overlap from stage to stage and the duration of each varies among individuals. Few people can clearly discern a formal beginning or end to each stage, especially while they are themselves bereaved.

Understanding stages of bereavement to be real transitions facilitates adaptation in two ways. First, it helps each person understand that what is happening is *normal*. Widowed men and women feel uncertain and at times frightened by the power of grief; unfamiliarly strong negative feelings like rage or revenge may enter their conscious minds. It is thus comforting to understand that such feelings are a predictable part of bereavement, and that they will lessen over time.

Second, the notion of stages of bereavement may help a widowed person to place him- or herself, gaining a perspective on grief. For example, a widow who is still experiencing numbness or depression after a year can consider her grief prolonged. Looking at bereavement as a stagewise progression can also give those who provide support and help to widowed people an indication of how the widowed move through bereavement, and when they should be encouraged to seek professional help.

STAGE 1
Encounter

Beginning with the death of the spouse, the first stage of bereavement is encounter, the initial confrontation with the new phase of life called widowhood. Encounter is characterized by emotions ranging from numbness to deep sadness to anger. Widowed men and women in encounter may experience depression, shock, rigidity, constant or frequent crying, rage, a desire for revenge, loss of appetite, or insomnia. They must be watched closely, especially if there are expressions of—or wishes for—self-destruction, perhaps wanting to "join" the deceased spouse. The importance of caregiving—watching carefully and sensitively over widowed men and women—cannot be overstated. While three months to one year is the commonly cited amount of time a widowed person needs to move beyond the most intense feelings of grief, there is really no rule of thumb that can suggest how long caregiving must continue. The first days and weeks are certainly critical times.

Shock, disbelief, and denial are characteristic feelings during this first stage, and they set in simultaneously with, or shortly following, the death of a spouse. Above all other sensations, numbness is the most frequently reported emotion (or absence of emotion) of the early encounter stage. Beginning when widowed people first learn of the death of their spouse, numbness can last from a few minutes or hours to a few days or weeks, depending upon the circumstances of death (such as whether it was anticipated or unexpected). Widowed women whose husbands die accidental (unexpected) deaths have initially stronger grief reactions than those whose husbands' deaths are due to illness (anticipated). On learning of the death of their spouse, both men's and women's reactions are marked by confusion, panic, denial, a lack of recall, and numbness:

> When the police came to tell me my husband had been killed, I screamed at them and tried to push them out of the house.

> Thank God the children were at school—I was a ranting madwoman! The next thing I knew I was crying at the hospital. I don't remember a thing after I pushed the police out my door.

> I was positive it was a mistake when the doctor told me they'd lost my wife. *How* can you "lose" somebody because of a routine operation—they do a million of those each year! I thought the doctors were simply *wrong*. They had the *wrong* woman, and they were telling the *wrong* husband!

> It was like I was suddenly turned into a robot. I felt nothing—like I had died. It was like a dream, and I actually kept pinching myself. He would soon be home from work and we'd have dinner, and we'd both laugh about my silly dream. God almighty, I knew it wasn't a dream . . . or *was it? Where* was my husband now that I needed him more than ever?

Attacks of panic, crying, and headaches are common, often continuing past the first days of numbness and sometimes past the first stage. Many widowed people are unable to read printed matter like newspapers or magazines, for concentration is impossible.

At or near the beginning of bereavement, most widowed people are zombies, unable to focus on television, conversation, reading, or normal activities that were once routine. The American Psychiatric Association calls this a part of "uncomplicated bereavement," the early, normal reaction to the death of a loved one, characterized by such symptoms as poor appetite, loss of weight, and insomnia.[1] Zombie behavior is—and should be—temporary:

> I thought I'd never smile again. For weeks I was a robot, just going through the motions. I forgot things very easily. When I was introduced to new people, I forgot their names as quickly as I was introduced.

> In the beginning, I was really a nitwit—no other word is as precise. I started cooking supper and would go off to another room. Next thing I knew, the pot was burned black and the kitchen was filled with smoke. I overfed the dog, forgot to pay the mortgage, and would confuse my children's names. All I remember was thinking about him from the moment I got up until the minute I went to sleep.

> Being a widow was six months of "space-cadet training" for me. I was an absolute ninny, like that character Amelia Bedelia, the one in kids' books where they tell her to sow the seeds and she takes out a needle and thread to "sew" them! Words didn't mean much to me; people would talk and I'd agree, and they'd think I was really listening. But I wasn't. I was just being polite.

Gradually, as encounter proceeds, the reality of the loss begins to penetrate, which can result in an obsession with the deceased spouse. It is not unheard of for widows to spend all their waking hours preoccupied by thoughts of the deceased; this can carry over to dreams. For those who are not obsessed, thoughts of the deceased occur frequently. Some widows' preoccupation is so intense that they attach meaning to events that at other times would have had no special significance. For example, a few widows recalled violent thunderstorms the nights their spouses died, briefly wondering if there was some "meaning" to those natural events. Some surviving spouses try to continue communicating, interpreting natural phenomena as "signs" that the deceased was "watching" or dwelling nearby, absent yet somehow present. Other widows describe seeing men who resembled their spouses, restraining—with great effort—a desire to confront the stranger.

A health checkup is vital as soon as possible following the death of the spouse. The physician is a potential source of valuable support, one who can help the widow understand which physical symptoms are normal and which are not. (Physicians have an especially crucial role when extreme reactions to the death of a spouse are considered: There is evidence that physicians tend to be the helping professional most likely to be seen by potential suicide victims, and other evidence shows that suicidal patients will admit their intentions if asked by the physician.[2]) In fact, all helping professionals and volunteers who work with widowed people should as a matter of course encourage and direct widowed men and women to see a physician for a checkup.

During encounter, widowed men and women (who do not yet see themselves as "single" adults) may perform certain behaviors out of habit, as a way of resisting the disequilibrium that has marked their lives. Numerous widows I interviewed said they continued to cook the same amounts of food as before, and some continued to launder the clothes of their deceased spouse ("They were getting so dusty in his closet"). Others set the table as they had done before their spouses died; one man told me how he kept picking up the phone at work to call his wife, automatically dialing their number before remembering she had died. Some widows attempted to do jobs around the house formerly done by their spouses, not only because those jobs had to be done, but as ways of helping them avoid the reality that the spouse was indeed gone. Sometimes, widows worked especially hard to maintain personal equilibrium through the illusion of domestic stability. I was no exception.

After my wife died I spent great amounts of energy trying to keep things as they were, and this included keeping the house in pristine order, despite the fact that there was only one person now to do it instead of two. One night shortly after my wife died I noticed how dirty the kitchen floor had become. Reacting ("it never looked like this before"), I washed it. When finished, I scrubbed it again with a brush, and then scraped the floor with a razor blade to remove tiny bits of who-knows-what. Last, I dried it with clean bath towels (who's to complain? I did all the laundry), before finally waxing the floor. Finding nothing but test patterns on Vermont television at four o'clock in the morning, I then collapsed on the sofa.

During encounter, widows may psychologically "fuse" their individual identities to their marriage identities. Even though illusory, retaining the marriage identity can be comforting as it permits the widow to continue to perform *as if still married*. It serves to bolster the widow temporarily, like a bumper jack holding a car for a tire change, until she has moved further in the reformulation of her personal identity. The degree of fusion of widowed men's personal and marital identities is often unclear, because men define and speak of themselves primarily in terms of occupational status instead of their marriage relationships. In addition, their sometimes-marked dependence can be confused with marital closeness.

Fusion allows the widow to postpone addressing the "Who am I?" question. Indeed it prevents that question from fully crystallizing because the fused identity is so powerful that there is no need yet for the widow to fully acknowledge her new status as a single woman. It is not uncommon for widowed women in encounter to speak of their spouses in the present tense, for example, "Harold hates when I go off on tangents like this!"

Widowed women (and sometimes widowed men) show a close identification with the deceased spouse by occupying their spouse's place in bed, taking over his or her seat at the dining table, wearing the spouse's wedding band, or performing roles formerly done by the deceased spouse. Widowed people will defend this behavior by saying, "I couldn't *bear* to stare at his empty seat!". Others make no effort to deny the continuing close identification: British researcher Colin Parkes quoted one widow who claimed, "My husband's in me, right through and through. I feel him in me doing everything." Fusing one's personality to, or closely identifying, with the deceased spouse is part of an "equally mystifying . . . loss of self which is reported by many widows."[3]

American researchers have also reported a type of lifelong fusion: an ongoing experience of spouse "presence" and an emotional identification with the dead husband that some women continued for years after they became widowed.[4] Ninety percent of young and middle-aged Japanese widows whose husbands died in motor vehicle accidents reported a sense of the deceased husband's presence,[5] while 80 percent of a group of British widows younger than sixty years of age (who had lost husbands through various causes) reported sensing the presence of the deceased,[6] as did half of an earlier sample of seventy-two younger British widows.[7]

Through the early days and weeks of bereavement, some widowed men and women engage in an intense form of pining for the deceased spouse. Widowed men and women told me how they acted on this by going to the cemetery, feeling comfort there (despite the intense grief they also experienced), and still others set up a regular schedule of visits to the cemetery, to pray over—and be near—their deceased spouse.

After the death of a spouse, widowed men and women are driven by the urge to recover the lost "love object," which is characteristic of all human grief. Some will engage in "searching" behavior, emotionally seeking the lost spouse for up to one year following the death.[8] In addition to the cemetery, widowed people can be drawn to visit other places that—to an observer—have no logical purpose. Yet searching can provide the widow with temporarily comforting ties to the life that once was: a college, church, beach, store, city where they first met, or a bar where they first drank with each other. Physical objects, too, can provide those ties, including clothing, books, toiletries, jewelry, and possessions favored by the deceased spouse. People (especially children) can become treasured "objects" because of a favored status they enjoyed with the deceased. Searching behavior can also lead widowed men and women to identify characteristics in other living persons that remind them of their spouses. Because the widowed person is preoccupied by the memory of the lost spouse, he engages in a sort of mental "matching game," noticing a gesture, a glance, a speech defect, a precisely correct hair color or style, or even a twinkle in the eye of someone else that evokes a mental image of the deceased spouse.

> A strange thing used to happen whenever I'd go out shopping or to the city—I'd see a man, and something about him reminded me exactly of my husband! If I ever met that person, I was always disappointed, because it would dawn on me that it *wasn't* really him.

Since they are still trying to make some sense of what has happened, it is not unusual during encounter for widowed men or women mentally to reexperience the circumstances and events surrounding the death of the spouse.

Although fusion fades near the conclusion of encounter, searching may continue through the next stage, because the utterness of death cannot be rapidly internalized by the widowed man or woman. But as bereavement progresses, the widowed person will gradually internalize the death of the spouse, and over the first months of bereavement the deceased spouse's presence will gradually fade, replaced by the demands, tasks, and enjoyments of present life.

Over two thousand years ago, the Chinese philosopher Confucius said: "Let the mourning stop when one's grief is fully expressed." Bereavement cannot be assigned a specific amount of time. Yet for some depressed widowed men and women, the grief is never fully expressed, and the mourning does not stop. Although most widowed people eventually come through bereavement and resume living productive and satisfying lives, some widowed men and women experience such prolonged or severe grief reactions—like depression—that therapy is indicated. Caregivers must be especially attuned to signs of severe or long-standing depression and deep distress in widowed women and men and arrange for appropriate professional therapeutic intervention.

Depression, which affects over ten million Americans each year, is not a sign of weak willpower, nor is it a hopeless condition. According to Lewis L. Judd, director of the National Institute of Mental Health, depression is "a real disease, just as a heart attack is real." Although the disease may be hard for individuals to distinguish from the normal sadness of bereavement, Judd suggests that the duration and severity of the symptoms should guide one in seeking the help of a professional. The symptoms of depression include a mood that is persistently sad, anxious, or "empty"; a feeling of loss of life satisfaction, pessimism, or hopelessness; feelings of guilt, helplessness, or worthlessness; an inability to give or accept affection; a loss of interest in daily activities including sex; waking early, oversleeping, or insomnia; a gain in weight or change in appetite; physical symptoms including pains, extended crying, hyperactivity, irritability, or restlessness; low levels of energy, slowed thinking, or fatigue; an inability to concentrate, decide, or remember; or thoughts of suicide or death.[9]

How serious should depression be before a widowed man or woman seeks help? While even professionals may not always agree, Dr. Judd advises that if one suffers from four or more of the symptoms of depression for longer than two weeks, one may be depressed and in need of professional intervention. Even if one's symptoms seem vague or transient, if one is uncertain whether or not one is "really" depressed, it is better to talk to a professional. Widowed people may not be aware that they are experiencing symptoms of depression. Thus, it behooves caregiving family and friends to be alert and to take action without delay.

Further complicating the picture is the tendency for the widowed man or woman in encounter to *appear* to be doing well after the initial impact of the death of a spouse and following the funeral or memorial service. This makes it more likely for others to miss signs of depression. Unfortunately, friends and family usually rely on outward signs of restoration of stability: returning to work and resuming old eating, dressing, or socializing habits that—when viewed by themselves—can be misleading signs of "progress" on the part of the widowed person. They fail to reveal the continuation of grief that comes from the sense of lost identity. Spending time with—and listening to—the bereaved person can be the most significant caregiving.

Depression differs from grief because the latter is a realistic reaction to the loss of the person and the relationship. Grief is normal when it is proportionate to the loss, while depression is "a morbid sadness, dejection, or melancholy" that is out of proportion to the loss.[10] In addition, "in grief reactions there is not the loss of self-esteem commonly found in most clinical depressions."[11] There are at least two "scenarios" where self-esteem can be affected in widowhood, causing grief to turn "disproportionate" to the loss.

First is the crisis of identity discussed earlier, which confronts some widowed people beginning and during the encounter stage. Grief can intensify as the widow begins asking the now-more-urgent question of "Who am I?" a question that cannot be satisfactorily answered during the first stage because there is not yet a clearly perceived replacement for the marital identity. Especially for a widow whose personal identity has been closely bound up with her marital identity, it is not a simple matter to separate the two and rapidly "become" an unmarried, single woman. If the widowed man or woman urgently presses the question of "Who am I?" it may be immediately answered by the reply, "I'm a nothing." The great gaping hole that was a husband or wife can almost be tangible, and grief can intensify. Therefore, holding on to the marital identity through the role of widow may be the least threatening and best choice for the newly widowed person. Until the question of one's new identity can be answered, the negative identity provided by "I'm a widow" is better than having no identity at all.

The normal, healthy reaction to the death of a spouse should be "I have lost both my spouse and the relationship that meant so much to me. But I cannot permit this loss to overwhelm my life, for I will compensate for that loss, even if it takes much time and effort." Depression can arise when the statement becomes: "I have lost both my spouse and the relationship that meant so much to me. I have lost everything and therefore have little or nothing left."

Another source of depression during bereavement can be anger. Thoughts of sadness and longing are normal to all widowed men and women, but they may become overwhelming, giving rise to feelings of deeper regret, self-blame, longing, sadness, and ultimately to anger, which is common in the first stage of bereavement. Those who have examined human bereavement reactions in different societies have noticed how universal a reaction anger is.[12]

Although anger may be a common reaction early in bereavement, its expression can be startling to the nonbereaved, because anger—seen by itself—is usually considered a uniformly destructive emotion. A newly widowed woman told me how horrified her sister became upon hearing her say, "I'm so angry that he left me all alone! If he was here now, I'd really let him have it!" Other widowed people verified how widespread anger was in their early grief:

> When I first heard about my husband's death I was more angry than numb. "How could you do this to me?" I kept asking him. "How could you leave me alone with the kids, this house, your stupid truck, and your damned relatives?" I thought it was a real dirty trick for him to leave me.

> I stayed up for nights and nights. Nothing helped. I took walks, I cleaned the house until I collapsed, I baked I-don't-know-how-many coffee rings and put them in the freezer. But I was *mad* as I did all these things. And I knew I was mad at him for leaving me. As I rolled out dough, I pressed so hard my hands kept going through it I was so angry. Even the way I walked, it was like I was getting ready to clobber someone.

> I was the nastiest SOB you could find for days. I still have half my family either mad at me or afraid of me! I snapped at them when they tried to comfort me, and I dumped a whole bottle of Scotch they were drinkin' down the drain. They had some nerve sitting there drinkin' while my husband was lyin' there dead!

While it is true that destructive behavior sometimes accompanies verbal expressions of anger, verbal expressions by themselves are not necessarily destructive in the early bereavement of widowed men and women, and they do not necessarily predict destructive behavior. Expressions of anger may serve a healthy purpose if the bereaved is allowed to acknowledge her feelings and receive acceptance and reassurance that they are normal and do not reflect badly on her.

But anger must dissipate as bereavement continues. Dissipation usually comes about through a refocusing of energy on a constructive endeavor. If negative feelings do not dissipate over time, widowed men or women may become angry at their inability to stop feeling bad and angry at their lack of control over their situation—angry, ultimately, at themselves.

When anger is turned inward, it results in depression. Women may be more susceptible to this type of depression, reinforced by a lifelong pattern of considering the expression of anger inappropriate and unfeminine, a sign of moral or psychological inadequacy. Feeling both hostility toward and love for the deceased spouse, a widow may feel guilty about her hostile impulses and turn them inward, saying in effect, "I hate not my deceased spouse but myself; I am a bad person and do not deserve the esteem of others." Combined with an uncertain identity, this can plunge widows into deep depression.

While both widows and widowers may turn anger inward, the result is different: for women introjected anger will tend to result in depression, while for men introjected anger will tend to result in self-abuse or self-destruction. For men aggressive behavior—inner or outer directed—is almost characteristic of Western civilization. Indeed, it is not a threat to a man's sense of masculinity to act out anger by engaging in violent acts. Unfortunately, the individual price paid for this is high: It accounts for part of the exceptionally higher violent crime and suicide rate among men, and a high suicide rate among widowed men in particular. Anger directed at others does not necessarily preclude it from being self-directed, as seen in prison suicides and suicide attempts.

One of the problems facing bereavement counselors and others who would help widowed men and women is deciding how much depression is normal in widowhood and how serious it must be before being treated. It is almost obvious that a man or woman whose spouse has died will experience grief. But the fact that grief is experienced by all widowed people should not lull us into confusing *common* with *normal* or *acceptable*. When grief continues, or is so strong that it interferes with the widowed man or woman's daily living and normal relationships, it is time for intervention. Extreme (severe) or chronic (enduring) grief does not "go away" by itself. But there is hope for depression that is treated. Approximately 90 percent of depressed patients recover when treated. Without treatment, depression can go on for a long time, sometimes ending, unfortunately, only with the death of the grief-stricken person.

Emile Durkheim attributed suicides occurring during the crisis of widowhood to the "domestic anomie" resulting from the death of a spouse, which in turn results in "less resistance to suicide."[13] Durkheim's "anomie" refers to alienation and personal disorganization, a precipitator of suicide. This is not to suggest that widowhood inevitably leads to a predisposition toward suicide, yet feelings of loss can be so overpowering that depression may become severe. Indeed, widowed men and women (especially younger widowed men) are at greater risk of physical illness, suicide, and early death.[14] Throughout the bereavement process, and most notably during encounter when grief is usually most intense, the heightened risks to widowed people are formidable. About five days after my wife died, and while I was still quite numb, deep in that numbness I briefly contemplated suicide. Fortunately, the feelings soon dissipated; I remember hearing one of my sleeping daughters call out from upstairs for a glass of water as I buried my face in the sofa cushion. I got up to give her water.

Sometimes the feelings do not dissipate. Dr. Edwin Shneidman, founder of the American Association of Suicidology, identified the following characteristics common to people who are likely to commit suicide: (1) a feeling of unendurable psychological pain; (2) a sense of frustrated psychological needs for security, achievement, trust, and friendship; (3) seeking a solution to a life crisis; (4) attempting to end consciousness and stop awareness of the pain in one's life; (5) feeling helpless and hopeless; (6) perceiving limited options; (7) equivocating—being ambivalent, even over suicide itself; (8) communicating intent to others (four out of five suicidal people give clear clues); (9) previous escaping behavior; and (10) demonstrating lifelong coping patterns consisting of "previous episodes of disturbances . . . the person's way of enduring psychological pain and to a penchant for constricted 'either-or' thinking." Shneidman emphasizes the importance of familiarizing ourselves with this information, noting that general public and professional "awareness of the suicidal ways of thinking may be the most effective suicide prevention."[15]

While a fleeting thought of self-destruction is not unusual in the grief that accompanies early bereavement, it should not be lightly regarded or dismissed. *All* thoughts or feelings about suicide should be discussed with a friend, a relative, a doctor, or other professional or confidant. A widowed person's expressions of self-destruction should be taken seriously. Thoughts of suicide sometimes do not "just go away" or disappear by themselves. For those who cannot turn to friends or family to assist them in seeking professional help, there are toll-free numbers (sometimes called suicide hot lines), and the state department of health or mental health may have one as well. If none of these is available, hospitals and police departments have specially trained professionals who can listen and give advice. Again, if widowed people have thoughts of suicide, they need to *talk* to someone and get help. A friend or neighbor can be helpful by providing empathic reassurance that life gets better no matter how bad one feels.

STAGE 2
Respondence

During encounter the widowed person's behavior is essentially passive: He or she receives the blow dealt by the death. It is primarily a time of impact and immediate, often instinctive, reactions to the blow (sometimes these are life-threatening reactions). As numbness fades, the widowed person begins the first coherent responses to what has happened. This next phase, respondence, is characterized by more active and thoughtful response to the death of a spouse. Respondence marks the beginning of separation of the widowed person's personal identity from the marital identity. In sum, the difference between encounter and respondence is one of degree of active response and comprehension of what has happened. Together, encounter and respondence comprise the widowed person's painful confrontation with—and response to—the movement through widowhood.

In this second stage of grief, as the protection provided by numbness gradually wears off, the reality of being a not-married, widowed adult creeps in—slowly, because widowed men and women who valued their marital identity have great difficulty this soon in the grief process seeing themselves as a single man or single woman. At the beginning of respondence, widowed persons begin responding to and interacting with other people and events, gradually moving away from their obsession with the past in general and with "that day" in particular. But some reactions and feelings continue from the first stage, including an inability to sleep or concentrate, absent-minded behavior, sensations including restlessness, lethargy, hypersensitivity, desperation, and for some a continuation of numbness and shock. There is a growing awareness that the spouse's death is real, permanent, and irreversible. Since numbness has gradually dissipated (though it may not have fully disappeared), feelings and sensations are reemerging, no longer dulled by the shock and impact of encounter. The growing understanding that death has occurred moves the key question from "What happened?" to the more wrenching and plaintive: "Why did this happen to *me*?"

Seeking an answer to that question may arouse other troubling emotions. As during encounter, the widow can experience feelings of anger. Restraining herself from directing them at her deceased spouse for leaving her, she will feel guilty, possibly directing the hostility toward herself, which will result in depression. Or depression can arise when anger is initially self-directed, when the widow blames herself for the death, perhaps because she failed to take some action (seeing a doctor in time, making him take his pills, and so on) that might have prevented the death. Additionally, widows may compare themselves to other women whose husbands are alive and healthy, and conclude that—since they are widowed—they are "losers": One woman told me at a conference, "Everything I touch turns to crap anyway."

A widow may face additional problems that will magnify this sense of identity loss. As she comes out of the initial numbness and begins to reflect on her loss, she may regard her grief reactions (even those so obviously normal as crying) as signs of weakness. If she lives among people who prize unemotionality, she may consider her grief reactions to be "abnormal," conclusive proof that she is "nothing without her spouse." If she has never before experienced grief this strong, she may be frightened by its intensity and persistence.

Perhaps while she was married her spouse was uncomfortable when she cried. Not knowing how to react to her expressions of emotion, he may have asked her to stop, or he may have disdained her "lack of self-control." Or she may have been made to feel silly—that she was crying over nothing, fretting over something insignificant.

In support-group meetings of widowed persons, recently widowed women (who assuredly have something to cry about) may apologize as their voices break, unable to continue speaking. Emotion may be filled with self-castigation ("I *hate* when I do this!"). Others reveal that their self-punitive attitude had been reinforced by their spouses: "My husband always said I loved to cry." I remember one elderly woman reproaching herself, shaking her head as tears came to her eyes: "Look at me. Sixty-eight years old and crying like a baby!"

Respondence can be the most emotionally painful phase of widowhood, because the earlier numbness of encounter no longer protects widowed people from the pain of loss. Without the protection of numbness, respondence is an intensely turbulent phase of widowhood. The wrenching experience of grief felt during early bereavement can be especially devastating because it heightens a sense of helplessness; it illustrates our lack of full control over life and leads to feelings of despair. Respondence is also painful because we are fully confronting the personal needs that are now unmet: needs for attachment, social integration, nurturance, alliance, guidance, and reassurance of worth that the widowed person once derived from the marriage relationship.[16] Ultimately, the sense of helplessness coupled with the unmet needs results in an overwhelming sense of loneliness—loneliness that the widowed person still believes can be relieved by only one person, who is no longer alive.

Typically, widowed people experience ups and downs during respondence, feeling that just when they have noticed some progress, all of a sudden things begin to go badly again. This phenomenon continues into the next stage, with some widows comparing it to "riding a roller coaster," because of swings of emotion and moving back and forth between the "me" and the "us." Insomnia is not uncommon; a series of naps or short, unsatisfying periods of sleep substitute for what was formerly a full night's rest:

> I came home from work exhausted, but I still couldn't sleep at night. I wound up asking the doctor for pills to help me sleep. They helped but I woke up with a hangover in the morning.

> At the slightest sound outside on the street I woke up. I didn't just wake up, though. I *bolted* up even if it was just the cat jumping on my bed. I expected to see Will next to

me or somewhere in the house. Then it would hit me that he was gone. This happened almost every night for months.

Hypersensitivity may emerge, too, in seemingly bizarre or irrational, overreactive behavior in the course of routine activities.

About three weeks after my wife died, I stood in line at a busy supermarket with about eight items to buy. As is usually the case in busy supermarkets, the lines leading to the cashier were not well-defined, and as I stood holding my red plastic basket, a woman with a shopping cart full of food and kids pushed in front of me, brushing me back. Silently I stared at her, and she snapped at me, "*I* was next!" I shrugged my shoulders. "No problem," I said, backing off. As she began to pile her things on the conveyer, I stood there silent as tears came to my eyes. I didn't move; I was angry as hell. . . . How selfish that woman was to do that to me! As if to insulate myself from her, I turned to the person behind me and said, "Go ahead—I'm waiting for someone" (no lie there!). I let the next person ahead, too, and the next one as well. One by one the line moved around me until I stood at the end. Finally, I turned and replaced each of my eight items on the shelves and walked out.

When I related this incident to other widowed people, they identified incidents in their bereavement that were similar to my highly emotional reaction to what is to a nonbereaved person just a routine confrontation of daily life: One widow told me how she panicked and burst into tears after her car was stopped by police for an expired inspection sticker. During respondence, widowed men and women focus more closely on their life and environment, observing events and actions more closely than before. Widows who earlier accepted "fate" now begin to question it. Along with a heightened awareness of the fragility of life, the widow's own sense of vulnerability increases, too. Many leftover emotions and experiences from encounter continue, permeating the respondence stage, including periods of anger, loneliness, a reliving of the circumstances of the spouse's death ("It plays and replays over and over again in my mind like an endless videotape," said one widow).

One of the factors making respondence a particularly difficult phase is the change in behavior of those who previously supported the widowed man or woman. Relatives and friends begin to think that "he's okay now," or "she's over the worst of it," and the calls, invitations to dinner, and attention begin to drop off, especially if the widow appears to be doing well. This is the second time support drops off: The first time is a few days after the death of a spouse when the widow or widower's entire social circle has descended on the house. Within one week (usually corresponding to the end of the funeral service or Jewish *shivah* period), that highly focused and widespread attention drops off, leaving a circle of relatives and perhaps a few close friends. But in respondence, the intensity of focused support shrinks again, leaving those widowed men and women who have no close personal friends with no regular caring contact. This is the time social isolation can set in, especially for elderly widowed people.

Widowed people with close personal relationships can find a curious role reversal taking place at this time: Believing that the widow is over the worst of it, family or friends may lean on the widow, who then finds herself in the role of supporter:

> At one point I began to wonder, "Who is helping whom?" I mean, it seemed like *I* was the one constantly trying to make *everybody else* feel comfortable whenever they tried to comfort me! "Oh, don't worry about me, I'm fine," I would say, knowing fully well that I wasn't. My family tried to help me, but my sister would just burst out in tears whenever she saw me, and I'd wind up reassuring *her,* even though *I* was dying inside!

Respondence is the time when most begin to reach out, however tentatively, to the world again. Interest in joining a support group heightens, fortunately synchronized with the drop-off in support from family and friends. While some widows in the encounter stage attend support groups and find them valuable, most are still too numb to be able to listen to and profit from sharing another widow's story. Widows who seemed to profit most from support self-help groups were those who began attending no earlier than the respondence stage of grief:

> Going to the THEOS group was the best thing I ever did after my husband died. At first I didn't want to go, so I kind of sat in the back. No one made me participate, which is why I came back. The group discussed things, some people

cried, but the best part was that they *laughed* sometimes. Can you imagine how good it felt to be able to *laugh* again?

During respondence, the widow engages in spouse sanctification, idealizing the image of the deceased spouse in her memory. Sanctification is a vital step in the bereavement process, because it permits the widow's previously fused identity to become separated. Sanctification initiates a separation that is both comfortable and safe, because by elevating his memory to near or total perfection, the widow is not "casting off" her spouse. Widows who say they have had unsatisfactory marriages are less likely to engage in sanctification of their deceased spouses than those who have had fulfilling marriages and strongly positive memories. For some, sanctification is transitory and hardly noticed, while for others it is a consuming, passionate undertaking that may mark the beginning of sealing themselves off from any future romantic involvements.

When it does not become so extreme, sanctification is not the unhealthy or trivial activity that others may consider it. On the contrary, sanctification can facilitate movement through widowhood. Practically, it provides the widow with a respite, allowing her to go about her business by moving the deceased to "an other-worldly position as an understanding and purified distant observer."[17] The widow is testifying to the goodness not only of her husband but of herself in choosing him.

Sanctification serves as an emotional milestone for the widow, for it opens the way to eventual acceptance of her spouse's death. Although it does not signal her arrival as an unmarried adult, it allows the widow to justify pursuing her own interests because her spouse has gone on to a larger, better, or simply another level of existence. Ultimately, the widow takes comfort in feeling that her spouse is not only not suffering but is in fact "sainted."

However, like widowhood and bereavement, santification should be a temporary phase, not a way of life. Once the image of the deceased spouse becomes more distant, the widow should refocus on her present life. If sanctification is prolonged it can become "canonization," which can immobilize the widow, making her unable to move ahead with personal identity reformulation.

Canonization involves extreme attention and devotion to the deceased and his memory. Some widows attend church twice a day, performing rituals such as avidly lighting candles *to* (not *for*) the deceased spouse. I noticed more extreme behavior as well. In her home one widow proudly showed me her "basilica": Her deceased spouse's bedside night table and dresser had been turned into altars, complete with an array of photographs, candles, mementos, ribbons, medals, and personal effects like wallet and keys. "It is just the way he left it," she proclaimed proudly.

> In our support group there's this widow who is obsessed with her husband! All she talks about is how much they adored each other before he died. I worry about her sometimes.

> After being widowed for exactly one year, I went back to the cemetery. But this time things felt better. I knew he was at peace, and I stopped pleading with him to take me, too. I never told anybody this because they'd think I was crazy. But I used to pray to him every day. I still do once in a while, but if I miss a day I don't go to pieces like I used to. It was like a mortal sin.

> My poor children! They put up with me so patiently after their father died. I was a wreck, constantly after them telling them "not to touch" this, and "keep away from" that. If they so much as went near something that he owned, I'd go crazy. The house was like a museum . . . nobody could sit in "his" chair, and it even bothered me when they sat on the side of the sofa he liked, and crossed their legs just like him.

What can make sanctification turn into canonization (and thus turn unhealthy) is if it is so severe or long standing that the widow is obsessed, directing her energy toward an activity that can provide little ongoing fulfillment. As "a religion of one," it is a pretty lonely religion. Canonization robs a widow of time and energy that could otherwise be devoted to activities that can provide reciprocal rewards. A living human being can smile and say thanks for kind words, help, or a joke, but a deceased person's jewelry just sits there.

Canonization is also a barrier to future romantic involvement. As described by one man seeking to begin a relationship with a canonizing widow: "Her attitude seems to be, 'See if you can possibly make me like you—I doubt that you can, but I dare you to try.' "[18] Even attempts at nonromantic friendships can be difficult because of the "no one can compare with her/him," attitude that is part of canonization. As a result, widows can be sealed off from new relationships. For some the isolation is temporary, for others, permanent.

There are canonizers who manifest their continued focus on their deceased spouses by actively seeking in others specific qualities their spouses possessed. They evaluate others by the ways in which they are similar to or different from their deceased spouses.

Thus, a widower may regard a new woman in his life simply as one who is "not my wife," instead of a new person with her own unique qualities. And for the duration of his canonization, no other person can be "my wife," because *my wife* describes only one very specific set of characteristics: weight, height, skin color, personality, and intelligence. From the most minute to the largest detail, the new friend is compared to his deceased spouse. One widowed man I met actually wrote a list of qualities he sought in a wife. Neatly typed on a slip of white paper, he proudly showed it to me while we listened to a speaker discuss remarriage after widowhood. He wasn't too choosy, for there were "only forty-one qualities" that his ideal woman needed to possess. Coincidentally, his first wife happened to have possessed all forty-one of those qualities. To canonizers like my list-making friend, the comparison is always to the disadvantage of the newcomer, because "no one could compare to Helen":

> This sounds ridiculous but each night I'd take my wife's coat out of her closet and sniff the collar. I could smell her hairspray and perfume on it, and it made me feel better. I pitied women who didn't use the same hairspray, and all other women smelled like they had cheap perfume on. I mean, it was very strange, but it helped in the beginning. If I'd lost her coat or somebody took it from me, I would've been unable to go to sleep at night.

> Once, I went through the Sears Catalog—the one called "The Wish Book"—and picked out the men who looked the most like Bob, and the ones who smiled like Bob! I had this idea that I would write to Sears to find out the names of their

> models, because there was also this one guy in their "Big and Tall Catalog" that looked *exactly*—and I mean "exactly"—like Bob! Talk about wishes! All I wanted for Christmas was Bob. But I'd settle for the next closest Bob Sears could send me!

Almost completely opposite to the style of canonization, some widowed people submerge any feelings of sanctification, and—driven by intense loneliness—seek a replacement for their absent spouse with amazing rapidity following the death. They latch onto others with a tenacity and grip that resembles the behavior of a voracious barracuda:

> I got married three months after my husband died. It was the worst mistake of my life, because my new husband just used me. He thought I was rich; boy, was he in for a big surprise! Why did I get remarried so quickly? I was lonely. Very lonely. We got divorced six months later. He still thinks I hid my money before we got married! What a jerk!

> After my wife died—and this is the God's honest truth—I used to pick up women at the Post [local singles bar]. If I went home alone, I went crazy all night long. I must've had sex with thirty different women before six months went by. After that, I just answered the personal ads in the *Voice* [a newspaper], and met I-don't-know-how-many-more women that way. I couldn't get enough, but I never stuck with anybody more than one night. This lasted almost a year, and then I got married. I got sick of all the one-night stands. But I didn't lie—I used to tell all of them that I was a widower, and that I was "sex-starved." It worked, I guess.

> All of my friends were divorced, so I used to go out with them. We'd go dancing, and every time I danced with a guy I felt guilty. Like I was torn. I didn't want him to let go of me, but at the same time his arms and all just didn't feel "right." I was forty, and I felt like I was over the hill, so to speak. And I was so hungry for someone to care about me that I just wasn't very particular. You're a widower. You know what it's like to be lonely, don't you?

The few widowed men and women who become barracudas are avoiding the natural grief process, seeking a replacement rather than a relationship, trying to avoid the reality that growing beyond widowhood cannot be avoided through substitute relationships. Widows who remarry do so within a median period of approximately four years following the death of a spouse (compared to approximately three years for divorced women).[19] But there is no correct amount of time that must pass before a widow or widower should remarry. In the United States there are two million remarried women who were once widows, and almost half remarried within three years of the death of their previous spouse. However, there are no indications that these remarriages are better or worse than those made after three years have passed. While conventional wisdom counsels widowed people to avoid hasty remarriage,[20] clearly one's reasons for remarrying are more critical to successful remarriage than the mere amount of time between widowhood and remarriage. If the primary reason for remarrying is to secure a substitute for one's missing spouse, that marriage will probably not flourish regardless of the number of years that may have passed since the previous spouse died.

The key to moving through respondence comes with the widowed person's understanding that holding on to the past must give way to living in the present. This cannot simply be "told" to the widowed person—it must be personally experienced. Nor can moving through respondence be left to the passage of time, for time by itself does not heal. Instead, the widowed person's understanding must derive from concrete experiences of satisfying human interaction. The majority of widowed women I interviewed felt that other people—family, friends, children, or neighbors—were "most important" in helping them survive since their husband's death. While simply "being there" is important advice for those who wish to help the widowed person in encounter, the widowed person in respondence needs more active social support. That support should be aimed at meeting needs for attachment, social integration, nurturance, alliance, guidance, and reassurance of worth. Although other individuals cannot replace the lost spouse or meet the widow's needs in exactly the same way, they can meet at least some needs, providing limited but vital respite from the pain. That temporary reprieve can initially bolster the widow, gradually evolving into a more consistent source of support. A widow's loneliness, caused in part by her unmet needs for attachment and reassurance of her worth, can be counteracted by her active involvement in a stable family that loves her. Although family membership cannot provide the especially intense attachment or reassurance of unique worth provided by a marriage relationship, family members can help meet needs that are otherwise unmet.

There is perhaps a "hidden potential" in the pain of respondence: Through needs that are being met in new relationships or activities, the widowed person may discover others that were never (or only poorly) met during marriage. Although respondence is usually too soon for the widowed person to acknowledge new relationships as being "better than" or more fulfilling than the past marriage, those new relationship(s) can become a foundation for a new, different life that may promise even greater fulfillment of personal needs than did the past life.

As I said earlier, moving through respondence is not simple: The widow or widower may find it more challenging to meet personal needs through concrete experiences than to face the external problems of daily living. But as difficult as it may be, moving through the beginning stages of encounter and respondence is an accomplishment that can help widowed men and women realize that successful movement beyond widowhood is possible. After encounter and respondence, the worst is over. Despite all the moments of grief and discouragement they have experienced, widowed people begin to gain momentum, enabling them to continue moving through bereavement, because small changes soon reveal more growth and life satisfaction.

CHAPTER 5

Growing Beyond Widowhood

Emergence and Transformation

The strongest principle of growth lies in human choice.

—GEORGE ELIOT

After the intense grief of respondence has dissipated, the energy and attention formerly focused on the deceased spouse become redirected toward the present, and the widowed person begins to move toward a fullness of being. The movement beyond widowhood holds a new set of challenges and uncertain times for widowed people. Following the death of her husband, Franklin D. Roosevelt, Eleanor Roosevelt described her apprehension as a newly widowed woman:

> I rode down in the old cagelike White House elevator that April morning of 1945 with a feeling of melancholy and, I suppose, something of uncertainty because I was saying good-by to an unforgettable era and I really had given very little thought to the fact that from this day forward I would be on my own. I realized that in the future there would be many important changes in my way of living but I had long since realized that life is made up of a series of adjustments.[1]

Obviously, some widows are set apart from most by wealth and social position. Nevertheless, they experience most of the same difficulties, sadnesses, and disequilibrium as do less prominent widowed women. Whatever a woman's fame, fortune, or social position, she will experience bereavement when her husband dies, and she will be challenged to grow through widowhood. As Eleanor Roosevelt left the White House for the last time following her husband's death, she said, "I had to face the future as countless other women have faced it without their husbands,"[2] And Jehan Sadat expressed what could be echoed by millions of widowed women:

> I wore only black, and when the traditional period of mourning ended, after a year, I continued to wear black. Every morning when I opened my closet I saw nothing but black and felt nothing but black. I had no desire to put on colors, to wear jewelry or makeup. Some women can just snap their fingers and say that their period of mourning is finished. But I could not. Something inside of me had died.[3]

Yet the pain of being widowed has not prevented some notable women from embarking on productive careers following the death of their prominent spouses. For example, Mme. Sadat, the widow of President Anwar Sadat of Egypt, turned her attention from the assassination of her husband to study for a Ph.D. in literary criticism. Corazon Aquino ran successfully for the presidency of the Philippines following the assassination of her husband. Other widowed women take on unfinished business begun by their famous spouses. Coretta Scott King, Bess Truman, Muriel Humphrey, "Lady Bird" Johnson, and Rose Kennedy each continued in some way the work of their husbands.

While economic or social advantage can affect the circumstances of moving beyond widowhood, such movement is by no means limited to the rich or the famous. The way widowed women and men define or interpret the fact that their spouse is gone from their lives determines how quickly and how satisfactorily they will grow through and beyond widowhood. For example, a widow who views her husband's death only as a personal rejection—even if it was a freak accident that took his life—will have a more difficult time returning to wholeness than a woman who more realistically views her husband's death as the unfortunate result of an accident or illness. A widower who sees his wife's death as a form of punishment or retribution may continue to live a guilty and repentant life. Only when the death of a spouse is understood as an event that is now completely part of the past can the widowed person truly move beyond it.

STAGE 3
Emergence

Stage 3, emergence, is the central goal of bereavement: It is the end of mourning, and it signals the beginning of the growth beyond widowhood.

Questions from the previous stages ("Did this really happen?" or, "Why has this happened to me?") may still be only partially answered. Yet during emergence the widow turns toward a more focused consideration of her future, drawing on the past and present to determine the direction in which she will move. Because of the time that has been spent on grief during the first two stages of bereavement, and as a result of having reflected on and responded to the texture of life without her husband, her life has achieved more equilibrium.

Entering emergence does *not* mean that the widow is "her old self again" (she will never be that), nor does it mean she is "the new me"—not yet:

> I knew I couldn't go on thinking Ned would come back to me. Too much had already changed; the kids even seemed to be adjusting better. Although I still didn't let a day go by without thinking of him, I *knew* I was alone. And I knew I had to get a job. The question was, "Who would hire me?"

Emergence is a time for "growing out of" the weariness that has become almost routine. It is a time for making contact with the world to a fuller extent than was possible for a numb, angry, and lonely person. This contact with the world is very healing, but it must be gradual and unforced. Trying rapidly to sever ties to the deceased spouse can precipitate symptoms of grief similar to those experienced earlier in bereavement. Enjoying the company of another single adult is very beneficial, but a widower who sees dating as a way of helping himself "get over his wife" is actually highlighting his continuing attachment to her. If the widower (or widow) can say, "I'm looking forward to being with this new person, and I will impose no expectations on her [or him]," then the widowed person may be capable of discovering—and enjoying—new qualities in this "new" person. Otherwise, dating will only serve to emphasize what has been lost, instead of what can be gained by new relationships. The passage of time can help by providing an emotional "distance" between past and present.

As time passes, thoughts and memories of one's spouse become less constant parts of daily life. Early in bereavement widowed people fight against the tendency of memories to fade. But as weeks and months pass, keeping a dim memory in sharp focus takes more and more energy, and it eventually requires more energy than does living in the present. Consequently, it eventually takes greater exertion *not* to grow beyond widowhood—to continue living in the past. Thus, emergence is inevitable for those who live in the present, focusing instead of memories on contemporary experiences.

Experiences are always important because they give shape to our lives. With each experience our lives are changed. To achieve or maintain a satisfying life, our experiences should logically meet our personal needs. But we must have a reasonably good idea of what our needs are before we can attempt to seek experiences to meet them. The numbness and almost single-minded focus on a gradual return to the realities of daily living characteristic of the first two stages of bereavement—encounter and respondence—enable widowed men and women to avoid facing this basic question. Those who emerge from widowhood have spent time asking themselves "What will I do?" and have come up with at least some tentative answers. Perhaps they have discussed the question with close friends, family members, children, or professionals and have incorporated aspects of their past lives that had provided fulfillment into a plan for their present and future lives. It is important to articulate one's needs in positive rather than negative terms: Saying "I know what I don't like to do" provides no help in defining needs because life is *doing,* not *not doing,* especially when emerging from widowhood. Emergence demands action.

Nevertheless, the secret to getting human needs met lies in knowing the difference between the possible and the impossible; between those areas of life we can control and those we cannot. Thinking we have control over matters that are really *not* in our control causes frustration; not choosing in matters over which we *do* have control makes us, at best, passive participants and, at worst, victims. Obviously, neither is helpful in growing beyond widowhood. To move beyond widowhood, we must make choices in those areas in which we do have control, that meet our needs and enrich our lives.

As they move through bereavement, widowed people come to realize that death is a natural outcome of life, one over which we have little control. This realization not only "prepares" the widowed person for future losses, it also facilitates the present movement beyond widowhood. Since they clearly perceive what cannot be controlled (death), what *can* be controlled (where I go, what I do, with whom I spend time) thus becomes clearer, standing out in sharper relief than before, when loss was but an abstraction.

Realization of loss is different from resignation to loss; the latter is a defeated, negative interpretation of the meaning of death on one's life. Resignation is: "I have loved someone who has died. Since death lies at the end of each person's life, there is no point in loving someone who will die." Realization is: "I have loved someone who has died. Even though death lies at the end of each person's life, I am alive and capable of loving and living until I die." With realization, widowed people can make changes they postponed during the early stages of bereavement, such as moving to a new home, making a large purchase, or effecting a career change. Some emerged widows use realization to follow up on activities or interests pursued before marriage, leading to the resumption of a career or the search for professional advancement through study or brushing up on specific skills. Choices made now are usually wiser ones than those made earlier during encounter or respondence.

Realization is part of the psychological *acceptance* of the death of the deceased spouse. (I vividly recall one widow just shrugging her shoulders: "I gave up fighting it. I said to myself 'He's gone,' and that was it . . . did I have a choice?"). Although the question of whether or not we can ever truly "accept" the death of a loved one remains debatable, during emergence widows accept death in the sense of admitting to themselves that it has taken place, that it is final and irreversible, and life must now be faced alone. (Eleanor Roosevelt immediately understood that her husband's death meant a major life change. According to friends and White House aides who helped her relocate, her adaptation within two weeks of his death demonstrated extraordinarily rapid growth, typical of a person widowed many months or longer.)

Acceptance of the death of the spouse is the key issue of emergence, hence it arises frequently in widows' descriptions of their experiences: "Once I accepted the fact that my husband had died, life became clearer to me." Acceptance is the end of a relentless questioning process that begins at the death of the spouse (and sometimes before death, when the spouse is ill), and continues to the point of "verification."

During emergence the widow stops questioning the reality and the meaning of her spouse's death. Verification marks the end of that psychological "searching" that began early in encounter, when the widow set out on an emotional (or actual) search for the deceased spouse. By the time they are in emergence, many widows have become conscious of their "searching" behavior, sometimes dryly sharing stories at coffee breaks in support-group meetings.

There is one final task that must be faced before emergence is complete: A "critical conflict" must be resolved. While acceptance and verification are issues tied to the past relationship, critical conflict is a question rooted in the present. It calls for the widow to take a clear stand on her role as an unmarried person. The widow must now elect to remain defined and confined by her widow identity or to opt out of it. "Am I to be a widow for the rest of my life?" is essentially the question of critical conflict.

Throughout bereavement, friends and family may bolster one or the other side of this conflict: To save her feelings (and perhaps their feelings as well), they may encourage her to move the deceased out of the center of her attention: "Come, let's get your mind on other things." But the widow must simultaneously confront forces that pull her in the opposite direction: Friends, family, and society often encourage the widow to keep alive her deceased spouse's memory.[4] They pull her back into sanctification, talking about "that sainted man," and "Yes, he was wonderful . . . the salt of the earth! No man was as good as George!" Often motivated by a desire to "speak well of the dead," associates of the widow may unwittingly lead her down the path of lifetime widowhood if they persistently surround her with images of her past relationship. Some may push her back even further by encouraging permanent fusion. This may be motivated by a wish to prevent her from violating the singular-love fantasy our society holds so dearly: "You can truly love only one in this life." Jealousy, competition, and a mistrust of the motives of this newly single person may contribute to "saving her from doing something foolish," urging her to accept permanent widowhood as her lot in life. As a result, some "choose" not to undertake new tasks, adopt a new point of view, or enter new fulfilling relationships. In effect, they remain widows for the rest of their lives like "viduates," an order of widows in the early Christian church.

As a goal of bereavement therapy, this kind of "adjustment" to widowhood falls short. Adjustment to widowhood without a movement *beyond* it can be a "life sentence" for the widow. Grief counselors should help the widow work toward putting things in perspective and putting the past behind her. At the same time, the therapist must take into account how far along in bereavement the widow is before advocating a course of therapy. Some widows need the temporary security provided by the role of "widow." They are not yet ready to put their pasts behind them. Hence, efforts to move such grief-stricken widows beyond widowhood would be useless, and perhaps harmful. Others are more deeply disturbed: Their depression may be long standing or so severe that immediate professional intervention is necessary.

Insistence by family, friends and others on continuing attention to the deceased often implies an all-or-nothing choice between memory and forgetting. In fact, not dwelling on the spouse's memory does not necessarily mean a total forgetting, nor does it demand the widow's denial of his existence.

Healthy mourning (and successful emergence) demands that the bereaved only temporarily keep the deceased spouse at the customary central place in her life. Fully emerged widows shed widowhood and see themselves as *single, unmarried people,* focused on pursuits and relationships more relevant to the present and future than to the past. A widow can still honor the memory of her deceased spouse without spending so much time dwelling on the memory that it detracts from her present life. Widowed people can keep their spouse's memory alive by establishing philanthropic foundations, scholarship funds, resuming activities they shared with their spouses, or continuing some work their spouses began. Jewish families keep alive the memory of the deceased by customarily naming newborn children after a beloved, deceased relative.

By the conclusion of emergence, an "unmarriage" takes place. Although the marriage physically ended at the moment their spouses died, widowed men and women remain psychologically married through the first two stages of bereavement. Unmarriage is the point of closure to that psychological marriage, and it is the culmination of emergence. Sometimes unmarriage is sought through remarriage, but some widowed men and women and their new spouses have paid the price for engaging in such "psychological bigamy."

The movement beyond widowhood that begins at the start of emergence can be an intense, painful, and frustrating ordeal, for it involves both risk and change. As the widow moved through widowhood, she had to discard—almost one by one—each obsolete behavior pattern. When married, these behaviors had meaning and purpose, and they served some necessary function in the relationship. The casting off and discarding of obsolete behaviors can precipitate a sense of disorganization and despair, which may lead to depression.[5]

British author and literary scholar C. S. Lewis described his casting off of behaviors that had been comfortable when his wife was alive:

> I think I am beginning to understand why grief feels like suspense. It comes from the frustration of so many impulses that had become habitual . . . now their target is gone. Thought after thought, feeling after feeling, action after action, had [my wife] for their object . . . so many roads once; now so many "culs-de-sac."[6]

As behavior patterns are cast off there is a risk that what is there to replace them may not prove to be as satisfying as the memory of the obsolete behaviors. Some widows become "professional widows," frozen in incomplete emergence. Although they have understood and even accepted the death of their spouse, they do not relinquish widowhood itself, finding comfort in the "cul-de-sac" (dead-end street) it has become.

Some of the most helpful, warm, and caring widowed people are "professional widows" (PW). Comfortable with their widowhood, they are fixed on it, incorporating the fact that they have lost a spouse into their permanent identity. PWs convert a transitional role into a fixed and permanent life-style. While this means they have effectively stopped their personal movement beyond widowhood, PWs usually devote a great deal of energy to supportive enterprises for other widowed women and men, serving as discussion-group participants or self-help-group leaders:

> I've become a "career widow," I guess! My husband died over fifteen years ago, but I'm as active as ever in the church's support group. We call it the "Save-A-Soul Mission," like the one in *Guys and Dolls!* I found a very rewarding career helping other widows get over their losses. And I guess I'll do this for the rest of my life.

> You can call me an all-purpose counselor. I've been single, married, divorced, remarried, and widowed. If there's something else I can be, I haven't found it yet! But it helps me. I teach the "death and dying" course at the community college. No, I never really get tired of it. I learn something new every time I teach the course, and this is the tenth year—twenty times altogether I've taught the course—that I've been doing it.

> What I like best about going to these Wednesday meetings is the social life. I must be strange or something, but I feel like I *belong* here. I started this group in 1967, and it's been going strong ever since. How many support groups do you know of that have been around for seventeen straight years?

Of course, there is a difference between professional widows who focus their own lives and identities on widowhood and those who are active volunteers without a deeply personal stake in widowhood per se. Those who have lived through a personal crisis often have a unique perspective on helping others through the same issues they've faced. Alcohol and drug abuse counselors, for example, are often willing and able to share insights they have gained through the personal challenges and trials presented by their addiction, now that they have moved beyond the life crisis brought on by that addiction.

Similarly, widows can help other widows, but they can help them best when they have moved fully beyond their own bereavements. (In fact, the Widow-to-Widow Program of AARP has a standing rule that widowed outreach volunteers must have experienced the death of their spouse no less than eighteen months prior to serving.) Widows who have placed distance between "that day" and the present and who are no longer so intensely focused on their own losses are in a better position to listen to others, and to advise from a point of view that is more objective.

Although PWs often make great contributions to the community in general and to widowed people in particular, they often lose the critical balance in their own lives. Giving of one's time and extending support to others facing a life crisis can be part of one's path in moving beyond widowhood and performing a valuable social service at the same time. However, PWs forestall completing emergence, which would enable them to move beyond widowhood. Although they have put their grief behind them and in every other way are living productively in the present, PWs permit the temporary identity of "widow" to continue to be an integral part of their permanent identity. Instead of becoming unmarried single persons, PWs reach emergence but fail to emerge fully from widowhood.

Perhaps the most appropriate suggestion to help the PW achieve a sense of balance is the simplest: Take time for yourself. Take the final step and move out of and beyond widowhood when you're ready. If it takes you twenty years, and you're helping others along the way, you certainly deserve praise. But your personal relationships may be hindered if your identity continues to be "widow" instead of "former widow," because the former implies a large presence of "someone else" in your current life. One can help widowed people as a "former widow" just as effectively as one can as a PW.

Ultimately, the beginning (or reestablishment) of satisfying new interpersonal relationships can only take place following successful emergence from widowhood. There is no alternate shortcut through bereavement and widowhood.

STAGE 4
Transformation

At the completion of emergence is the fourth stage, more accurately described as a plateau because it signifies an arrival rather than a turning point. The essence of transformation is captured by the French idiomatic expression *l'échapper belle* ("the fortunate escape"), because transformation embodies a departure from and movement beyond widowhood.

Widowed people who experience transformation have moved completely past the widow role and developed a clearer and more enduring identity enriched by past experiences but also by present ones. Author Alan Paton described transformation beautifully as he related his feelings after his marriage of forty years ended with the death of his wife. Paton's words capture the essence of the fortunate escape not from love or life but from widowhood.

> Once before I wrote that my grief was done, and then it suddenly returned. . . . But now it will not return again. Something within me is waking from a long sleep, and I want to live and move again. Some zest is returning to me, some immense gratefulness for those who love me, some strong wish to love them also. I am full of thanks for life. I have not told myself to be thankful, I just am so. . . .[7]

Some, like Alan Paton, rise above and beyond the devastation of widowhood, aware of the unique changes occurring, fully welcoming them, and looking forward to a life that had earlier seemed of little importance. Observing the transition through grief of English widows, Lily Pincus stated that "there are widows who blossom out after their husband's deaths and find new meanings for their lives," adding, "It is these women who hate the term 'widow.' "[8] In the language of support groups, transformed people are simply called survivors: ordinary women and men who are extraordinary in the degree of personal growth they have experienced in their movement beyond widowhood. This degree of personal growth makes transformed men and women less likely to appear in the groups of widows from which most research samples are drawn, or even to agree to participate in studies of widowhood, precisely because they no longer consider themselves to be widowed.

As I looked more closely at differences between emerged and transformed widows, I noticed that what distinguished the latter was an additional two-part transition they underwent following emergence: metamorphosis and rebirth. They went "from grief to growth," as one widow expressed it.

Typically during transformation some widows—fully aware that their intense grief was winding down—began to realize that something was changing in their lives, something they perceived as positive change. Metamorphosis was a time of reflection where the widow "knew" that although life had changed greatly during bereavement, there was still something missing—a question arising not from grief but from an aroused curiosity: "My life is good [again]. I'm not totally sure things will stay this way, but it *won't go back* to the way it was." Metamorphosis is a stepping past emergence:

> I couldn't *wait* to go back to school! All my life I had wanted to graduate with that little white nurse's cap they wear! My family told me to wait until the first year was over, until I was "myself" again. "Myself?" I *knew* what I had to do. I paid my dues by taking good care—and I mean *good* care—of my husband, so I didn't feel one bit guilty about kicking up my heels and going back to college to get my diploma.

These widows were aware of a new direction that their lives had to take; of an exciting new movement toward a fullness of a new, changed persona they had not previously known. The growing anticipation of that persona set the stage for an awareness of a new life that the former widow would enjoy:

> I couldn't put my finger on it, but so many things started to matter again in my life: It had been only four years since my husband died, but here I was: getting my master's degree, moving to California to a new job—my friends thought I was crazy like some widows who do stupid things! No, I knew what I was doing because there were a hundred things I always wanted to do and never did them. Now it's *my turn* to live.

> I work for Metropolitan Life here in Detroit and I'll never know what gave me the courage to apply for this job! But I read the paper, sent them a résumé, and here I was! Yes, I

> think they did feel sorry for me. But my husband used to say, "If it works, use it!" Boy, would my husband laugh if he saw how much they pay me. It's unconscionable! But I'm worth it. You know, I got this job only six months after he died, and I've been here almost eight years. Not to put down other widows, but it sure beats sitting home and moping. . . . Maybe I should thank *my husband* for leaving me with nothing but a mortgage to pay?

Self-improvement was a recurrent theme among transformed widows, and this often entailed continuing education. I found a significant positive connection between adaptation among widowed women and their level of formal education. In general, the higher a widow's level of education, the better was her adaptation. Widows with more formal education enjoyed an identity facet that was not "damaged" by the death of the spouse, and it opened doors that were not available to their less educated counterparts.

Like education, an occupation can provide an added dimension to the widow's identity and self-worth. For men, occupation has traditionally been the source of self-definition, and it can continue to serve this function in widowhood. Women—especially older women—however, have had fewer opportunities outside the home. Those who have spent many years at home may have difficulty entering or reentering the job market. Yet the potential benefits of doing so can be great. Besides providing an additional facet of identity and reassurance of one's worth, a job provides welcome financial resources, which can ease worries about making ends meet and facilitate the pursuit of other rewarding activities. Isabella Taves, author of *The Widow's Guide,* called work "the widow's solace and salvation." She cites the advice given to widowed women by Mary Ellen Gordon, a successful widowed friend who had faced widowhood with few skills or work experience:

> Act. Walk out of the house and go to school, or to an employment agency, or to a counseling service, or whatever. It's the most difficult thing in the world because of fear. But in action the momentum carries you through and it gets easier. Don't just fantasize, do it![9]

It may not even be necessary to leave the house; widows who prefer to remain at home to care for children can also find ways to earn income and create an occupational identity for themselves. A professional or technical skill like word processing or graphic design is one basis for a home business. But women have turned all kinds of interests and talents, from child care to piano playing, into financially and emotionally rewarding occupations. After her husband died, a widowed friend of mine began a day-care center in her home. Though the income from the venture was minimal, it also helped her to focus her need to help and nurture others in a constructive way.

Metamorphosis is change. Metamorphosis is not something that happens to some lucky widowed people; it is something that they *do* to bring about positive change in their lives. Occupation and work facilitate metamorphosis because they provide the newly single adult with a facet of identity that, in our society, offers financial and emotional rewards. These will ultimately help her grow toward independence and the fulfillment of her needs that were formerly fulfilled through marriage. She is seeing how much she has—or can potentially have—not only in material terms but in emotional satisfaction.

Completing transformation, metamorphosis ends in a rebirth that is not unlike that of the mythical phoenix arising from the ashes. In fact, two widowed women used the analogy of being reborn from fire:

> You know, I felt like . . . the animal . . . which rose from the ruins, born again. I looked younger; I felt younger. I lost *tons* of weight . . . you sound like a dear young man and I'd like to talk with you more, but I can't right now, I'm getting packed for an Elderhostel trip to Mexico. Give me a call again next month.

> [My husband] would never—in a million years—recognize me if he bumped into me on the street! I'm different, and I'm glad. I loved him like crazy, and I still think of him fondly now and then. But I could never have that kind of marriage again because I'm just a different person. Frankly I don't even know the Olivia I used to be! The memory is faint. So faint . . . and, you know, I probably wouldn't even recognize [my husband] if he popped back into my life tomorrow. I might date him or live with him, but marry him? Not this time.

> I'm almost embarrassed to say this, but after being a widow for three years I tossed my black skirt and black blouse in the woodstove! If I had a black bra I would've burned that too! I went to Boston and brought home the most colorful clothes I could find. You know, I never felt better in my whole life, and it's not only the clothes that have changed!

> After all the tears and questions, I knew that my life was good again. And it wasn't just good in money or success or finding a gorgeous man or forgetting about my husband. I knew I was changed, and that I was still changing. But I felt there was a direction to it, and the direction was *good*. Real good!

Having unmarried, transformed people are—in the words of one widow—"the same book but a revised edition." Some continue their jobs, some switch careers, others devote their time to family or other pursuits, while still others carry on the work of the deceased spouse. What they all have in common is the fact that their pasts have been put into perspective, neither hindering nor handicapping them, and they have created new identities for themselves.

Like all who are no longer restricted by an imposed role, transformed people are faced with numerous choices. Just because the grieving is over does not mean that life's questions have been resolved. They *know* that life is a series of continuous changes (for they have lived through and are living through change), and they know not just intellectually but emotionally that transition is necessary for growth. Transformed people can look back to that day and grasp how far they have grown since the time they thought nothing would ever again make life worthwhile. In fact, they are only beginning:

> As I look back, there were times I thought "I'll never make it." My first two years were the hardest, and I wouldn't wish what I went through to happen to anyone—even my worst enemy. I have enough, Lord knows, in my life to keep me busy—my church, my sons, my grandchildren. I'm still alone, but I'm not lonely anymore. There's a big difference between being alone and being lonely.

> I went back to school right after [my husband] died, and it was the best thing I ever did. I met all kinds of different people, younger folks. This helped me stay young. Can you guess how old I am? I'm seventy-one!

> My daughter's husband and my husband died within a year of each other, and then she wanted to move in with me. I certainly don't mind, but at my age and with all the things I have to do I can't start being her parent all over again. . . . Would you like to meet her? She'll be back around five o'clock. I think the two of you have a lot in common.

Transformed people rise to new heights in their flight beyond widowhood. While emerged widows have moved through bereavement and begun to live full lives, transformed people have gone even further. They have begun to achieve life dreams previously undreamed or submerged during marriage when they confined their energies (and limited their identities) to taking care of a husband and/or raising children. Those who remarry do so under different terms from their original arrangement, seeking and attaining a more fulfilling life involving spouse, friendships, career, and a pastime.

I met transformed widows who were young, middle-aged, and older. Regardless of age, what distinguished them was their enthusiasm to *do* and their passionate interest in *being:* to live, to grow, to be with others, and to be alone; to read, dance, sing, sleep, laugh, make love, cry, get married, or—like one fifty-year old woman—"go steady." Their relationships were different from other widowed peoples' relationships because they brought to them a sense of self. That renewed sense of self (and not necessarily just the freedom from a husband or wife) allowed them to exert a greater control over their lives, perhaps for the first time realizing the difference between what can be controlled and what cannot. I did not meet one transformed widow who seemed upset over what she could not control; nor did I meet one I would characterize as interested in controlling others' lives. Like the butterfly described by Nobel Prize recipient Sir Rabindranath Tagore, who "counts not months but moments, and has time enough,"[10] transformed widows seemed involved with people and things of the *present,* having (barely) enough time to do and be all that they wish.

In transformation, men and women become more "their own

person," but because the traditional sex roles ascribed to men and women are different, the common ideal of becoming one's own person is approached from different directions by each sex. For example, women traditionally invest more of their identity in marriage, but transformed women are less dependent on a husband and marriage for a sense of personal identity. Men traditionally rely on their spouses and marriage for intimacy and emotional closeness, but transformed men can get their intimacy needs met without dependence on a wife.

Despite this apparent advantage in becoming one's own person, successful movement beyond widowhood is not so common in men as women; few widowers become transformed. The reasons for this discrepancy are intricate, but three factors may be significant. First, widowed men are more likely to remarry—and remarry sooner after the spouse's death—than are widowed women. Because they can traditionally select from a larger age range, and because older single men are vastly outnumbered by single women (three unmarried women to each unmarried man in the age group older than forty-five years), they have a larger pool of potential mates from which to select. Men who remarry thus spend less time as widowers than women, which means they spend less time working through bereavement. Hence, many men may short-circuit their transformation by quickly reverting to a familiar role (marriage) instead of pursuing self-development that may lead in other directions as well.

Second, defining the masculine individual as one who is autonomous, separate, and self-reliant makes it harder for men to derive emotional closeness and intimacy through interaction with others (notably, other men or married women). To become transformed, a widower must either oppose part of society's definition of masculinity, or he must remarry.

Finally, growing beyond widowhood holds no particular identity-enriching opportunity for men. For a woman transformation promises a new personal identity that may be freed of dependency on men and freed from a man's dependence on herself, but a man's transformation is different. Since he did not identify *being married* as a key component of his personal identity, being widowed now causes no loss—on a cognitive level—of that identity. Like a widow, he has lost—on an emotional level—a "part of himself," and feels it acutely. Unlike a widow, he is not as easily able to see his deep attachment (because he has been raised to think of himself as an autonomous individual), nor is he able to see his dependence on his spouse as an unhealthy aspect of that marriage. Men do not admit their emotional dependence on women, and they certainly do not see it as something to be "grown out of" when the relationship ends.

If transformation demands that a man free himself of his emotional dependence on women (which it does), he must free his wife or partner from the obligation to do more than love him and share with him. He must free her from meeting the depth of emotional need he cannot meet by himself. This is very difficult, for it involves acknowledging (perhaps for the first time since he was similarly dependent as an infant) that without a wife he is incomplete. It would highlight what is empty in his otherwise superior, independent identity. Growing beyond his socially prized identity into a new identity—one that, to himself and his friends, lies in uncharted, feminine waters—is risky if not downright frightening. It is easier (and safer, considering the risk involved in being perceived as "feminine"), therefore, for a man to remarry than it is for him to work toward a reformulated personal identity.

In sum, given the prevailing definition of masculinity, although remarriage is more available to men, the options for personal growth that lie beyond emergence for widowed men are fairly limited. As more and more women free themselves from dependent relationships and form cross-sex friendships that are more egalitarian, men will benefit as well.

It is characteristic of transformed widows to be oriented toward the present: They do not speak of their past lives as if they still existed. Some told me of times when they thought about their former spouses, but the memory associated with that recollection was warming rather than searing. And although some frankly admitted they missed their spouses, not one yearned to have back the life she had had instead of her present life.

> If you said ten years ago that I'd be running my husband's business, I'd tell you that you were nuts! Who ever thought I'd own a meat distribution company! You know, I'm proud to say that our assets are almost twice what they were when he was alive, and we're opening a firm down in the "States."

> I have no major goals in life, like many women do today. I'm just happy to have my kids, my friends, and my religion. Working in a greeting card store is fine for me, at least for now. I get to meet good people, and it gives me a chance to get dressed up. For eleven years I lived with an abusive husband. Compared to that nobody I used to be, I'm a somebody now. You know, I'm sad for all the suffering that my husband and my children went through, but I've gotten past the anger I used to feel toward him. But believe me, when you run with the wolves, you begin to think like a wolf.

> I thank God for each day, and I take each day one by one. The biggest change in me is that I look forward to each day now, and I worry a whole lot less. When I was married, there were so many pressures on me that I never had a chance to sit down and think clearly. I can honestly say that I'm finally finding out who I am. And it feels good. My whole life is divided up into fourths: for the first twenty years, I was a girl. For the next twenty, I was married. Now I'm almost done with the third twenty, which I spent as a widow. My last twenty will be the best!

Thirteen years after the death of Franklin Delano Roosevelt, Eleanor Roosevelt described her transformation from widowhood:

> I had few definite plans but I knew there were certain things I did *not* want to do. I did not want to run an elaborate household again. I did not want to cease trying to be useful in some way. I did not want to feel old—and seldom have.[11]

Continuing, she acknowledged that the movement beyond widowhood did not proceed along paths that were smooth or well marked:

> In the years since 1945 I have known the various phases of loneliness that are bound to occur when people no longer have a busy family life. But, without particularly planning it, I have made the necessary adjustments to a different way of living, and I have enjoyed almost every minute of it and almost everything about it.[12]

She describes how her life had consisted of previous adjustments and readjustments, and these had helped greatly in preparing her to be on her own. In addition, her husband's illness—along with a recognition of other changes—prepared her for the larger task of facing her life without him. Although she described normal feelings of loneliness after he died, Eleanor Roosevelt was never really alone. Maybe the most important clue to her movement beyond widowhood is contained in this: There is not one page in her autobiography that is not filled with the names of people—friends and relatives.

Sometimes a successful confrontation with widowhood involves overcoming more than the loss of a spouse. Jane Smith's ten-year-old daughter Samantha captured headlines in 1983 when she received a letter from Soviet President Yuri Andropov, responding to a note Samantha wrote expressing her fear of nuclear war. When Andropov invited Samantha and her parents to tour the Soviet Union, the Smith family was bombarded with media attention. Samantha soon became a symbol of the hope of post-nuclear-age youngsters for a better future. Soon after her first Soviet trip in 1983, Samantha made almost thirty television appearances, wrote a book about her trip, and won a part in a weekly television dramatic series. On a return trip from filming in London in August 1985, both Samantha and her father Arthur were killed when their plane crashed in Maine.

Jane Smith was waiting at the airport. She learned that she had not only lost her daughter but was now a widow as well. "After the crash, people wrote to me saying 'I know you don't think you will survive, but you will,' " she said recently. "That never occurred to me. I knew I would survive. It was just a matter of how."[13]

Using the donations sent by sympathetic well-wishers, Mrs. Smith joined with friends to establish the Samantha Smith Foundation, created to keep alive Samantha's ideals and to foster international understanding. In a separate effort funded by the people of Maine, a statue of Samantha was erected outside the statehouse in Augusta. At the unveiling, Jane Smith remarked, "The statue will help remind all people, especially children, that ordinary people can make a difference."[14]

Recently I had the good fortune to meet Jane Smith, and I immediately asked her not about Soviet-American relations but about her survival as a widow. She seemed surprised by my question; I got the clear impression that Jane Smith was not accustomed to thinking of herself as "a widow." After a moment's hesitation, she acknowledged that while her situation "wasn't typical" because of the celebrity Samantha had attained prior to her death, Jane said, "I'm a practical woman, and I tend to look ahead instead of backward. I had many opportunities and this (the foundation) was one of them."[15]

Following Samantha's and Arthur's deaths, Jane Smith found notepads imprinted with mottos among her daughter's effects. One said, "A peacock who sits on his tailfeathers is just another turkey"; the other, "So much to do—so little time," which crystallized for Jane what her work and new life now involved. Having resigned her job as a social work administrator to work with the foundation, Jane Smith reflected on her recent past:

> It's been amazing. For so long it was a thrill-a-minute and for a while after the crash, I felt like I was in a fog of unreality. There are times when I still get sad and have sad moments but there are still other good things to life. I am moving on.[16]

In moving beyond widowhood another widow traveled a totally different path, yet she too demonstrates a heightened level of purpose and deep satisfaction with her life. Instead of sinking into bitterness and depression after the assassination of her husband Dr. Martin Luther King, Jr., Coretta Scott King moved beyond herself and her loss. Her determination to "rededicate" herself to the goals they shared is inspiring:

> I feel strongly that Martin's work must go on. In the same way that I had given him all the support I could during his lifetime, I was even more determined to do so now that he was no longer with us. Because his task was not finished, I felt that I must rededicate myself to the completion of his work. . . . I believe that this nation can be transformed into a society of love, of justice, peace, and brotherhood where all men can really be brothers.[17]

More than simply carrying on the noble work of her deceased husband (which some widows do in the emergence phase), Coretta

Scott King was now directed toward making her own contribution, a hallmark of a transformed woman:

> Not that I can do what Martin did; but I hope to make my contribution in my own way. In some small way, perhaps I can serve, as he did, the aspirations of oppressed people of all races, throughout the world.[18]

Emmy Award–winning actress Betty White has come a long way from 1949 when she was the first woman disc jockey in Los Angeles. Having starred in numerous television shows (most recently as Rose in NBC's "The Golden Girls"), she has been a widow since the death of her husband, Allen Ludden, after eighteen years of marriage. Reflecting recently on being widowed, Betty White said:

> When you're a widow, you're a fifth wheel, you're an odd number. I'm the wrong one to answer your question, because in show business you are so taken care of you can't equate with the real world, except that I watched my mother go through the same thing. It's tough, sure it's tough, for a widow.[19]

She feels, however, that it probably is easier for widowed women today, because they "can shift into second gear," having alternatives that women of her mother's generation, for example, did not enjoy:

> The survivors are there . . . if you've got any drive, sure, you lose the other half of your life. And sure, you're dragged to the bottom. But somehow you pick it up and you put it together. There are so many women out there now who are doing that who never thought they could . . . when my mother was widowed, and was lost—she had no friends, because she had devoted her whole life to her husband—there were opportunities for her that she didn't even know were there.[20]

When Betty was asked specifically how she'd advise other widows to move through bereavement, she echoed a theme common to all who move successfully through widowhood:

> You call on what you had before. You reach around and you see other people—because when you get to a given age there are a lot of other people in your world. Somebody reaches out a hand, somebody grabs it, somebody reaches over here, and somebody grabs it. And pretty soon you find that . . . you're freer than you ever were before.[21]

If there is a "secret" ingredient to her growth and success in later years, it is probably contained in her description of how she fared after Allen died. Betty White felt that her life is "more interesting with every day that passes" because of the "great Superfriends to glue it all together. They understand my alone times . . . and I have the comfort of knowing they are *there*."[22]

There are Superfriends for each of us, and there are challenges that—when we face them with others—become surmountable. Like mountains that must be climbed "because they're there," millions of widows survive successfully simply because they *must*. Sometimes when a marriage ends

> . . . and all of a sudden the lady is thrown out into the deep water, and she learns to swim. And suddenly she finds she swam to something she would never have swum to before.[23]

Transformed people are indeed fortunate: No ghosts keep them awake at night; they have rejoined the human race by day. Transformed people provide important role models for other widows who are not so far along in bereavement; they are proof that life does get better again after the death of a spouse. Perhaps the greatest value of programs like Widow-to-Widow lies in sharing successfully adapted widows with other widows—real examples that successful movement beyond widowhood can be achieved. Widowed people must fully understand that life without a beloved spouse is *possible*. Later, it is to be hoped, they will see that it can be *good*. But *possible* is the beginning of *good*. When they have looked back over their movement through the stages of bereavement, widowed people can see how their lives have become different, in many cases better than they ever were before.

TABLE 1 Stages of Bereavement in Widowhood

Growing Through Widowhood

Stage 1. Encounter: Characterized by fusion (oneness with deceased spouse), numbness, shock, anger, depression, feelings of guilt, self-blame, sadness, rigidity, lability, denial, rage, physical symptoms, sense of "presence" of deceased spouse, mystical-spiritual experiences, passive or aggressive behavior, searching for lost spouse.

Stage 2. Respondence: Characterized by sanctification (deification of deceased spouse), sadness, hypersensitivity, continued numbness, insomnia, lethargy, first attempts at reaching out, flashes of hope that "it's all a dream," desperate feelings, restlessness, inability to concentrate, beginning of separation of marital identity from self-identity. Searching continues.

Growing Beyond Widowhood

Stage 3. Emergence: Characterized by verification (end of searching), critical conflict (decision to unmarry), conclusion of searching, less intense self-blame, reduced questioning, "emotional roller coaster," anguish more limited, moments of doubt, thoughts of the future, completion of unmarriage.

Stage 4. Transformation: Characterized by Metamorphosis and Rebirth (*l'échapper belle*), cessation of self-perception as "widow," closure of mourning, concern with present and future, past marriage integrated into flow of life experiences, acceptance of role as single adult.

CHAPTER
6

The Value of Personal Relationships

More psychotherapy is accomplished between good friends at coffee every morning at ten o'clock than all day long in doctors' offices. A good talk with a close friend can solve problems, or at least put them in some perspective, before they become overpowering. One of the problems we face today is the scarcity of good friends.

—Dr. Joseph D. Matarazzo,
Pres., Am. Psychological Assn.

When I was brought to the hospital the day my wife died I collapsed in vague consciousness in an emergency room chair. Not a violent collapse, just exhausted, numb, and in tears. I will never forget the faces of those on duty: They looked rapidly at each other, uncertain of what to do with me. After dashing around for what seemed like a half hour, someone produced some sedatives, another offered a paper cup of water. I asked for more; they gave me more.

However, what was far more therapeutic than the sedatives was simply their human presence—the fact that they were there. Even in my distraught and anesthetized state, I derived comfort and reassurance from the understanding that these people were doing something for me, regardless of what they were doing and why they were doing it. When I tried to stand, a hand was there. Perhaps it was John's hand, maybe Agnes's. As if I was a child afraid of the dark, someone walked with me to a chair, led me to a bruised baby calling "Dada." As I held my baby someone put an arm around my shoulder. In my numbness little made sense. But I distinctly remember a strange comfort from both that arm around me and from the baby's nuzzling of my neck. They helped quell a monster deep down in a part of me I remembered only vaguely from childhood. This comfort touched me at a most instinctive level. As alone as I felt at that moment, my experience in the hospital was actually not at all unique. All human beings (and even animals) require intimacy or at least close contact with another to survive,[1] especially when threatened by highly stressful situations.

As I moved through the early days of widowhood, at first people did things for me and later, with me, but in either case, their human contact remained more important to me than what they did. In retrospect, I saw that contact with friends and family provided me with a great deal of protection from depression. In the early stages of bereavement, when widowed people are experiencing the strongest grief, they are more vulnerable to depression and psychological distress than those in later stages of bereavement.[2] Newly bereaved men and women are lonely and worry about being lonely forever. They are troubled by their constant sadness, and they wonder how life can go on without their spouse. Hence they need support in two forms: companionship and nurturance.

Human contact is critical in counteracting loneliness, the most predictable consequence of widowhood regardless of sex, age, income, or race.[3] Loneliness is particularly prevalent among older widows and widowers, whose decreased mobility and financial resources restrict social opportunity. They are at greater risk of being socially isolated than those who are young or middle-aged. One older widow I interviewed consistently answered my questions with long, rambling responses, followed by questions of her own. When she asked me to stay for coffee and then for lunch, I realized how isolated she was. She told me that I was the first "living person" she had spoken to since three days earlier, when the boy who delivered her newspaper came by to collect his money.

The pain of loneliness is accompanied by fear. When one's

spouse dies, a perception of personal vulnerability to illness and death is heightened. Bereavement therapist Beverly Raphael suggested that:

> Death of the marital partner, or the dyadic partner of an intimate bond, brings death very close and, inevitably, touches the bereaved personally, reminding him that he too may die.[4]

Adults have a more accurate mental picture of death than young children do. They know that death is a final, irreversible event. Yet, as "accurate" as this adult understanding is, it is still not a deep understanding, perhaps remaining "a thin veneer, barely covering the concrete or fantasy conceptualizations that evolved through . . . [the adult's] childhood."[5] When one perceives a threat to one's survival, fear is the normal instinctive response. Living free of fear is impossible for any sane human being undergoing severe stress, whether from illness, divorce, war, or the death of a spouse.

However, in our culture, which prizes fearlessness, fear is considered a sign of weakness. "Don't ever let them see you sweat" is the watchword not only of football coaches urging coolness under pressure, but of Madison Avenue advertisers as well. Our society disavows fear, advocating the autonomous, "fearless self" originally an ideal for adult men but now an ideal for both sexes and children as well.

When men, in particular, experience the fear attendant on widowhood, they are torn between the need to express it to obtain reassurance and the pressure to conceal it to avoid appearing weak. The pain of this conflict is exacerbated by the recognition that the one person in whom one would have confided—the one most likely to listen to and accept it without ridicule—is gone. The inability to express fear contributes to the early emotional isolation and loneliness experienced by widowed men and women, especially those who have no immediately available close friend or relative.

There is another way that fear can increase the loneliness of widowhood: On some level, others may be afraid of being near the widow or widower. As if they had a communicable disease, widowed people can be shunned. In *The Survivor,* Terence Des Pres points out how the survivor is at times avoided by those who try to keep intact their illusions that death happens only to anonymous others. Close contact with a survivor can jeopardize that illusion.[6]

Many widows told me they felt snubbed by people who were once their friends, especially those whose spouses were still alive. A few widowed people told me they were also feared because they represented a "threat" to married people, some of whom were formerly close friends. Some widows were openly accused of flirting with or trying to "steal" another's spouse. Among married people a widow's presence can both threaten their illusion that their marriage is endless and, in some cases, represent unwanted "competition."

These perceptions of the widowed person as a threat are less prevalent among close family members and close friends, who provide immediate and dependable support to newly widowed people. Although their relationship with the deceased was not identical to the widow's, family members are also personally affected by the death, at times as profoundly—though in different ways—as the widow. Perhaps the most powerful emotional support they can offer is by "bearing witness to" the death of the spouse. By sharing the loss, others can help the widowed person safely affirm and ultimately accept what has happened. Close family members can provide a bridge from early denial and numbness to an acceptance of the death, providing a secure, consistent environment for the widowed person.

In addition to providing emotional support, family members often provide significant practical support. They can "step into" specific roles once occupied by the deceased person. For example, they can help the widowed person manage finances or child care. Or family members can help by performing specific tasks like food shopping, maintaining lawn and garden, or doing home repair tasks. Despite controversy over the effects of its "breakup," the American family has nevertheless been identified as one of the most important factors in facilitating successful movement through bereavement.[7] Throughout my interviews and meetings with widowed women and men, the most consistent theme was the value of emotional and practical support received from the family. Women usually spoke of supportive children; men typically spoke of a supportive daughter or other female relative:

My son and daughter-in-law checked on me each week. They brought me whatever I needed and were always asking me how I was doing.

If it were not for my teenage daughter, I would not be alive today. Because of her, I'm not alone in the world. She needs me, too.

Other societies with a longer history and more homogeneous and entrenched cultural tradition than the United States provide a better-orchestrated and more coherent system of familial support for widowed members. But that system usually entails a clearly defined, even rigid, role for the widowed (typically, widowed women), in which there is little or no opportunity to grow beyond widowhood. One exceptional group is a tiny, displaced Samoan community in California. After a death, the family continues to function smoothly because of a well-defined series of supportive actions, dictated by tradition, that come into play. Interviewing widows of victims of a 1964 fire in a social club that claimed the lives of seventeen Samoans, researcher Joan Ablon remarked, "By all accounts, Samoans as individuals and as family groups appeared to have absorbed the disaster amazingly well."[8] She attributed this to specific supportive customs, such as a ritual exchange of goods and donations of money that pay for the funeral and burial and for the food needed for the series of involved social events that take place following the death. There is an immediate gathering of family and friends in the house of the deceased; they come from Samoa and Hawaii, moving "with studied efficiency to take the burden of decision- and arrangement-making off the shoulder of the surviving spouse."

Some of the Samoan widows—like the survivors of the tragic 1942 Cocoanut Grove nightclub fire in Boston that killed 491—still reacted fearfully to fire and had continuing dreams about it. (Both fires occurred at a social club; both had been celebrations that turned into disaster.) Yet the Samoans "listened with wonder to the description of such symptoms" described by Erich Lindemann after the Boston fire, unable to identify with the symptoms of acute and morbid grief he described among Cocoanut Grove survivors.[9]

For the Samoan widows, cultural tradition made moving beyond widowhood an expected course. Two young widows were pregnant; each remarried less than fourteen months after the death of her spouse. An older widow with six children did not remarry but built up one of the few Samoan-owned businesses in the United States. Each Samoan widow was grief stricken when her spouse died, yet her bereavement, once concluded, was then dismissed. Widows were not only free to remarry but were encouraged to do so by the community. A young widowed woman, badly scarred by burns, feared "no man would want her" because of her scars. Yet she, too, remarried fourteen months after her husband died. Neither her burns nor her ten-month-old child served to deter the powerful cultural advocacy of remarriage for widowed women.

Ablon attributed this to a unique attitude toward "replacement" of the deceased person:

> Samoan attitudes toward death and the acceptability of replacement of individuals in family roles serve to preclude the acute trauma of bereavement experienced by many Americans. Samoans view death as one of the natural events in the experience of the living.[10]

In addition to their smooth and systematic insertion of new persons into vacant family roles, Samoans attach great significance to accepting death as a normal result of "God's will." They do not hide death from children or adults, thus Samoan children grow to regard death as a normal event that ends life. Many Americans, on the other hand, have neither the accepting attitude toward death nor an "automatic cultural solution to the problem of replacement."[11] Thus, when her spouse dies, the American widow must rely on the personal support network that she has created (and continues to maintain) to help her move through bereavement. An American widow must map her own way, confronting at times varied and unpredictable pressures and attitudes toward shedding the role of "widow."

Rituals and traditions are not the only means by which families can support widowed members. In large societies like ours, cultural background and rituals are of less significance than the support provided by individual members of the family.[12] Many widowed people I interviewed verified this:

> My father was always special—he was my favorite and I guess I was his. He has meant everything to me, especially now that I'm alone.

> I come from a big family, and after the funeral, my brothers and sisters were all arguing over who would take care of me! I said, "Cool it! I'm taking care of *myself!*" But it was nice that they made a fuss!

> I live under my parents. Their apartment is right above mine. I guess it's been helpful having them so near now. I would like a little privacy, but for now, I can just go upstairs instead of cooking, or I can send the kids up when they get rambunctious.

One particularly powerful type of familial support is the widowed mother-daughter relationship, in which sharing a common grief engenders a special mutual supportive bond. Widowed mothers and their daughters tend to have especially close relationships—characterized by less conflict—than relationships between divorced mothers and their daughters or married mothers and their daughters.[13] When their parents divorce, daughters are likely to feel pressure to take sides, form an alliance with one parent, or rebel against the parent seen as the initiator of the divorce. But when a father dies, daughters see their mothers in a different, sympathetic light. On becoming a widow, a mother may show a vulnerability that was previously invisible to her children, and this will act to diminish interpersonal discord.

Widows with grown children say they receive emotional support from "my children" or "all my children" when responding to general questions about the sources of support they receive. However, when asked about how much active support they receive, they report that their daughters provide more comfort and companionship than do their sons. Widows also say they are closer to their daughters than to their sons, although they acknowledge their sons' contribution toward their feelings of security.[14]

Support for a widowed man or woman can also come from parents. If the parent is also widowed, he or she can provide empathy as well as sympathy. Parents—widowed or not—can be sources of security and refuge. Like recently divorced adults, widowed people may "retreat" to the home of a parent. By occupying the familiar role of dependent son or daughter, the widowed person can derive the comfort needed to counteract loneliness. Of course, the widowed person should regard this retreat as a temporary refuge and not as a permanent asylum.

Neighbors, including casual friends and acquaintances, can provide a substantial amount of assistance, especially early in bereavement, providing food, temporary care for young children, or transportation. In most situations, widows I interviewed praised the help they had received from neighbors, who often became closer friends as a result of that supportive contact:

> I have a big family, and . . . they were great. But my friend Yolanda—she lives in the apartment across the hall—Yolanda was a *saint*. At night she'd tap on my door and brought me in her apartment to play cards, talk, and drink coffee until all hours. And she had a husband to take care of, too.

> I have the most wonderful neighbors living right here in this complex. Since that night that it happened they are extra nice to me. They ask me if I need something at the store, or if I'm feeling well. I didn't go out of the house one day, and late that night one of my neighbors rang my bell just to see if I was okay.

Those who seek to comfort and support widowed people early in bereavement should keep in mind how important their simple presence is in protecting against extreme reactions to grief. Trying to decide on the "right" thing to say to the widow ("What do I tell her when I see her?") places too much emphasis on the healing power of words by themselves. Caring words can comfort a widowed person, but there are *no* precisely right things to say that can significantly change, reverse, or rectify what has taken place. Far more important than what is said is how it is said, and the feelings and actions of support that back up those words:

> People need to understand their roles in times of grief. Our task is not to explain. Our task is to be there. All we have to do is just be there. We do not need to say anything at all. Our presence and a hug go farther than all of the explaining in the world.[15]

The hug is important, for it gives a hurt person a tangible, physical support when in pain—a shoulder to cry on. This allows the widowed person the freedom to not have to fight back expressing feelings caused by the pain. However, it is worth keeping in mind that any words may have a limited effect on newly widowed persons. Numbness and preoccupation with thoughts of the deceased render most people relatively insensitive during the first hours and days of widowhood. Even those who appear to be "remarkably composed" may nonetheless be totally unable to focus on conversation. When my wife died numerous people visited, especially before the funeral. But I remembered little of what was actually said to me, even as soon as it was spoken.

Secondly, widowed persons know there are few variations to saying "I'm sorry" and "I share your sadness." By the same token, although there are few words that, by themselves, are hurtful, there are many inappropriate ways to behave toward widowed people. Nevertheless, widowed people assume they were not spoken out of malice; thoughtless or inadvertent, perhaps, but not meant to sound that way.

Maybe the most common problem is infantilization, in which the widowed person is treated as though he or she is incompetent. Parents, close friends, brothers, sisters, and even children are all potential offenders:

> They would not let me out of sight. Maybe they thought I'd do something drastic if they left me alone. But they drove me crazy and I couldn't wait until they all went home.

In an attempt to spare the widowed person's feelings, or because of a desire to run the show, there may be some fairly assertive friends or family members who will try to exclude the bereaved person from decisions connected with the funeral, burial, cremation, or memorial service arrangements. Unless the widow or widower specifically asks another to decide, she or he must be consulted and included in planning and carrying out arrangements. Doing too much for the widowed person can cause frustration. It can also rob him or her of a valuable opportunity to begin working toward emotional acceptance of the death of the spouse. Denial that the spouse has died is a normal feature of early bereavement. Yet if the widowed person is kept from participating in the ritual separation from the spouse, denial will take a firmer hold and will last longer.

Intrusive or coercive behavior of any kind is rarely welcome.

When I went upstairs to rest the night my wife died, it bothered me greatly that someone had removed a large wedding picture of my wife from my bedroom wall and placed it in the dresser drawer. After rummaging around the room, I found it and immediately put it back on the wall, simply because that's where I wanted it. I wasn't angry, because I instinctively knew that someone was trying to protect my feelings. Nonetheless, I resented the intrusiveness of someone touching that picture.

In sum, caring words can comfort a widowed person, but considerate behavior will be more valued than flowers, and tangible, practical support is far better than vague promises. During the first weeks after my wife died, two of my friends took my two young children to their house to stay overnight with their children, thus allowing me to get some needed extra sleep. I awoke feeling better, still numb but able to perform certain tasks that had to be done without being overwhelmed by having to attend to diapers, prepare food and get them dressed at the same time.

My experience was quite typical. As I interviewed widowed women and men, I learned that caregiving and nurturing usually begin immediately, and they take many forms: Widowed women and men receive visits, telephone calls, invitations to dinner, cards or letters, offers to clean the house or cut the grass, gifts of food, religious items, reading materials, flowers, or candy. One widow even received a mammoth crate of oranges from Florida.

Perhaps the most characteristic American custom is calling on newly widowed people, who respond in various ways to this flurry of personal attention. Some may consider the gathering a celebration, while others may feel that sadness is the only permissible emotion to express. Some quietly retreat to the periphery, while others position themselves in the center, in an attempt to bring a kind of normalcy to the situation. By acting "normally" (usually as a "social director"), the widow can direct her energy toward the goal of helping callers be comfortable. The widow's hostess behavior conveys implicit permission to callers to behave socially: to talk about subjects other than the deceased, such as the weather, home decor, dinner, or politics. Or they may discuss the deceased in an objective, detached manner.

While social conversation may be easier for some widows and their guests alike, it must not restrict or prevent the widowed person's expression of grief, especially early in bereavement. All callers should take cues from the surviving spouse and the immediate family: If one is greeted with a smile and laughter, one can respond in kind. If one is met with tears, a hug is a far better response than a clever word or anecdote. Meeting the newly bereaved person is never a time for making believe all is well, even if the bereaved person looks well. Every widowed person needs time to grieve. But crying and expressing the full measure of one's despair is not easily done in the presence of a large group of people, and their full grieving is postponed until only one or a few close friends or family remain. Hence, callers who are not close friends of family should limit their stay. They should greet the widow(er), and before leaving they should make certain that a family member or close friend will remain.

There is another reason why callers should limit their stay: Widowed people, close to exhaustion within the first forty-eight hours after their spouse has died, are in desperate need of rest. Human company is vital, but too many people at once, or an endless stream of callers, can overwhelm.

When the callers have gone, taking with them the distraction provided by social conversation (which is usually more comforting to callers than to the widowed person), the widow or widower experiences a surge of grief. This is why it is especially important for the primary caregiver to stay with the widowed person during the first two days of bereavement, possibly longer depending on circumstances. Newly widowed people sometimes invite close friends or family to stay for a few days to help. If no one is invited to stay, someone—preferably the closest relative or friend—should probably offer to do so or at least raise the issue. But it is not wise to force oneself on a widow who prefers not to have company. Ultimately, all decisions should respect the wishes of the widowed person, unless he or she appears seriously self-destructive. And even then, it is important to tread with care, and in consultation with a mental health professional.

Friends and family should not expect reciprocity in their interactions with widowed people early in the bereavement process. At that time, all widowed people are highly self-focused. And at times they can even be apathetic or hostile toward others. Social graces normally taken for granted cannot be demanded from them. They need human contact and nurturance but are often temporarily incapable of putting aside their own feelings of grief, fear, and anger to respond graciously when others express concern. It is even possible that nothing that a friend or family member can do will please the widowed person, yet this too should not be misinterpreted as rejection or disapproval. The newly bereaved widow or widower is simply not yet capable of reciprocating or of attending to the emotional, psychological, or physical needs of another person, no matter how beloved.

The role of professionals in the support of newly widowed people is quite important. Funeral directors have traditionally been the most visible and helpful source of professional support, capable of providing services beyond the disposition of the body. Others, such as physicians, nurses, clergy, social workers, and hospice staff, also provide valuable support early in bereavement. But generally speaking, family and friends' support is the most comprehensive, personal, and consistent at the beginning of bereavement and during the first two stages.

As widowed people move through bereavement, the type of support they receive changes too. By the end of respondence, although grief has not disappeared, the most intense grief has subsided. This means that widowed persons need the freedom to reach out to others outside the family, and the permission to grow away from the strong dependency on the family that may have developed during early bereavement. Later, during Emergence widowed people fully shift their focus, becoming more concerned with financial and interpersonal issues, redefining goals, surviving as a single adult or as a single parent, and building new relationships while maintaining established ones. Therefore, support for widowed people should focus less on sympathy and comfort and more on helping them build new relationships and reestablish a sense of equilibrium in their social lives.[16]

Eventually, support from friends and colleagues becomes more significant than family support in facilitating movement beyond widowhood.[17] Generally speaking, after the first year of bereavement the family is still central in the support network of the widowed. But its power and presence must recede as the widow begins to move through emergence, or it can become suffocating. This is especially true for a widowed person seeking to build a life quite different from his or her past life.

Intense involvement with the family can result in dependency on the family. A widow can become so tightly enmeshed in the needs of others that reestablishing herself as a single person can be difficult, perhaps even harder than when she first established herself as an independent woman. This is perhaps more of a potential problem for widows than widowers, because of the different roles assigned to men and women. When an adult returns to the "child" role by moving in with his or her parents, the role of "son" allows more freedom and opportunity to meet others; more restrictive expectations are placed on widows in the role of "daughter." Caring for the family, nursing ill relatives, and performing different domestic tasks and child care can take up much of a dependent widow's time, leaving her with little to pursue interests of her own. A widow's emergence may come as an unwelcome surprise to a family that is not ready to accept (or may never accept) her movement beyond widowhood. They may be unprepared for the end of her mourning, or for her new, close and/or intimate relationship with anyone other than the deceased spouse. Many families consider a deceased son-in-law or a daughter-in-law to have been an esteemed family member ("She had to be a saint to marry our son!"), and will not release the memory as quickly as their widowed daughter or son may desire; an entire family may sanctify the memory of the deceased in-law.

The widow in that situation must communicate with her family, enlisting their understanding that she must emotionally (and physically) move away from them, without that movement being taken as a sign of rejection or disapproval of the family. They must understand the difference between support and dependency. The family must give the widow her freedom, allowing her to contribute to the family again as an independent, healthy adult instead of as a chronically dependent widow.

Having spent the majority of their lifetimes as married people, married to one person, widowed people confront two social challenges. First, although they are single, their social circle is different from the social circle of single people. Except for older widowed women (whose friends tend to be widows), the friends of most widowed persons tend to be married and the widowed person often feels "like a fifth wheel" when socializing with them. In addition, it may be difficult for both the widower or widow and friends to achieve a comfortable way of interacting. Some of my married friends focused on the past by continuing to talk about things I did with my first wife, while others wanted to rush me into another relationship. I became acutely aware of the powerful social pressure to marry (and remarry) when I became widowed. The pressure can be magnified if married friends try to arrange "matches" for the widowed person. After my wife died I was invited to more than one dinner to discover that the only other dinner guest was a single woman about the same age as I was . . . "someone I thought you'd like to meet. She likes Mozart, too!" Eventually I accepted few dinner invitations except those from my closest friends—those whose surprises were limited to marvelous homemade chili.

Matchmaking can be painful because, by raising the issue of "a new person," it keeps the widower's attention focused on the absence of his spouse. Conversation can be awkward, especially in front of "new" people. For example, to be a single man who begins a conversation saying, "You know, my wife was saying the same thing last week . . ." can be embarrassing, because a hush invariably falls when "my wife" is mentioned. Being single again after years of being married, I immediately became aware of the social "protection" marriage provides, especially in cross-sex interactions. Even light banter with unmarried women now made me uneasy, for I wondered if my behavior might be interpreted as romantic interest. Thus, matchmaking for widowed persons is best delayed until later in bereavement.

Widowed persons are also faced with a time warp: Their skills for dealing with new people may not be up to date. Widows may be surprised at how "forward" single men appear to be. Similarly, widowed men characterize single women as being less inhibited than they remember women being when they were single. Those who work in a therapeutic capacity with widowed people (as well as those who befriend them) must realize that to widowed men and women being single means an image of themselves when they were first single, prior to marriage. Thus, their reactions to being single will reflect values, generalizations and stereotypes that were formed at an earlier time and reinforced over years of marriage. A widowed man or woman may miss the sexual relationship enjoyed while married, yet may feel uneasy about meeting that sexual need outside of an intimate, committed relationship, or outside of marriage. Even widowed persons who experience relief after the death of a spouse will require time to readjust. As one widowed friend told me:

> When I met [my new husband], I only knew how to act like a wife . . . I thought being a woman meant you take care of men, that you serve them and stroke their egos. But he was really different. I saw that he needs me for myself and not what I do for him. Before I met him, I thought all men were the same. They aren't.

Forming and maintaining individual friendships is especially essential for widowed people. Particularly important throughout the bereavement process are "confidants," significantly close personal friends with whom one can safely share one's deepest concerns and joys. In my evaluation of the importance of the many facets of widowhood, I found that widows who had a confidant relationship had higher levels of well-being, showing more satisfaction and less distress than those with no confidant.

Ideally, confidants strike just the right balance by providing support and nurturance yet at the same time encouraging the widowed person to pursue actively activities and relationships—both new and old—that are fulfilling. Confidant relationships provide an ongoing exchange of emotions that affirms and renews our worth as human beings. They bolster us against the loneliness that not only diminishes happiness and feelings of self-worth but also provokes anxiety and fear, which undermine health.[18]

Confidant relationships are so important to widowed people because they provide intimacy, a basic human need encompassing the needs to be accepted, valued, and loved by another human being. The importance of intimacy, as distinct from social contact, is evident when we look at widows who have an active social life but no close confidant relationship. They are more likely to be depressed than are inactive persons who have confidant relationships.[19] Intimacy provides hope: a promise of personal renewal through close friendship or romance with another. Numerous widowed women in my investigation had close confidant friendships with other women (and sometimes with men) when their husbands died. These friends were still important sources of solace and comfort years later. Widowed women with a "new" confidant (one not known before the death of the spouse) had significantly higher levels of well-being and less distress than widows with no confidant, and slightly higher levels than widows with an "old" confidant. Perhaps widows who are happier and more self-confident are more likely to attract new friends or confidants. Or perhaps those widowed people with new confidants are more easily able to function as "new people" themselves, while those with "old" confidants may feel some obligation to live according to the way things were before their spouse died. New confidants are to widowed people what tailors were to George Bernard Shaw. In *Man and Superman,* Shaw's character John Tanner spoke of the difficulty he faced when his old friends clung to their fixed perceptions:

> I had become a new person; and those who knew the old person laughed at me. The only man who behaved sensibly was my tailor; he took my measure anew every time he saw me, whilst all the rest went on with their old measurements and expected them to fit me.[20]

The gender of the confidant is also important. Almost five out of every ten widowed women in my investigation had other women as their closest confidants, while two out of every ten widows had men as their closest confidants. (The rest had no confidant or were not particularly close to one person.) Widows with male confidants adapted better than those with only female confidants, probably because of the value they—and society at large—place on heterosexual relationships. It is also possible that some of these relationships offered the possibility of marriage, enhancing feelings of well-being among those who sought to be remarried.

Nevertheless, having a confidant is of itself more important to adaptation than is the gender of that confidant. A confidant can help a widow move more smoothly through bereavement, toward a more positive adaptation. Nevertheless, it is important to emphasize that the confidant him- or herself does not cause the widow's growth through and beyond widowhood. The restorative power lies not within the confidant but in the relationship itself. Other investigations have also emphasized the importance of friendships in the healthy adaptation of young, middle-aged, and older widowed women.[21]

The age of the widow plays a key role in predicting her likelihood of having a male or female confidant. Among the group of middle-aged and older widows I interviewed (that is, those forty and older), few had male confidants at the time of interview, while almost half of all widows younger than forty named a man as their closest confidant. As discussed earlier, these differences are understandable because far fewer single men are available to middle-aged and older widows, and older widows might simply be less inclined to seek relationships with men even if the number of available men were greater. They offered differing reasons such as being "too old" to remarry, being satisfied with their situation, and thinking there were too few worthwhile single men at their age. Some said they felt pressure against remarriage (mostly from their adult children), while others were afraid of the task of tending to the needs of an ill person. Most answers were pragmatic; unlike young widows, few older widows expressed idealistic reasons for or against new relationships. Unlike middle-aged widows, older widows appeared relatively unconcerned with "what others might think" if they began a relationship with a new man. Older widows seemed generally satisfied with their friendships, which usually were with other widows. Indeed, although married women typically are more satisfied with their lives than widowed women, in very old age widowed women surpass married women in level of life satisfaction.[22] Having a confidant relationship for widows—even very late in life—represents a buffer against loneliness.

Although remarrying may be an important goal for those women who value being married, remarriage has more auspicious implications for men's adaptation. Because marriage is so valuable to men's health and longevity, formerly married men are an especially high-risk group, especially widowed men in the middle and older years. Unlike widowed women who derive support from their networks (children, parents, lovers, friends, family), middle-aged and older widowed men often suffer from the absence of interpersonal relationships.

Widowed men explained that they did not develop many or close friendships with other men (or women) while married, lending support to the notion that many men rely on their wives as their exclusive source of meaningful social interaction.[23] For most widowed men, remarriage is the most likely route to a confidant who can provide the self-validation he cannot derive from friendships with others. Lowenthal and Weiss of the Human Development Program of the University of California also found that:

> Widowhood is often more traumatic for men than widowhood for women, and we explain this on the basis that men are less likely to have other persons with whom they are

intimate. In fact, men name their spouses as confidants far more often than women do.[24]

Even after the death of a spouse, men rarely go to self-help and support groups. Leaders of those groups attest to the difficulty they face getting men to show up for meetings, and the further difficulty they see men having in "opening up" once they do attend. Widower Bob Allan found talking about his wife's death almost impossible until he met other widows at the Widows' Network in Lafayette, California. Allan analyzed the plight of widowed men quite accurately: "When a man is widowed, nine times out of ten his men friends give him a strong handshake and a steely look in the eye and say hang in there. And women friends hesitate to give real emotional support because of the sexual hang-up. A man goes without hugs."[25]

But despite their intense need for interpersonal closeness (that can evolve into dependency in some marriage relationships), many men adopt culturally accepted and approved ways of masking that need to others and to themselves. There are numerous ways in which men talk and act as though they have no need for—or interest in—intimacy. "Gene," a tall, good-looking computer programmer widowed eight months, exemplified the difficulty some young and middle-aged men face in becoming aware of—and sharing—their feelings. At a Cleveland support group's open house, he and I were two of only a few men attending along with at least thirty widowed women:

"Don't let these women kid you. They're here looking for a husband. That's why they keep joking about how men aren't here," he said. I asked Gene if he was looking for a wife.

"Me? Naw. But I am looking to enjoy myself. After Sandy died I had this feeling that I wanted to get married again right away, but it was a foolish idea, you know? Let me show you something." We walked out to the parking lot and Gene unlocked a brilliant black Pontiac Trans-Am. We sat inside as he told me about its engine, how much it cost, and the various options.

"This is my new toy. We'd been socking away money to buy a house, but after Sandy died I went crazy. That first year I almost went broke buying things—a new stereo, a VCR, an IBM computer—the XT—the three-thousand-dollar one, not the PC, but I couldn't resist this baby," he said as he patted the steering wheel.

"You know what's the hardest thing about losing Sandy? It's this: whenever I meet somebody, they go like this when I say I'm a widower," and he slowly drew his hands together and exhaled air in the manner of a balloon losing its air.

"Forget it. Never tell a girl you're a widower. When you go out and meet somebody they go, 'Oh, wow. Sorry to hear that,' and they politely walk away. And these support-group widows are just as weird. They're 'casserole ladies.'" I asked what he meant.

"They just want to feed you and feel sorry for you, but they don't even want to get involved with anybody. Even if fifty men showed up they would say none of them measure up to their Freddie or whoever." Gene told me Sandy died of a brain tumor; it was totally unexpected. Fortunately, he said, they had no kids. I asked him what he was planning for his future.

"Well, I'm probably never going to find another girl like Sandy—I was lucky—so I don't know if I ever want to get married again. Even though we loved each other, we had our own lives, you know what I mean? She was getting her master's and all that, so we hardly saw each other. Say, listen to this!" Turning up his digital stereo to a ear-splitting level, Gene sat there grinning, tapping his steering wheel. He stared straight ahead through the windshield and nodded.

"Yeah. From now on, I tell the chicks I'm divorced. They can relate to that!"

Despite his cocky, carefree manner and all the outward signs of cynicism, Gene was advertising his loneliness and need for affiliation. His conceptualization of relationships was simplistic: His feelings were so submerged that he defined the "hardest thing" about losing his wife not in terms of loneliness (He couldn't say, simply, "I miss her" or "I'm lonely as hell!") but in terms of how his consequent status as a widower was detrimental to his chances of meeting a new woman. And he spoke of a search for a new relationship not in terms of the wish to give or receive care, friendship, or love but simply in terms of the "correct moves" or strategy of the chase. Gene was able to express his loneliness and desire to establish new ties with women only indirectly and ineffectively.

Like Gene, many American men are "on the run" from intimacy and often do not perceive—and thus cannot acknowledge to themselves or others—what they are missing by fleeing. As I discussed the loss of intimacy with widowed men, most interpreted my word *intimacy* as *sexuality,* and "sharing intimacy" with a woman meant "having sexual relations" with a woman. Whereas to women I interviewed, intimacy encompassed a sharing of feelings, close contact, confiding, sexuality, and a feeling that their particular relationship was unique—a special relationship not devoid of, but not so highly focused on, sexual fulfillment.

Without the emotional support that is so essential for survival, young widowed men who do not remarry often increase their consumption of alcohol, tobacco, and tranquilizers, or they experience sleep, appetite, and weight disturbances.[26] Widowed men appear more predisposed toward self-abusive habits than other men, most notably alcohol and tobacco abuse, poor diet, and lack of exercise. (In contrast, widows smoke less than single, married, divorced, or separated women.[27]) Widowers' self-abusive and self-destructive behaviors, most notably their high suicide rates,[28] are health issues that must be addressed.

Research must examine mens' dependence on marriage and its implications for their—and their wives'—quality of life. Support services for widowed men must by nature be of the outreach type, where clients can receive services at or near their homes, because most widowed men will not seek support. The components must include a medical examination, health counseling, psychological evaluation, and a professional one-to-one contact, similar to Widow-to-Widow, in which a nurturing man who has successfully moved through widowhood (or other serious life crisis) maintains regular contact with a newly widowed man. A paid, professional position, it would encourage even remarried former widowers to participate and attract nurturing men from a very limited pool. It would provide an alternative to men's utter reliance on marriage for confidant relationships and would at least provide intensive support until other ongoing support can be arranged. Although intimacy is not a cure-all, any social program that intends to ease the plight of widowed men in any age group should capitalize on our knowledge of the benefits of ongoing, caring, personal contact—especially for those stoic men who appear to need it least.

CHAPTER 7

Remarriage
Obstacles and Satisfactions

I need to feel, to be alive *with* someone, no longer alone—to *share* thoughts, love, hate, all the emotions in the world. To touch someone *mentally,* not just physically. I want to create and be created. Not stifled, not ignored, not rejected. I need someone who will *say* to me when I hurt so powerfully "I am sorry you feel pain, I care." Someone who will *share* my joy, my happiness and sadness, who will listen to my doubts, delight in and laugh at my silly fantasies *with* me and accept them as a part of me.

—NANCY MYERS, *"Surviving the Loss of Self-Identity"*

At a weekend retreat for widowed people in Maine one of the presentations was "Relationships and Remarriage." As I stood outside the room awaiting the discussion group leader, a few women walked by and one—pointing to the word *remarriage* written on a sign near the door—was aghast:

"Remarriage?" she spat. "*Who* can think of remarriage? I'm still trying to get over my last marriage!" Her companion sounded even more indignant: "I think this has no business being here. I didn't come to get remarried; what do they think this is—a singles bar?" But a third widow, who appeared to be the oldest, disagreed: "I'm going in. My boyfriend is constantly after me to get married. Maybe I can learn something here," and she walked in, leaving the other two to attend a different seminar. I walked in behind her and said, "It seems like 'remarriage' is almost a dirty word to some people." Turning to me, she said "Oh, some of these widows feel like they *have to* say that they don't want to get married again, because it would sound like they were disloyal or hungry. But most of them would jump at the chance to get married if a nice man came along."

Ambivalence is one of the hallmarks of bereavement. It is highly likely that those objecting to the presentation were at the same time drawn to the subject of remarriage. Conversely, those openly interested in the subject harbored uneasiness; uncertain, perhaps, whether or not enough time had passed. Despite feeling lonely and wanting a close relationship, widowed people may feel compelled to disavow interest in remarriage for many reasons, including a need to appear or remain "loyal" to the memory of their deceased spouses or out of fear of losing a spouse again. After years of marriage, it is not easy to sever ties to their spouses. It is even more difficult for some openly to *admit* their intentions of doing so. Unfortunately, there is still a vague "unseemliness" about remarriage—and new relationships—among widowed people.

But this attitude is becoming less prevalent. Almost 45 percent of all contemporary marriages involve at least one partner who is remarrying, compared to 31 percent of all marriages in 1970. Historically, the vast majority of American marriages ended at the death of one spouse. But since the 1930s, the divorce rate has increased dramatically while the rate of widowhood has remained constant. Hence, most contemporary remarriages are made by those who have been divorced: 87 percent of all remarrying women have been divorced and 13 percent widowed; of the men, 89 percent have been divorced and 11 percent widowed.

While the remarriage patterns of divorced men and women are fairly similar, there is a substantial difference between widowed men and widowed women. Widowed men remarry at a rate almost identical to the remarriage rate of divorced men and divorced women. In middle adulthood (thirty-five to fifty-four years of age), the remarriage rates are high for all three groups: 71 percent of widowed men, 80 percent of divorced men, and 71 percent of divorced women remarry. Yet fewer than half of widowed women (49 percent) remarry, and that percentage decreases with age: Fewer than 5 percent of widows older than fifty-five ever remarry.

One reality that limits the likelihood of widows' remarriage is that they outnumber widowers throughout the lifespan: 2 percent of all males older than fourteen years of age are widowed compared to 12 percent of all women, but that difference is not constant. Due to the shorter lives of men (especially single men), this scarcity is especially pronounced for older women. At age twenty-five, widowed women outnumber widowed men three to one; at age thirty-five that ratio has grown to eleven to one. Although the difference moderates toward middle age, there are never fewer than five widows for each widower throughout the balance of the life span.[1]

This discrepancy is magnified by the tendency for men to marry younger women (or *not* to marry older women). Thus, by the time a woman reaches old age, there are few eligible men in her age group. But there are indications that the significance of this demographic fact may be changing, because the "younger man–older woman" pattern is far more common today than previously. In addition, potential marriage partners can come from the ranks of the never-married or divorced men as well: I have heard widows discuss the scarcity of "marriageable men," yet single, never-married men outnumber single, never-married women in every age group between fourteen and sixty-five years of age.[2]

Secondly, older widows considering remarriage to people their own age must often contend with difficulties posed by differences in health or energy level. A frail widow may not be able to sustain a relationship with a more active man who enjoys extensive travel and exercise. On the other hand, widowed people who have lived through years of caring for an ill spouse may not wish to repeat that experience. Widowed women who express relief often cite the burden of caring for a highly dependent spouse who had a serious or terminal illness that required home care for a period of time. Thus, an older widow or widower considering remarriage must also accept the possibility of illness and physical dependence of one or both partners.

Another consideration faced by widowed persons contemplating remarriage is the presence of dependent children. About nine out of ten young children and adolescents living with a widowed parent live with the mother. Widowed women are more likely than divorced women to have had children, and widowed women are also more likely to have had larger families. Only one out of every four widows with three or more children ever remarries.

Men may be hesitant to take on the financial support of a widow's children (since there is no ex-spouse to send support payments), especially if they themselves have children to support from previous marriages. Furthermore, even if children do not deter a potential mate, widows with children have fewer opportunities to meet men and develop relationships with them. Widowed men's social lives tend to be less constrained by children because men are more likely to pay for help with child care than are women. This probably reflects men's greater financial resources, their sense that child care is most appropriately "woman's work," and their doubts about their own abilities to care properly for children.

Forty percent of the widowed women I interviewed stated that they wanted to remarry, while 31 percent clearly said they did not. Almost 80 percent of those younger than thirty-nine wanted to remarry or were at least open to the possibility, while this was true of only 47 percent of women older than fifty-five. Although most older widows ruled out remarriage, only 17 percent of widows between the ages of forty and fifty-four said they did not want to remarry; the remaining 83 percent wanted to remarry or, uncertain of its likelihood, were hesitant to predict.

In addition to factors like the presence of children and the disparity between the number of single men and women, the widow's unique experience with her previous marriage will influence her decision to seek—or avoid—remarriage. I heard a couple of widows aver, "I'll never make that same mistake again." At the other extreme were widows who were "hopeless romantics"—"in love with being in love."

Widows who remarry enjoy several kinds of advantages over those who do not. For older widowed people, being remarried leads to longevity, better health, and higher morale.[3] In a study of four hundred Canadian widowed men and women ages fifty-five and above, Judith Stryckman found that those who remarried had a higher morale and a better self-image than those who did not. As may be expected, widowed people who remarried were less dependent on their children and other family members, especially when it came to the decision to remarry. Of those who remarried, the majority relied on themselves alone to decide whether or not to remarry. Of those who remained single, half sought others' advice as they considered remarriage.[4]

Of all remarried widowed persons, 86 percent gave an unqualified yes when asked if they would make the same decision to remarry. Eighty percent said they were more content now that they were remarried. Mutual love was the most frequently mentioned reason for remarrying (38 percent), followed by a desire for companionship (25 percent). Although those who remarried were less well off financially than those who did not remarry, the remarried group reported fewer feelings of insecurity and less anxiety.[5] Older widowed women who remarry tend to say they are happy in successful marriages.[6] And while remarriage before the widowed person has been able to move beyond widowhood may result in an unsuitable marriage, it appears that widowed people who eventually remarry have a greater chance of marital stability (that is, a lower divorce rate) than those who remarry after a divorce.[7]

Comparing the responses of more than 4,000 Chicago-area widows of all ages who had remarried to those of over 74,000 widows who never remarried, Helena Lopata concluded:

> All the evidence presented thus far seems to indicate definite advantages of remarriage for those women . . . There are financial, service, social and emotional benefits for many women.[8]

Remarriage counteracts loneliness, the major problem faced by widowed persons. Although loneliness can also be moderated by a close friendship, remarriage implies a greater degree of commitment than friendship, and thus provides a more enduring sense of emotional security. Remarried widows' husbands provide more emotional support and contribute more practical support than widows' male friends. In my investigation, widowed women mentioned "to avoid loneliness" more frequently than other reasons:

> I'm very lonesome. I'd remarry if I found the right one, but I'd be bound to compare him to my first husband.

> Yes, I'm lonely. I tried to find a widowed group in this area, but there is none. My married friends ignore me and don't invite me any more. I'd consider getting married again.

> It's easier for a woman . . . who is married. A widow is left stranded at times for an escort. I'm not comfortable being alone.

> I'm not one to do things by myself. Socially, it's difficult to do things alone. I wouldn't remarry for the sake of marriage, but I'm outside the group of couples.

Remarriage provides an opportunity for the widowed person to achieve a fulfilling relationship, perhaps for the first time. By reflecting on their past marriage relationships, widowed persons may see aspects that were not particularly satisfactory. They may now seek, for example, a more trusting or expressive relationship, and remarriage may provide a second chance to have certain psychological, emotional, sexual, or intellectual needs met. Or, because they have changed since their previous marriages, they may now choose to have a marriage more egalitarian than the earlier one. Other widows told me they simply enjoyed being in love and saw a new marriage as the embodiment of that. A few women said they wanted to remarry for companionship, typically saying "I don't want to grow old alone!"

Remarriage can provide financial and emotional support for the widow with young children. Although single parenting has become more common and more accepted over the past three decades, raising children is still a job—one that is usually easier to manage when shared with another adult. Sharing the responsibility of child care and nurture with a stepparent can give the partner more time to pursue interests outside the home or workplace. Despite contemporary emphasis on remarriage as a means of providing an adult role model for children, few widows mentioned that issue. Most of those who sought remarriage for "the good of the children" also mentioned practical reasons such as financial support or someone with whom to share responsibilities. However, many were hesitant to endorse remarriage enthusiastically because of its unknown effects on their children:

> No, I don't want to get married, at least not now. I'm very close to my children, and I don't want marriage to hurt them.

> I want time to take care of my children . . . don't want the problems that might come with a new spouse. I don't know how it would affect my children.

In addition to another pair of hands, financial support and companionship, remarriage can offer a focus for at least part of a widow's new identity. Being able to give what another will need, enjoy, and value, and simultaneously receiving what one needs, enjoys and values helps each person's identity to become enriched and strengthened. One of the strongest predictors of remarriage happiness (and ultimately, of remarriage stability) is a clear sense of personal identity and self-esteem.[9] Remarriage provides an ongoing verification of that identity. Being valued by another person, one's own value (identity) is affirmed. In describing the significance of being loved by another, psychologist Ann Swidler identified precisely the same advantages enjoyed by widowed people who choose remarriage:

> In loving and being loved, people give themselves over, at least for brief periods, to intensely moving experiences through which they achieve new awareness of self and others. Love can make possible periods of crystallization or reformulation of the self and the self's relationship to the world. Beliefs about love permeate people's hopes for themselves, their evaluations of experience, and their sense of achievement in the world.[10]

But no matter how satisfying it may be, remarriage cannot substitute for a reformulated individual identity. Like first marriage, remarriage provides the most for both partners if they come into it with a reasonably well-formulated or reformulated sense of personal identity. As mentioned earlier, a few widowed men or women engage in "barracuda" behavior, seeking to latch onto a partner soon after the death of the spouse. Those who seek remarriage (rapid or otherwise) simply as a replacement for the lost marital identity or as a way of avoiding identity reformulation are less likely to be fully capable of helping another meet his or her needs in marriage. Or they may focus so exclusively on another's needs that their own remain largely unmet. For satisfying remarriage, a man or woman must define, create, and accept a *new* bond with the new person, instead of superimposing a familiar definition (that of the prior marriage) on the new relationship.

Despite the important emotional, social, and psychological benefits of marriage, some widowed persons are hesitant to remarry, often seeking to avoid bearing the burden of caring for a dependent mate, like their former spouse. Emotional dependence can psychologically and physically drain the one depended upon. I interviewed widows whose husbands had relied on them to buy their personal clothing, prepare all meals, discipline the children, and generally do most of the interacting with other people. While married, many of the women in those dependent-husband relationships accepted the situation as "the way things are." Once widowed, however, they saw their husbands' reliance on them not as flattering devotion but as unwelcome dependence.

Even very powerful men have been dependent upon their wives: Following the death of his first wife in 1914, former President Woodrow Wilson became severely depressed and saddened, almost totally unable to carry on his duties. One and one-half years following his wife's death, he married Edith Galt, a widow who reportedly brought happiness and security to their marriage. Edith provided immense support for the increasingly dependent president, literally guiding his hand in signing documents after his paralyzing stroke in 1919. Since the Constitution did not provide for successorship to an incapacitated president, and since Wilson did not give up the presidency, his wife filled the void. Woodrow Wilson left his bed only for brief movements and for simple, formal tasks, with Edith Galt Wilson performing most of the president's duties for the balance of Wilson's term of office.

Women too may become dependent upon spouses. Psychotherapist Jean Miller warns that women can become dependent when marital relationships grow into an unequal "leader-follower" relationship instead of a mutual and more egalitarian affiliation. Since they place a greater emphasis on affiliation than do their spouses, women may be perceived to be more dependent. This can also come about through their reliance on a significant other (such as a husband) to "affirm and confirm" their value and identity as a person. Such women may struggle with feelings that their achievements are worthless unless another person makes them worthwhile.[11]

While dependence is often viewed as implying a subordinate, powerless position in a relationship, it can function as a demand or expectation that the other do what one "cannot" or will not do for oneself. Thus, one spouse may depend on the other to perform a role or task such as breadwinning, cooking, cutting the grass, or taking care of children. If the spouse does not complete the expected task or behavior, that failure is interpreted as a personal affront: "I depended on him to . . . and he let me down." Since no man or woman is capable of working full-time to meet the needs of another no matter how much they may be beloved, dependence inevitably leads to disappointment. That disappointment may be translated into anger or resentment toward the spouse, or viewed as an indication that one is not sufficiently valued: "If he really loved me, he would have . . ." The dependent spouse may then conclude that something is wrong with her—that had she been a better person, more valued or lovable, the spouse would have performed as she desired.

Many widowed persons who consider remarriage are aware of this potential not only in themselves but as expectations to be placed on them by remarriage partners. They can then acknowledge and deal openly with the causes and consequences of dependency. A few widowed women reported that their spouses helped them become less dependent. One widow said that when her husband became aware that his illness would take his life, he began to "teach me how to take care of myself." She described how he sat down with her to instruct her concerning finances, paying bills, managing investments, and taking care of business matters that he had previously preferred to do by himself. This helped her feel more competent in these affairs after he died. Such preparation was not typical of most of the widows I interviewed.

Many clearly stated that they realized how dependent they had been on their spouses. Many became aware of their dependency only after their spouse died. Even if they did not acknowledge it directly, a fear of becoming dependent upon a new spouse was expressed indirectly:

> I like my independence. I have more confidence now in myself.

> I found out that I love to be alone. There has been a complete turnaround in myself. There's no more structure or supper hours, but I'm not a homebody anymore.

> I've made a lot of friends (since he died). I'm more independent and I have more opportunities.

Other women were aware of their new status, yet were not clearly sure they liked it better:

> I don't have someone to depend upon now. I have to fend for myself now.

> After my husband died, I had to go to work. Life isn't fun and games anymore.

In addition to considering issues of dependence, widowed persons should be aware of the related danger of framing remarriage as a treatment or cure for bereavement. Such a view casts the new spouse in the role of healer or savior, and it burdens the relationship as well, making it a one-way, therapeutic interaction: The doctor performs and the patient receives. While relationships can be healing, remarriage requires mutuality to be fulfilling.

Another consideration that dissuades some from remarrying is the prospect of becoming a stepparent, taking on a new web of relationships, forming perhaps a "blended family." There is little doubt that stepparents have been poorly treated, regarded as "cruel" in stories like *Cinderella* and *Hansel and Gretel,* and vilified in the popular literature from Hawaii to China to Iceland. But along with the historical disdain for stepparents is an equally ambivalent feeling by stepparents toward stepchildren:

> People go into second marriages with enormous hopes. They have failed once, or they have had their marriages broken by death, and they want everything to go right the next time. They idealize the new partner and then they find they have the partner's children to deal with as well and the idealization does not extend to the children. Far from it. The hostility aroused by the children jeopardizes the marriage. . . .[12]

When remarriage is not "just the two of us" a common issue that arises involves "my-mom-your-dad" feelings. The stepparent can be viewed as an intruder, one "trying to take the place of" the deceased parent. Children will also cling to the surviving parent because remarriage threatens a child's value in the family. The child resents competing with the new stepparent for the attention, time, and affection of his parent. It is also possible that a child will bring up the memory of the deceased parent in direct comparison to the stepparent. While fears of such situations should not prevent a widowed person from remarrying, they do need to be discussed before remarrying. Discussion need not produce a fully articulated strategy to "attack" the problem, but it should enable both partners to convey to the children expectations of respect and support for both the natural and stepparent.

Parents should discuss remarriage with their young children and adolescents. Without asking their permission, parents should try to get some feeling for how their children might view such a remarriage. The prospective spouse should not be present at this first discussion, to free children to ask the hard questions that may need airing, such as: "What do I call him? What would my 'real' Dad think about this?" It is normal for children to be self-focused. Given ample opportunity to discuss a parent's remarriage, children may still see no (personal) benefit in it or may downplay those benefits when weighed against the fear of another person "invading" their territory, competing for their parent's attention.

In addition to wanting to protect their self-interest in the family, children may also want to protect the natural parent from the new adult. Even among less demonstrative adults, remarriage involves an exchange of romantic gestures, words, feelings, and actions. Children are not normally willing witnesses to these even if they are not "sexual" by adult standards. They simply do not want to share their parents' affections with another adult or child. In addition, children are not comfortable seeing their parents as sexual or romantic beings, and not fully able to understand sexual or romantic attraction, they may protest by asking, literally, "Why do you have to get remarried? I don't want another Mom (Dad)!" Here too, both prospective partners should share their concerns with each other, understanding that it takes most children time to become used to new situations. It may also be comforting to keep in mind that, given the relatively high rate of contemporary divorce and remarriage, children and stepchildren of formerly widowed parents will have many classmates and neighbors who share their experience of living in blended families.

Because they are younger and their memories are not so extensive, infants and pre-school-age children will usually have less difficulty in accepting a stepparent as their legitimate parent. The older child's acceptance of the stepparent will be facilitated if the surviving parent can avoid immediately referring to the new spouse as "your new mother (or father)." That encourages a too-intense comparison with the deceased parent, condemning the stepparent to second best. Instead, the child should be able to spend time with a potential stepparent before remarriage takes place—permitted to get to know the new adult as an individual and not as a replacement. Forcing or bribing the child to accept another adult as a parent will not bring about closeness or respect for the stepparent. Only through the accumulation of positive feelings and interactions with the new parent over time will the child come to know, trust, and ultimately, love a stepparent. It takes time.

A desire to "protect" the widowed person from new ties seen as entanglements or threats is not restricted to young children. Sometimes, antiremarriage attitudes flourish among those who have provided the most support to the widow: family (including adult children) and close friends. These are the people who can and often do provide the strongest and most vociferous opposition to an intended remarriage. Usually driven by a sense of "loyalty" to the widow's deceased spouse, they may discourage the widow from seeking close relationships with new friends (specifically, with single men).

Older people face an especially strong societal discouragement of their remarriage,[13] and this affects widowed men and women equally. Writing for the Widowed Persons Service, James Peterson acknowledged that while younger adults in general contend with a high divorce rate and thus view any remarriages as risky, some widows' children view their own parents remarrying as "somewhere between a violation of the Ten Commandments and high treason."[14]

Adult children can provide the most strenuous opposition to remarriage. In the Canadian study reported earlier, widowed men and women who decided not to remarry explained their decision as mostly due to opposition from their children.[15] One widow's daughter became so distraught after the widow's return from her first date that the mother simply stopped dating. Another widow reported that her grown son and his family stopped visiting her completely to protest her decision to share an apartment with a widowed man. Unfortunately, it is not unknown for adult children to boycott the wedding of their widowed parent to a new spouse, staying out of touch with the remarried parent long after the ceremony. Widowed men and women must be especially clear-eyed in recognizing "emotional blackmail," realizing that children can be petulant even if they are forty years of age. If a choice develops between the approval of the child and the remarriage, the widowed parent would be wise to discuss this with the child but clearly reserve the right to make his or her own final decision.

One widow described pressure from her children—how her son and daughter opposed her remarriage, saying that it was "being disloyal to Dad." She responded to their pressure by capitulating; she refused to marry, and at the time we spoke she was "seeing him on the sly," hoping that her children would not "catch" her with him. Perhaps used to seeing their mothers in maternal roles, adult children may be disturbed seeing a mother dress differently, take up new interests or occupations, and generally live a new life. Widowed parents' friendships can be scrutinized by adult children who may wish to protect them from "gold diggers"—men or women "only after his money." Children may be concerned with losing their share of the family estate if a parent remarries. The prospect of a large business or cash holding being divided among stepchildren upon the parent's death may provoke anger at sharing Dad's or Mom's hard-earned money with "strangers."[16]

Financial considerations may also discourage many elderly people themselves from remarrying: An individual's income may decrease if he or she remarries. For example, spouses of U.S. armed forces veterans who have suffered "service-connected disabilities" continue to receive a stipend after their spouses have died. However, these stipends are withdrawn by the Veterans Administration if the veteran's widow remarries. This is also true for widowed persons receiving pensions from the Railroad Retirement System. Widows who receive survivor's benefits from Social Security lose that income if they remarry before age sixty-five. Fortunately, remarriage no longer reduces Social Security retirement benefits, and no Social Security benefits are taxed unless the widow has other income over a certain limit.

The Internal Revenue Service does allow a widow or widower to file as a "qualified widow or widower." This entitles the widowed person to use favorable "joint return rates" for two tax years following the death of a spouse, provided certain provisions are met, including the provision that the widowed person does not remarry. However, the current tax code does "taint" the widower or widow who has received a tax waiver on the sale of a family home. Since it is a one-time benefit, someone marrying a "tainted" widow stands to lose the capital gains benefits from the sale of a home they would hold jointly.

Of all obstacles to remarriage and to growing beyond widowhood, the most formidable lie within the widowed persons themselves and the significance of ongoing bereavement in their lives. Even two years after the death, many widows continue to experience episodes of grief. These are not necessarily signs of abnormality:

> I have known mourners who after the loss of their partners suffered from episodes of depression, despair, and regressive setbacks for well over two years and later made exceptionally good adaptations to a new life.[17]

Unless they are severe or endure for a long period of time, however, these episodes do indicate that the widowed person is not yet fully past bereavement. For some widowed men and women, grief can be particularly acute on holidays, birthdays, and anniversaries, which are rich with associations to past celebrations with the deceased spouse. Painful as they may be, these episodes of grief provide an opportunity for a widow to look back and gauge how much healing has taken place. They help us see how far we have moved from the early days of bereavement:

> Getting through my first Christmas without him was so difficult. So hard. I missed him so much I cried all day. But the second Christmas was easier.

> Holidays were the worst. I dreaded the thought that his birthday was coming. All the holidays were bad. Now, I still think of him, but it isn't with the same dreadful feeling.

At first, bereaved men and women mentally fight the closure of bereavement by focusing avidly on the deceased spouse. This focus is naturally very painful, because it is a constant reminder that the spouse has died. But as time passes, the memory grows dimmer and the bereaved person's consciousness focuses on other thoughts. As the widowed person becomes more concerned with matters of daily living and less focused on the memory of the deceased spouse, the relationship they shared becomes a fond memory, thoughts of which are no longer accompanied by intense pining or sadness. At this point the relationship is put to rest. The widow is unmarried.

Even when sufficient time has elapsed and the widow is basically "unmarried" from the deceased, the remarriage may be visited by the "ghost" of the deceased spouse. When one partner is formerly widowed, she, the new spouse, and the ghost of the deceased form a sort of marriage triangle. If both parties to a remarriage have been widowed, two interlocking triangles are created, in which both husband and wife may hold on to their old marriages as they strive to create a new one.[18] When they fear that they may not compare favorably to a former spouse, people who remarry create ghosts—idealized representations of the other's former spouse—to which they can never measure up.

Here are six of the most common "remarriage ghosts" that can be conjured up when comparisons are made:

Physical ghosts: "Was she prettier than I am? Healthier?" "Was he better looking?"

Competency ghosts: "Was she more capable than I? A better cook? Was she smarter than I?" "How do I compare to her first husband? He seemed to be very mechanical, and I'm all thumbs."

Sexy ghosts: "Was she more satisfied with him?" "Is he now missing anything he once had with her?"

Nanny ghosts: "Was she a better mother than I? Were the children better off with her?" "Was he a more loving father? The kids act like he was a god!"

Friendly ghosts: "Was she better liked by his friends? Do they compare me to her?" "Was he more sociable than I am?"

Mean ghosts: "Is his first wife mad at me for 'stealing' her husband?" "What would he say if he saw me with his wife?"

In any remarriage, there is a tendency mentally to compare the "old" with the "new" person, but formerly widowed people should be sensitive to the new spouse's fears of comparing unfavorably. Reassurance can help the new spouse understand that he is appreciated for who he is. Each partner can bring security to the remarriage by encouraging the safe discussion of feelings, especially those that may be disquieting. Reassurance defuses the power of "ghosts." Instead of hiding or avoiding one's past, a "sharing of the past may be supportive to the new tie; comparing with the past may be threatening to the remarriage."[19]

Sharing of experience must not be restrained by fear of ghosts, because such sharing is essential to the development of true mutual understanding and intimacy. There's nothing wrong with remarried couples sharing the grief they may have felt or the residue that remains. In the healthy sharing of past grief experiences, the survivor and his or her new spouse can together affirm that the grief is indeed past. Once the past is affirmed as being *past,* attention can be focused on the present and future, which belong to the new couple.

Writer David Gelman related a story of a couple who celebrated their fourth anniversary in a decidedly unique fashion. They had married each other following the deaths of their first spouses, and their story is a rather novel illustration of the "interlocking triangles" formed when two widowed people remarry. Here's how they humorously faced the ghosts of their first marriages:

> Last spring each of them would have been married to the original partner for 50 years. So on their own fourth anniversary they had a party and invited all their friends, old and new, and they had a big cake that said: 'Bill & Kay 50, Ted & Lil 50, Kay & Ted, 4.' I think that it was a wonderful kind of celebration.[20]

We should not confuse the love we shared in a past relationship with the present capacity to love again in a new relationship that is neither better nor worse but *different.* One's present happiness can never imperil or violate a past marriage; it can only serve as a tribute to what was enriching in that relationship. And just as one cannot rank one's love for mother, father, sibling, child, or other loved ones, one's present love cannot be compared to an earlier love. Remarriages can resemble prior marriages only in that they help one secure happiness, find fulfillment with life, and become one's "best self."

CHAPTER 8

Mutual Support Groups
Solace for Widowed People

Give sorrow words.
The grief that does not speak
whispers the o'erfraught heart
and bids it break.

—SHAKESPEARE, *Macbeth*

Over 150 years ago, Dr. Benjamin Rush, physician and signer of the Declaration of Independence, offered his best advice on helping grief-stricken individuals: He advised "liberal doses of opium."[1] Since 1835, we have come to realize that narcotics provide no cure for widowhood. In fact, there are no simple remedies. Despite tremendous advances in medicine and pharmacology since the days of Dr. Rush, the most effective "elixir" for normal bereavement is healthy interpersonal relationships that provide support for widowed people. When men or women become widowed, their family members or close friends provide the best immediate support, and as they grow beyond widowhood and reestablish interpersonal relationships with others, widowed people eventually interact more and more with nonfamily members.

But even the most supportive family and friends cannot meet all of the widowed person's needs or provide all of his or her support. Nor should they. While individual family members and close friends provide perhaps the most important support early in bereavement, eventually the widowed man or woman must reach out to the larger world again and reformulate his or her identity in order to move beyond widowhood. Individual adult identities cannot fully develop if they depend solely on friends or family for reflection.

Groups offer widowed persons opportunities to draw identity reflection from outside the circle of family and close friends. In addition, groups furnish a variety of positive reflections to individual members. And because of the sympathy and support they generate, groups are particularly important to individuals experiencing severe stress. For example, a recent study showed that the high level of social support available in the Israeli kibbutz may immunize members against the physiological consequences of stress.[2]

Although few Americans live in communities as cohesive and supportive as the Israeli kibbutz, we do have an abundance—perhaps half a million—of self-help or mutual support groups. There are three types of such groups: those that promote self-care or self-help (for people ill or suffering a crisis), reform groups (for addictive behaviors); and advocacy groups (to lobby for the interests of a particular social, ethnic, or racial minority). Regardless of the specific focus, "all mutual-help groups have the same underlying purpose: to provide emotional support and practical help in dealing with a problem common to all members."[3]

Mutual support groups are effective for widowed people primarily because those who attend are primarily other widowed people. As "prime mover" of the Widow-to-Widow program for widowed women, Phyllis Silverman noted that some professionals involved in giving care "were inadequate" in helping widowed persons:

> Not only did they have little understanding of what a widow or widower needs, but more often than not, they would withdraw, advising the bereaved to keep a "stiff upper lip."[4]

She was one of the first to emphasize how important other widows are in the mutual support process, mostly because they are "authentic role models" who can help widows learn new skills. Widows can (and do) provide substantial help to other widows, and they in turn derive benefits from those supportive relationships.[5] Researchers who conducted a major study of Australian widows in the first year after their husbands died found that widows reported other widows to be most helpful at that point in their bereavement.[6]

There is also encouraging research evidence that attendance and participation in mutual support groups increases the likelihood of a better adaptation to widowhood.[7] In a 1981 study members who regularly attended THEOS (a nondenominational support network whose acronym stands for "they help each other spiritually") meetings had better outcomes on four mental health indices. Active and former THEOS members showed the most improvement in depression, drug and alcohol use, self-esteem, and well-being. Particularly significant were the lowered depression and higher self-esteem scores. Compared to control groups consisting of those who never attended, or "shoppers" who attended only one meeting, those who attend or attended THEOS meetings and took an active part in social activities scored highest on all mental health indices.[8] However, there is no direct cause-and-effect relationship between attending a mutual support group and adaptation. Individual coping ability, identity strength, and the existence of other support systems (such as family and kinship) can affect adaptation irrespective of active membership in mutual support groups. There are people whose depression will be severe no matter how much social support they receive, and for whom professional help is needed.

Although there is no way to assess or predict the relative value of "inner strength" versus social support in growth through widowhood, there is little doubt that mutual support groups provide a valuable forum and an opportunity for widowed people, supplementing support from friends and family. The key to support, however, is self-help. Widowed people—like most people—profit most when they are active participants instead of passive subjects awaiting treatment. I've seen a number of skeptical widows who attended on the urging of a friend, only to remain skeptical on leaving, never to return. One widow noted that skeptics often come in with a "let's see what you can do for me but I doubt you can help me" attitude, and expecting little, they get little, leaving now fully confirmed in their skepticism of the value of support groups. "Go to a doctor or an auto mechanic if you want something repaired," said one widow. "If you want to share, heal, and grow, be prepared to actively become part of the support network. You can't get help or give help if you come just to sit on your butt!"

After interviewing and speaking with over one hundred widowed men and women, my distinct impression was that those who derived great help from the experiences they had in mutual support groups were active participants. Widowed persons who perceived themselves to be in charge of their lives were able to profit from the support available in self-help groups. They did things with the group. In addition, those who appeared to profit had a contribution to make to the group. The contribution may be simple: being an active listener, baking cookies for the group, arranging for a guest speaker, or contacting other widows to be members. In sum, widowed persons who profited did not necessarily need to be trailblazers or dynamic personalities. Attitude, determination, and motivation toward activity seemed to be of greater significance in growing beyond widowhood through mutual support groups. In every case, mutual support groups work best with emotionally stable adults who seek to share with others common concerns they face because of the crisis of widowhood.

On the other hand were those who reported little satisfaction with their lives since they became widowed, seeing themselves as "victims" instead of "initiators" of the circumstances that now touched their lives. Those who perceived themselves to be victims of circumstance consequently were less likely to make the types of changes in their lives that would bring them beyond widowhood. Although mutual help groups provide the opportunity for all who attend to realize the obvious truth that widowhood affects many other men and women, those who persistently feel "singled out" by misfortune are less likely to profit from mutual support group experiences.

Similarly, mutual support groups are not helpful for those who attend unwillingly. In most cases, only those who are open to receiving the support of the group will actually derive support from it. The decision to attend a mutual support group is often a difficult one. In deciding to attend, one is acknowledging that he or she is widowed. Widowed people should never be forced or cajoled into attending mutual support groups by well-meaning family or friends, or even by other widowed people or helping professionals. If they do not wish to attend, they are not yet *ready* to attend. They will profit more from a one-to-one evening with a close friend. It is far better for a widowed person simply to enjoy the benefits of being with another individual than to attend a mutual support group meeting unwillingly.

Finally, mutual support group experiences will not be very profitable for widowed persons in prolonged or severe grief. One who "stands out" in the nature or severity of his or her grief will come to the attention of another (perhaps the group leader) who can supportively guide him or her to secure professional help. For mutual support groups cannot take the place of professional and/or individual therapy.

However, for those individuals whose course of grief is relatively uncomplicated, mutual support groups can provide a very important affirmation of a new facet of their identity: that he or she is now a widow or widower. Indeed, for some individuals, mutual support groups may be the only available source of that affirmation. Although family and friends may be tremendously helpful in the course of bereavement, it may be quite difficult (or impossible) for them to provide the identity affirmation that the widowed person will need successfully to see himself or herself as such. Family and friends may not be in the best position to provide that affirmation because they have known the individual not as a widow or widower but as a parent, other relative, or friend. Or it may be difficult for family and friends to acknowledge that something so unpleasant has befallen one close to them. Nevertheless, affirmation that one is a widowed person must take place in order for the widowed person to begin accepting the new identity and ultimately to move on to a new, reformulated personal identity.

Mutual support groups are effective in providing at least part of that early affirmation in a nonthreatening context. Thinking of oneself as a widow can provoke fear, but to speak with, listen to, and witness the survival of, other widowed persons provides concrete reassurance that life does not end when one's spouse dies. Perhaps most fundamental, widowed men and women need the sense of hope that other widowed persons can inspire. Even if two widowed people have never met before, they can come together in a support group to "coverify" that the death of a spouse has not meant personal demise. This is the essence of hope that mutual help groups can provide. Widowed men and women I met at groups in the United States and Canada were effusive in voicing the benefits they derived from attending:

> For the first time since my husband died, I finally got to meet other people who'd also lost their husbands. I really

> thought I was the *only* one who was going through widowhood!
>
> At the support group I met a number of other people who went through worse things than I did. One man's wife committed suicide, and another man's wife and two children were killed in a car accident. Not that I felt better, but by looking at what happened to them I thought what I went through was almost nothing compared to what happened to them.
>
> I owe my life to THEOS. It has meant all the difference in the world for me. I used to stay at home and cry all day and all night. But my friend dragged me to a meeting.
>
> Going to my church support group made a world of difference. It made me feel *so* much better to know that other women were feeling the same feelings and going through the same anger as I was! I really had thought that I was the only young woman in the world who lost her husband at twenty-seven, and that I was the only one who lost a wonderful man. Was I wrong, praise the Lord!
>
> Nobody wants a widow. It's a married world out there. A widow is a fifth wheel. But at least here I'm not out of place. And it sure beats sitting home alone doing nothing.

Widowed people can provide practical help as well as emotional support to each other. Following the death of a spouse, widowed men and women are faced with many changes in their lives. They confront problems at work: how to manage the demands of the job when one is so preoccupied, how to respond to expressions of sympathy from colleagues or, in some cases, how to deal with their avoidance. For example, by sharing their experiences and the collective wisdom assimilated therefrom, they can help each other understand that—in this case—coworkers often do not know what to say to widowed people, or they may be afraid of saying the "wrong thing."

Sounding out others on how they are addressing particular issues in family or interpersonal relationships can also be beneficial: Having faced these questions themselves, other widowed people can suggest answers to "How can I talk with my mother? She just cries when I ask her a question," or, "How can I tell my friend to back off without offending her?" Problems related to financial investments, health, and children are also typical of the practical subjects addressed by mutual help groups.

The groups provide a less obvious benefit as well. They can serve as a safety valve, permitting the widow or widower to say things that can be said freely nowhere else. I once heard an obviously frustrated widowed woman end her question to a guest speaker by saying, "I wish my family would leave me alone! I need them . . . but I can't *stand* them!" Other group members reacted reflexively, nodding in unison, acknowledging that they knew and supported what she was feeling.

When a widowed person starts to attend, mutual support groups provide a needed "safe place to go." Early in bereavement widowed people avoid social events only in part because socializing may be viewed as unseemly. They stay away largely because they do not feel like socializing in ways they did before (which usually remain the only social opportunities that exist after becoming widowed). Early in bereavement, even though they may not yet fully identify themselves as "unmarried," widowed people are aware of being single in the company of married men and women. Fear of facing the discomfort or feelings of loneliness that such socializing can entail may lead the widowed person to remain at home, solitary and potentially isolated. Mutual support groups provide a place to go where they can engage with other people. Because of its specialized membership and focused agenda, the group is not threatening in the way that other social encounters may be. And it is different enough from old social outlets to validate the changed needs and new circumstances of the widowed person.

There are two types of organized mutual support for widowed people: institutional or "grass roots." Institutional services are well established, clearly defined, and are provided by a professional staff. Usually they are organizations of national or international scope that receive financial support from religious, commercial, or government grants. An example of institutional support in the United States is the Widowed Persons Service of the AARP.

Grass-roots support systems are typically smaller and arise more spontaneously than institutional supports. The "typical" grass-roots group for widowed people is founded when a few highly motivated people assemble and decide to meet on a regular basis with some common purpose in mind. Sometimes, grass-roots organizations grow to be institutional. In Washington State, eight widowed people gathered under the guidance of a counselor in 1974 and began a grass-roots support group. Now called the Widowed Information & Consultation Services (WICS), this Seattle-Tacoma-based group has expanded to serve over 6,000 widowed men and women in the Puget Sound area, and is funded by the United Way and Family Services of King County. Sometimes, grass-roots groups dwindle and disappear when the existing members' goals have been attained and no new members come to carry on the work.

There is overlap between institutional and grass-roots groups. In fact, most institutional support systems specifically provide training and other services to assist individuals and groups in setting up grass-roots support systems in their communities, with the larger national network available for consultation, networking, and occasionally, financial support.

One of the early North American efforts to help widowed people was the Widows' Consultation Centre, founded jointly by the Winnipeg, Manitoba, YWCA and the Great-West Life Assurance Company in 1972. This service began as a grass-roots-type pilot project, incorporating novel services such as a Visiting Widow service provided by trained widows who called upon newly widowed women for a one-to-one contact. A drop-in "widow's group" and individual counseling were also provided at the centre. With funding provided by the United Way of Winnipeg, a professional evaluation was conducted, in which the Visiting Widow service received the most strongly-positive feedback from widows. The evaluation concluded that a workshop format for teaching coping skills would be quite successful. This expanded into a series of New Perspectives workshops developed especially for widowed women who were ready to move beyond widowhood. The workshops' goals were "to help widows find direction and meaning in their lives, to set reasonable life goals for themselves, and to develop the self-confidence" to follow through on those goals. Evaluation of the program found both the workshops and the individual services to be highly effective.[9] The Centre is still flourishing.

Addressing a similar need in the United States, through a joint effort of the AARP and the National Retired Teachers Association, the Widowed Persons Service (WPS) provides a wide range of support services for widowed men and women. WPS focuses on five areas of support: outreach, where they provide volunteers who are widowed themselves to visit the newly bereaved; telephone service for information and assistance; group sessions that bring widowed people together for problem sharing and mutual assistance; public education services that call attention to the needs of widowed men and women; and a referral service that provides them with a listing of local services.

The Widowed Persons Service also sponsors the Institute for Lifelong Learning, which provides access to classroom courses, correspondence and home study courses, credit by examination, summer and weekend learning vacations (such as the popular "Elderhostel" program), external degree programs, discussion groups, and self-planned learning. For the older person who wishes to work beyond retirement or who wishes to find a new job, the institute provides career-planning assistance, information on starting a new business, and a hundred other supportive services for the older person.

While the Widowed Persons Service provides services directed mainly toward the older widowed person, THEOS seeks to meet the needs of young and middle-aged widowed men or women who face different circumstances. Though THEOS is an acronym for "they help each other spiritually" and happens to be the Greek word for *God,* it is a nondenominational but spiritually oriented network of mutual help groups throughout North America. Begun in 1962 by Bea Decker, who found herself a widow with three children and nowhere to turn for support and direction in building a new life, THEOS since then has grown but has remained grass roots, placing most of its emphasis on bringing widowed people together to form local groups that are part of a broad North American network. The British counterpart of THEOS is Cruse, the largest widowed persons' support network in Great Britain. Cruse, THEOS, WPS, Canadian YMCA–affiliated groups, and Chicago-based NAIM for Catholics provide the majority of mutual support services to widowed people in the English-speaking world.

Parents Without Partners (PWP) is a Washington, D.C.–based support network that has over 200,000 single, divorced, and widowed single parent members in 1,000 chapters in the United States and Canada. PWP provides a special community-based place for single adults with children to meet, socialize, and provide mutual support. Some even have support-within-support groups for children and adolescents of single parents.

Despite their successful record of providing practical and emotional support to widowed people, mutual support groups face various challenges. In July 1980, Sister Connie Charette started a four-week therapy group for widowed women and men in Bridgeport, Connecticut, which met three times a year. Out of overwhelming interest, it evolved into a six-week session, and it soon affiliated with THEOS. Sr. Connie soon led a vibrant, active, and self-supportive group that continues to meet two times each month. Her THEOS group now has spin-offs in other Connecticut cities, most notably highly active groups in nearby Norwalk and Stamford.

According to Sr. Connie, mutual support groups face four important challenges in meeting the needs of widowed people effectively.[10] First is the question of "ageism" in groups: Although widowed people in support groups tend to be considerate of each other regardless of age, there are times when a subtle distance is felt between the older and the younger widowed. This difference is particularly salient early in bereavement, during respondence, when younger widowed people are confronting different types of pressure and need different types of support than older widowed people. The age difference is also noticeable later, during emergence, when people gravitate toward different types of social activities. For example, younger people are more eager to remarry, and this is reflected in the kinds of social activities they pursue and the friendships they form as they move beyond widowhood. Perspectives and even basic values as well as social activities vary widely between young and older widowed people.

The second challenge is how to reach out most effectively to widowed men and women. Sr. Connie mentioned parish bulletins, newspapers, the visiting nurses association, the local hospice, and contact with social welfare organizations as avenues for recruiting new members, but she still sought a more effective way to involve isolated widows. Because older widows tend to have less social contact than others, as well as less money and less available transportation, *access* to mutual support services becomes the critical issue.

The third challenge Sr. Connie named (and one faced by most support group leaders) is getting widowed men to attend. Relatively few services are directed toward the needs of widowed men, and when those services exist, men usually do not utilize them. Outreach—bringing the support services to the person in need—is one alternative approach being explored. I spoke recently with a social worker who was working on a pilot project in California. The objective of this county-funded effort was to establish an outreach service for older widowed men, many of whom were living in isolation and were at high risk of suicide. It worked well for those men who agreed to participate, but she had been surprised by how hesitant elderly widowed men were to discuss their problems, or to accept help from social agencies. One Rhode Island support group leader jokingly suggested that the only way to get more men to attend was to have the group pay a "bounty" to each member who brought in a widowed man as a new member.

The fourth challenge facing mutual support groups is to provide training to widowed people in helping each other. There has to be a component that will extend the message of support past the limits of where and when the group meets. When I last spoke with Sr. Connie, she was working on a "community-based coalition," one that would organize and mobilize the resources of numerous area human-services groups, ultimately bringing support services to greater numbers of widowed men and women in southern Connecticut.

Ultimately, the best "elixir" for widowhood—both for men and for women—will emerge from increases in human support and support services. Support can soften the pain of loss and can provide encouragement and motivation for widowed persons to move on to new activities and roles. Individual relationships and mutual support groups provide the two most effective types of social support for widowed women and men—though not every widow would endorse this claim. Recently I met an elderly widow in Vermont. When I asked her about her sources of support, she peered at me through one eye: "Sir, in my day when a husband died, he *died*. There was no need for these therapy groups and psychiatrists!"

Her comment incorporated both a full acknowledgment of the utterness of death and an exemplification of the range of human variability. Certainly there are some widows and widowers who do not need or want support from others. Yet most do need support and can benefit from it. This is particularly true in contemporary America, where widows do not have a well-defined social network to provide financial or emotional support, and widowers do not tend to have the close friendships that can sustain them when their spouses die.

But support alone is not enough. Attitudes toward widowhood must continue to change. Widowed people and all who come in contact with them must be educated to understand that widowhood is only a temporary role. Thus, one of the key elements of effective support from others is encouragement of growth and change.

Perhaps the most outstanding advantage of an effective mutual support group is its flexibility. As widowed people move through bereavement, their needs for support change as well. While family and friends can provide a backdrop of ongoing support for other facets of the widow's identity, effective support groups can provide support for the evolving facets of the individual's identity. At first, this simply consists of an affirmation: "You are a widowed person. We are too. But none of us is alone in widowhood." But beginning with that early, safe affirmation of one's widow identity, the flexible mutual support group will go on to provide a means, setting, and encouragement for the individual to move ahead, discovering other facets of her identity, and ultimately, to move out of the mutual support group and beyond widowhood.

To achieve flexibility, the support group must function on two levels: one for the newly widowed person in the encounter and respondence stages and another for widowed persons in emergence, including a "launching" phase providing direction for moving beyond widowhood. For the recently bereaved the group provides solace: a safe place to express feelings—to cry, talk, and listen. While it allows the individual safely to affirm that he or she is a "widowed person," early-level support offers perhaps the widowed person's first glimpse of hope that a happy and full life is attainable. At THEOS support groups, early-level support typically means that a newly widowed person enters a smaller "coping" group (which one leader calls "intensive care"). A facilitator—usually a professional therapist—works closely with that group, which allows the widow to freely express grief and share personal experiences with other widows. Sometimes this early level includes an outreach component, in which other widowed persons past encounter and respondence are enlisted to make personal contact with a newly bereaved widow or widower outside of the small group. Formal lectures are never appropriate for newly widowed persons, nor are crowded meetings. Newly widowed men and women must have a chance to express their feelings, far more than they need information, factual material, or philosophical explanations.

When ready to do so, widowed people can begin attending regular, large-group meetings. Typically, these are ongoing and meet weekly, biweekly, or monthly. These meetings reflect a later level of support: Their content (topics of discussion) and processes (stimuli for growth) recognize that the widowed person has moved past encounter and respondence and seeks to emerge from widowhood. For example, each meeting can address a unique topic, led by someone with expertise in that area. Topics such as money management, single parenting, relationships, remarriage, health, leisure pursuits, educational opportunities, personal goal setting, and occupational advancement are appropriate and valuable to widows in the later level of support. Each widowed person should still have access to mutual help from others in the larger group. This can be accomodated by reserving some time for sharing at the close of each meeting. THEOS incorporates "plug-ins," in which widowed persons are matched with others of similar background and experience. Plug-in partners provide ongoing support, helping each other through difficult times, sharing concerns and strengths by telephone, by mail, and occasionally, in person.

In sum, the effective support group must address the differing needs of newly bereaved widows and those further along who are less focused on personal grief. A recent New England conference for widowed men and women recognized this difference by including a special session for the newly widowed person, called, simply, "What Has Happened to Me." While other widowed men and women attended workshops on topics ranging from dealing with adolescent children to defining career options, this session enabled newly bereaved participants to spend hours together simply sharing their experiences, which met their needs to express, to be understood, and to temper some of their deep loneliness.

At the very least, effective mutual support groups help the widow move through widowhood. But the truly successful group "launches" the widow, providing encouragement and direction for the individual to move away from the group; to move away from widowhood itself. This is done by including structured opportunities for widowed people to identify and redefine interests. These opportunities can become crystallized in the formation of smaller "splinter groups," initially centered around a common social interest. One splinter group recently chartered a boat for a dinner cruise; another group of five toured Europe. Ballroom dancing was the goal of another group of widowed women I met in New York City. These groups, which began as social in nature, can then set the stage for widowed persons to form new relationships, to meet new people, and to comprehend a range of occupational, professional and personal growth opportunities that lie past widowhood. Widows from the ballroom-dancing group began designing attractive embellishments for footwear, including some unique costume jewelry arrangements.

Those who move away from the larger support group are those who are doing the precisely healthy thing, because the purpose of engaging in a mutual support group is to enable a widowed person to become whole again, no longer in need of the specialized support that the group provides. Growing to a point where grief has subsided is only part of the aim of growing beyond widowhood; making one's life whole again is the important complement. An individual who no longer needs the support of the group is a testimony to a group's effectiveness, for that means that a widowed person has moved away from the identity of widow and on to new self-definitions and interpersonal relationships.

Such an individual is a fuller person not because he or she no longer needs the support of others but because a sense of balance has been restored: Support can now be given and received but it is support for new facets of their identities. Unlike the temporary facet of widow, the new facets are permanent ones that can provide ongoing satisfaction to the individual. Others profit as well, because as widowed men and women move away from the temporary identity of "widowed person," they become capable of sustaining relationships as adults in new roles as friend, lover, worker, husband, wife, or parent.

Sharing those joys and sadnesses in bereavement with other persons is perhaps the best practice and preparation for continuing to be part of the lives of significant others when one has moved beyond widowhood.

CHAPTER
9

Growing Together
A Family with a Future

Romance fails us and so do friendships, but the relationship of parent and child, less noisy than all others, remains indelible and indestructable, the strongest relationship on earth.

—THEODOR REIK, *Of Love and Lust*

Somewhere early in the first year of grief time stood still. I was tired each day—dead tired. It was difficult to fall asleep, and painful to awaken. As soon as I awoke I remembered: They died . . . really? . . . yes. That simple thought made it difficult to get out of bed. My first emotion in the morning was anger; by noon I had begun smoking my second pack of cigarettes. I was angry because they had died, but I was even angrier on behalf of them. As their survivor, I was experiencing the anger I decided they would feel if they were there. In addition to my personal anger and my anger on behalf of those who had died, I was perhaps most angry for my surviving children and for their losses. I saw what remained of our family not as a new family but as a fragment; we were victims of a vandalism that had torn life from our family.

Almost simultaneously with my deepest despair, two documents came by mail: I had been appointed legal guardian of each of my two children. At first I was indignant: "Who the hell are *they* to appoint *me?*" Then I cynically wondered if, had I been a mother instead of a father, I would have been spared legal certification of my status as a parent. Probate court assured me that guardianship was routinely certified when a parent of either gender died. This was indicative of the protective attitude the American legal system holds toward all children: All children are "at risk."[1] And when a child no longer has two parents who are alive, married to each other, and living in the same household, the state's perception is that the risk—of exposure to forces that will harm the child—increases.

Widowed single parents face many of the same economic, social, and practical issues and challenges faced by divorced and separated parents: Living in a two-income culture, one parent must now generate enough income for an entire family. And, much time is presently spent "juggling" tasks that can more efficiently be undertaken by two adults. There is still stigma attached to a household led by one parent: Regardless of the reason for the break, society still views the "broken home" to be less beneficial than the "intact" two-parent home. Finally, an active and fulfilling social life is not possible for many single parents, especially those with young children.

Yet despite these similarities with other single parents, widowed single parents face at least two distinctive realities that set them apart. The widowed parent must help the child move through bereavement of a loss more absolute than separation from a living parent. No visitation, shared responsibility, or shared custody is possible. And although widowed parents and their children are spared the hostility that sometimes emerges from divorcing parents, no hope can be held out for reconciliation or for support of any kind.

Nevertheless, just as widowed individuals move through widowhood and beyond to a new personal identity, a "widowed family" too can move through bereavement, emerging as a different yet fully functional and whole unit. Widowed parents can make a significant difference in making the family, once again, a salutary environment for children as well as themselves.

All children need a readily available, stable relationship with an adult who loves and values them. Usually, the child's biological parent will fill this role, but it can be filled by another adult in the absence or inability of the surviving biological parent to be the psychological parent. Even adults who are not biologically related to the child can become psychological parents, because the role is based on:

> day-to-day interaction, companionship, and shared experiences. The role can be filled . . . by any other caring adult—but never by an absent, inactive adult, whatever his biological or legal relationship to the child may be.[2]

A readily available, stable, and loving parent-child relationship is of particular importance to a child whose parent has died. This is because a young child's sense of self and personal value is embedded in relationships with significant adults in his or her life. Children assess who they are, and how good they are, primarily on the basis of the verbal and nonverbal messages they receive from parents and other significant adults. Therefore, the death of a parent—even if there was no strong psychological parent-child bond—is very intrusive and disruptive to the child's relatively immature sense of self. The loss of the parent feels to the child like a loss of his or her world. Although an adult's identity must be reformulated in widowhood, his or her sense of self as an independent being allows the relatively rapid development of a view of death that children simply cannot attain quickly or by themselves.

Because young children see the world only from their own vantage point, they react to death only in terms of its impact on themselves. They cannot see a mother's death as being a loss to the company for which she worked, nor can they empathize with the surviving parent's loss of a partner or helpmate. Instead, the child will wonder, "Who will cook for me now?"

The maintenance (or reestablishment) of a psychological parent-child bond after the death of a parent can help the child realize that he or she is still a wanted, valued person: "Even though Dad has died you have me and we have each other" is a powerful bonding message, one that all bereaved parents should convey to their children. With that type of strong message from the parent, the child can gradually relocate his or her attachment from the deceased to the surviving parent, and perhaps eventually to a new parent.

Accompanying one's child to the funeral or memorial service is one concrete, bonding action that will begin the child's refocusing. From the moment the child is told that father or mother has died (which should be done by the person who will continue to be the child's parent), there should be *no doubt* in the child's mind as to who will be available for reliable and consistently available love, reassurance, and solace. In the child's parlance, that adult must be "my Dad [or Mom] forever and ever." The availability of that attachment must be stable over time to be truly effective. Above all else, this demands the parent and child spend time with each other:

> The demand of love cannot be hedged or temporized. It necessarily and fundamentally means spending time with your child. You are either willing to pay the price of time, or you are not; the child knows instantly. No amount of material beneficence, not lip service or promises, not good intentions or favors or services rendered, not kisses and hugs, not a superior educational opportunity or material and social advantage—not anything will suffice to take the place of loving time spent with a child.[3]

But the time should not be spent merely sharing the same house, room, or television show. When they have lost a loved one, parent and child must spend time together in *communication*.

Crying is communication; mourning together is excellent and clear communication. Some of the most valuable time a parent can spend with a child is being with each other in sadness. Parents who wish to manage their grief and the grief of their children must effectively facilitate and encourage the mourning process.[4] This implies time spent together and permission granted to the child: "Talk to me. I will listen. I am very sad, but what you are feeling is very important to me."

Time spent talking with and listening to each other can be very reassuring to the child, and can provide moments of relief from mourning. Between three and four weeks after my wife died, I had an opportunity to talk to and listen to my daughters away from the sometimes chaotic house we shared.

As we sat at Burger King that day in July, five-year-old Aimee asked me "if Mommy can see us." As I began to think about that one, she asked me why if God really loved Mommy, He wanted her to die. I told her that I didn't think God "wanted" her to die. Aimee said someone had told her that her Mommy was a good woman, and she died because God wants all good people to be with Him. I felt it was important for me to be direct at this point, and I disagreed, saying that I was pretty sure God did not take away her mother. I explained that while

Mom was an especially good person, some good people die when they're young adults, and some good people die when they are older. I tried to reassure her that what had happened to us was quite unusual; but *I* intended to be with her and Katie for a long time. Not forever, but a long time. That seemed to satisfy her. Aimee looked at some huge potted ferns hanging under skylights and she asked me if the Burger King ferns will live forever.

"No, the ferns die, too. All living things die eventually."

"But why did God want Mommy? We need her more than God does."

"I think you're right, but I'm . . ."

"Can I get a Happy Meal?"

"This isn't McDonald's. Want a Burger King Kid's Meal instead?"

"What kind of surprise is inside?"

The first job of a parent is to build on whatever understanding the child already has about death. This means that the parent must spend time *listening* to what his or her child is saying. Death is not a subject that most families spend much time discussing; when a parent dies, a child will naturally be uncomfortable. Each child must therefore be given supportive permission to talk as comfortably as possible about questions and feelings. Building on the child's understanding means that the parent should avoid trying to teach or otherwise direct the child to think in a certain way. Instead, a listening parent permits and encourages the child to talk, responding in a way that shows interest: "I miss Dad, too."

Parents should avoid analyzing the child's perceptions; asking, "Why do you say that?" or, "Why do you feel that way?" is ineffective, for a child usually has little insight into his or her motives. It is better for parents simply to ask the child to "tell me more" or say "I feel the same way." Words are not even necessary; merely looking at the child and nodding can be helpful and effectively supportive, especially when a child sounds like he or she is hurting.

In discussing the death of a parent, I suggest that parents avoid intricate, philosophical, or clinical explanations. There is time later for the child to learn religious tenets. At this time of severe stress, hurt, and fear, keeping explanations simple prevents or minimizes confusion and provides a child with comfort. It also helps the parent clarify confusing explanations or mixed messages the child may get from other well-meaning adults. For example, a child's question on "where Daddy really is" may simply mean the child wants to be reassured that his deceased parent is not now still suffering the pain that the child may have seen before the parent died.

Although our children need to feel secure in their reliance on our wisdom, we do not have to have all the answers. There are many issues surrounding death about which the average parent has little knowledge, including anatomy, embalming, burial, and cremation. Children will not feel disturbed by a parent's honest, "I don't know." If an adolescent asked a complicated question about those issues, I'd encourage him or her to ask someone else—perhaps a doctor, teacher, or funeral director—for an explanation. If a young child asked, I'd answer to the extent of my knowledge, without frightening the child. There were times that I told my daughters "I don't know" when they asked me complex questions for which I honestly had no answer.

Parents should assuage children's fears. Teach them that death is not contagious. Because a parent has died does *not* mean that the child's death is at hand, nor does it mean the surviving parent will soon die. When they have lost a parent, young children are understandably afraid that they will lose their remaining parent. The surviving parent should reassure the child that although there are no guarantees in life, they are in good health and can expect to live a long, long time. Parents can point to an older member of the family as an example of longevity that can help the child visualize the surviving parent reaching a ripe old age. Concrete examples work best for children.

Furthermore, the child must be reassured that he or she did not "cause" the parent's death. Being self-centered creatures, children may connect death with something they did or wished for, concluding that they were ultimately responsible. By talking frankly about it, the surviving parent can break that magical connection young children may construct between themselves and the death.

Parents must avoid fairy tales like, "Daddy's gone on a trip." The child needs honesty. When parents begin with the truth ("Yes,

Daddy has died, but I'm still here"), it gets easier. Once death is openly acknowledged between parent and child, the worst is over. Similarly, death should never be called "sleep." If parents refer to death as "sleeping," children may be haunted at night, unable to sleep. Parents should not even compare death to sleeping. Meaning to convey a sense of painlessness common to both death and sleep, well-intentioned parents may say, "Death is like sleeping for a long time." But children will see only how alike they are despite the parent's perception that death and sleep are alike in but one feature. The child will take what is said quite literally, concluding that death and sleep are the same.

Instead, ask the child open-ended questions that will yield a fuller idea of the child's fears and misconceptions. For example, parents can ask a child to, "Tell me about the noises you heard last night," or an adolescent, "I have lots of time now, if you want to talk." Young children (kindergarten age or younger) do not fully understand that death is final. Older children often personify death, thinking of it perhaps as someone lurking in a closet, basement or elsewhere in the house. Preadolescents have a clearer idea of death but will nonetheless be fearful of dying themselves or losing the surviving parent, and so may cling to him or her. Children of any age, in fact, will become more possessive, perhaps not letting the parent out of sight. This is normal and understandable, because they are afraid. A parent's time, presence, and reassuring words are what they need above all else.

As parents support their children by those reassuring words, actions, and time spent together, they must also confront the fact that death has changed the work structure in the family. The amount of work that must be done has not diminished, yet there is one adult less to do it. Widowed parents are thus faced with doing the job of the deceased parent as well as their own.

No matter how I tried, I could not do what my wife had done as well as she did it. A minor but vexing example was my inability to do my daughters' hair. All the other neighborhood children had nice hair—ponytails, braids, banana curls. My daughters looked like aliens, because "doing" their hair ("Daddy, *do* my hair!" they used to say) with a brush and comb was beyond my ability. I might as well have used a rake. My attempts only reminded me how efficiently her fingers had moved through the girls' hair. When I dropped them off at school and they ran to their well-coiffed friends, I knew the other parents were thinking, "*He* doesn't do their hair like *she* used to—look at their hair! A disgrace!" As many widowed parents know, doing a job *as well as* it was perceived to have been done previously is extremely critical to the surviving parent.

Everyday events can present the most vexing practical problems. For example, since so many single parents are mothers, few realize the problem single fathers face when they need to use a restaurant's public restroom. Does he leave his children sitting at a table by themselves? I did not feel safe leaving a five- and a two-year-old alone. I wondered why it is okay for mothers to bring little boys into a women's room but absolutely verboten for fathers to take girls into a men's room. Not that I wanted to do that, but it was an example of something I never thought about before my wife died.

"Aimee, you wait right here and hold Katie's hand. I'll be right out." I raced in, listened to hear their voices, and in a minute I was out again, thinking that maybe I should have just asked someone to watch them. Although these "daily hassles" may appear terribly minor, especially compared with the magnitude of parental death, those minor issues are the tangible and persistent reminders of how life has changed.

But perhaps more significant than the jobs she had done, the *roles* she had performed became extremely challenging for me to carry out by myself. Although all single parents (and even some married parents) must confront being "both mother and father," none of us receives preparation for taking on another person's complete set of roles. (Indeed, such an undertaking may not be humanly possible.)

Fathers have traditionally been less involved in child rearing than mothers. Taking over such an enormous role is a staggering thought to most fathers, which is why so many widowed fathers immediately seek support by hiring or marrying a woman willing to raise children. I felt fortunate that we had actively shared responsibility for child care when my wife was alive. Had I not been involved at all, it would have been a much more daunting task suddenly to assume the entire responsibility. Nevertheless, it was still not easy for one parent to fill a role that had formerly been shared.

Recognizing the impossibility of carrying out all the roles she had performed, I focused on specific jobs that had to be done. For example, I could not take over her role as "family doctor and nurse," so I pinned a list of my children's inoculation needs to the bulletin board along with a list of telephone numbers of our pediatrician, family doctor, and other medical specialists. When I did not know if the baby thermometer was oral or rectal, I called my next-door neighbor for advice. If my child had a temperature, I called the medical center for guidance, prepared to bring her in if warranted. Reflecting on my behavior as I recorded it in my journal, I did a lot of barking of orders as well:

> Stay outside! I'm waxing the floor! (Response: "Do we hafta?")
>
> Stay inside! It's raining! (Response: "But I *like* rain!")
>
> Sarah, share that toy with Katie! (Response: "But I had it first!")
>
> Time for lunch! (Response: "Oh—I don't like this. My mother puts *honey* on peanut butter sandwiches!")
>
> "Mona, use your fingers on the piano, not cars!" (Response: "They're not cars, they're trucks!")
>
> And it was I who had to hear (and respond to):
>
> Dad, what's on television?
>
> "Mister D, I feel sick."
>
> Dad, can you send Sarah home? She's swearing!
>
> "Mister D, my Mommy said I can't eat this hot dog because we're veterinarians now."
>
> Dad, by mistake Michelle went on the bathroom floor!
>
> Mr. D, did your wife crash into the truck, or did it crash into her? Mary said that her mother told her that . . ."

Parents' roles are not the only ones that change—and must change—as a result of the death of a parent. Children's roles change as well. By enlisting the child to carry out some of the jobs formerly done by the deceased parent, the parent meets two needs: First, it reduces the amount of work he must do alone. Second, there is a psychological payoff for the child. Not only can he or she take pride in making a concrete contribution to the family, but his or her sense of competency is strengthened as well. Every opportunity to build a child's self-esteem—especially at this time—is beneficial. Because the child takes death personally ("Mommy left us"), boosting the child's self-esteem can help offset some of the blow.

Widowed parents I interviewed enlisted their children to carry out numerous jobs around the house. These ranged from dusting furniture to picking up. Some jobs, shared with other family members, included repainting bedrooms and planting gardens. One woman gave her teenage daughter responsibility for reconciling her checkbook with her monthly statement. Although my daughters were aged two and five, I insisted they help with the laundry. I gave them laundry baskets they would now bring downstairs. But I did not demand perfection. Insisting that the job be done precisely as it may have been done before by an adult is unfair to the child and will serve to discourage her from continuing. It is far better that she do the job and acquire competency at it as she goes along than that she do it "right" the first time.

Problems may also arise when bereaved parents try to avoid conflict that might add tension to their already somber home. Because of their own distress, vulnerability, and loss of support from the absent parent, their authority may be weakened. As a result, they may be susceptible to resistance from children or teenagers. Yet despite the aggravating circumstances, some forms of resistance (such as complaints about performing chores) must be steadfastly repudiated. A widowed woman with perfectly healthy teenage sons may expect to hear complaints ("Mom, why do I have to do this?"), but she should not try to compensate for their loss by relieving them of the responsibility. The *best* thing she can do for herself and for her sons is clearly to expect them to carry their share of the load, even if it has now increased. Discussing these matters honestly and directly with the child can be more effective than demanding, badgering, or giving in to the complaints. Children—especially older children and teenagers—must understand that although all are trying to maintain stability and comfortable sameness to life, some changes are necessary. Each person must therefore pitch in.

Widowed parents should also reflect on the new family structure, being particularly careful that one child does not take over a larger than appropriate share of the jobs done by the deceased parent. Identifying with one's parents is healthy for a child's self-esteem, yet too imitative or intense an identification is not. It is not in a child's best interest to become a "clone" of his or her deceased parent, nor is it beneficial for children to see themselves as "replacements" for the deceased spouse. A child may come to feel guilty about standing in for the parent, perhaps wondering if he or she achieved this position by wishing for it at some earlier time. Or the child—still physically small and relatively unskilled and powerless—may realize how inadequately qualified he or she is in comparison to the deceased parent. A parent who can dole out jobs that must be done without attaching messages of it being "Mom's work" or "Dad's work" is helping the child avoid the competitive implications. It is better for the child to identify with the deceased or living parent than to strive to replace the deceased.

A widowed parent should seek to assign and clarify job responsibilities in the new family structure without also assigning "messages" from or links to the past. When performing a job the focus should not be on memories of Dad who used to do it, but on its contribution to the family's welfare. Helping a child to live in the present, and to find it at least reasonably fulfilling, will further the emotional development of both child and family.

There will be times when the family—as individuals or as a unit—must reach outside itself for support. For example, as a widowed single parent, I sought neighbors' help with my daughters' hair. When I returned to full-time work, I hired someone to do some of the housework; another person helped with child care. The support was for me and for my family to help us avoid compounding the normal stress of bereavement with worries about accomplishing household chores. Instead, I could look forward to a weekend activity as a time for the rest and relaxation we all needed.

Sometimes widowed parents must reach outside the family to secure additional help for children who do not appear to be dealing satisfactorily with the death of the parent. Some authors caution that a "denial" of death can be devastating. Bereavement counselor Dr. Earl Grollman claims that "the inability [for a child] to mourn leads to personal disintegration, the upshot of which is mental illness."[5] A fine line exists between normal and disordered bereavement. As with adult bereavement, the duration and intensity of a child's grief are key indicators of unhealthy bereavement:

> It is a *continued* denial of reality even many months after the funeral, or a *prolonged* bodily distress, or a *persistent* panic, or an *extended* guilt, or an *unceasing* idealization, or an *enduring* apathy and anxiety, or an *unceasing* hostile reaction to the deceased and to others.[6]

No two children will experience bereavement in precisely the same way; no two children will rebound at the same rate. Some children have mourned other deaths prior to their parent's death, others have not. Some have discussed death with their parents or have had a chance to spend time with their dying parent, while other children have been denied this chance. Talking with other widowed parents (perhaps in mutual help groups) can help parents get an idea of what behaviors are common among bereaved children. An alert and sensitive parent is a bereaved child's best ally; nonetheless, a loving relationship cannot take the place of professional intervention if the child shows indicators of unhealthy bereavement.

Professional consultation is especially indicated where death of a parent may have occurred under violent circumstances. For example, a child whose parent has committed suicide (particularly if the child has witnessed the suicide) is at especially high risk. Children whose parents committed suicide related those suicides to themselves and their misbehavior:

> Coming home late from the playground, a bad report card, another fight with the boy next door, and even getting another bad cold were all stated as causes of the parent's committing suicide.[7]

Teachers can be another source of help for both the bereaved parent and child. Parents should talk to the child's teachers not to seek their sympathy (which they will get), but to make them aware that the child is going through a stressful time. Teachers can give parents valuable feedback on the child's achievement and behavior, and can monitor the child over a period of time. They can describe any changes in a child's disposition, schoolwork or behavior, point out adverse reactions they may have seen, and suggest ways of addressing problems that may arise. Through the school system, parents can enlist the expertise of support professionals such as the school physician, social worker, guidance counselor, nurse, and school psychologist.

Adolescents need reassurance just as surely as do young children, but of a somewhat different kind. Early teens may be embarrassed by the death of a parent because it sets them apart from "everyone else." The teen years are a time when peers play an enormously important role in their lives. The adolescent is especially sensitive to the opinions of—and possible rejection by—his or her associates. Therefore, although the family and friend support network works well for younger children, they may be less effective for teens. Thus, parents may find that schools, community support services (sometimes church or synagogue sponsored), or counseling offered by hospitals and hospices offer forms of help acceptable to otherwise reluctant teenagers. A reluctant teen may decide to attend if a friend accompanies him or her. Like Widow-to-Widow programs, some mutual support groups in larger cities have special programs for adolescents. Peers provide a clear sense of normalcy that is comforting for a bereaved teen. Adults must remember that "normalcy" means *acceptance* by, and being the same as, one's peers. Thus, if the death of a parent is an event that sets one apart, peer support can help maintain the adolescent.

This does not mean that parental support is not needed. Widowed parents can further marshall the resources peers can provide by making the home a place where a teen's friends are welcome. After my father died, I remember that my family's warmth—and perhaps the plentiful food—made my adolescent friends feel especially welcome in our home.

But no matter how warm and tolerant parents are, it is nonetheless normal for teens to distance themselves from parents. Adolescents whose parents have died may seem unwilling to talk about their feelings, especially about the deceased parent, with the surviving parent. Parents should not badger their teens to communicate but should seek to spend time with them even if few words are exchanged. On the other hand, teens must also be free to spend time away from the family. For they may be better able to share their feelings with friends than family members, and adolescent friendships are critical to the development of identity. As always, widowed parents should continue to be alert for signs of illness, fatigue, or symptoms of drug abuse by their teenagers.

Being a single parent is tough under any circumstances. Managing these challenges while trying to cope with death in the family can seem overwhelming. As a newly single parent, I was unsure and angry. For the first time in my life I experienced depression. But the need to help my daughters became paramount, and they helped keep me focused on the activities of each day. When one is directly confronted with death, life is changed totally. Yet we soon learned to focus less on what was gone and more on what continued. I became gradually less preoccupied with the unanswerable question of "Why?" and more attentive to the family I now headed, viewing it not as a bitter fragment of the past but as our own small family unit that had a future.

In many ways, I am now a different person, having emerged from the trance and pain of widowhood and bereavement. I abandoned "shrines" along the way. Like millions of other widowed men and women, I hid away—in a top drawer—a whole stash of relics: perfume, leftover deodorant, earrings. Like a smoker who hides a cigarette "just in case," I hid her cherished broken figurine. But gradually—over perhaps the first two years after her death—I gave away all those relics to people who would use them. I took my wife's last bottle of bath oil and last bottle of cologne out of my dresser, filled the tub for my daughters, dumped in the sacred lotions, and let them have a "smelly bath." They loved it. And I too felt cleansed.

For the first six months, I thought about her *constantly*. After one year had passed, I no longer cried each night. Before the second year had passed, days would go by when I—often guiltily—did not think about her. By the third year, I had removed pictures from the walls, gave away the last of her items, and felt comfortable thinking of myself as an unmarried person. When I thought of her it was with warmth accompanied by no guilt. I enjoyed being with other single women and men. Aware of this, my daughters seemed distracted as I read them a story one night. One looked up at me and said, "Dad, I don't want a different Mom. Are you going to get married again?" I laughed (because it was one of those questions young children raise totally out of the blue—what did it have to do with *The Cat in the Hat?*). "Maybe," I said. "I'm not sure. But if I do, it'll be someone nice." My answer was an important step for her and for me. She had to know that I have a life to live not only as a Dad but as an individual. And she needed to trust me.

From the earliest time of my despair and depression, I remember one minor event that was the first particularly clear turning point as I moved through widowhood.

One morning as my two daughters played in the living room, I tried to keep the floor clear by picking up after them. I vacuumed the rug, pushing toys into a corner with the head of the vacuum cleaner's nozzle as I went. Nevertheless, toys and clothing still seemed to be all over the place and the phone was ringing. Absent-mindedly, I stuck the nozzle under the sofa and inadvertantly sucked up the unattached head of a Barbie doll. It stuck fast, just out of my finger's reach.

I banged the nozzle against the floor. I gave in to the ringing phone. It was my friend Paul, who asked me how I was feeling. I felt like throwing in the towel. I told him I sucked up a Barbie doll head into the vacuum cleaner. It sounded as if he'd fallen off his kitchen stool laughing. I shone a flashlight into the nozzle. Blue eyes twinkling, Barbie smiled at me.

It was ridiculous. I laughed so hard tears came to my eyes. It was the first time I had laughed since they died. My five-year-old daughter Aimee heard me and came into the room. Not used to hearing me laugh, she looked at me inquisitively. When I showed her the object of my laughter, she asked, "Why did you put Barbie in there?"

Seeing the humor in one of life's daily frustrations signified a major step for me. While laughter by itself did not herald a miraculous recovery, it provided my first concrete evidence that at least momentary respite from constant sadness was *possible.* But it wasn't a doll's head or even the situation that made me feel better. It was answering the phone to hear the voice of a person who cared about me. I would not have laughed had he not taught me that what was happening at that moment was funny and silly, not sad and aggravating. I remembered how good it felt to hear him define that moment; I liked his definition better than mine. It helped me find a moment of happiness even at the lowest point in my life. More important, it gave me early insight into some keys to understanding my bereavement: Laughter is not the "opposite" of crying; felicity does not "violate" grief. Happiness is possible—and permissible—even when one is in the throes of sadness. Although bereavement is a time of mourning, and crying and feeling sad are normal elements of mourning, neither crying nor sadness are the hallmarks by which successful bereavement can be judged:

> Successful grief . . . is really coming out better than you went in. It's coming out enriched and a better person because you have lived through all of that pain, because you have assessed your life, assessed your marriage, and assessed yourself. You become more sympathetic with people and have a greater joy in joy. You sense the preciousness of time. You are focused on what is important. In sum, you not only survive; you are much more alive.[8]

Widowhood is not an illness or disease, nor should it be regarded as a chronic condition or permanent status. It is a time of transition; of crying until there are no more tears; of feeling pain until the strongest pain is a sobering but distant memory. It is also a time of taking, and of giving; of laughter and of, eventually, increasing measures of joy. Regardless of one's age or any other circumstance, successful widowhood is coming away from bereavement not simply a full person, but one *fuller* than ever before. Successful widowhood is becoming more clearly and securely one's self, yet a self that is woven deeply into the fabric of living humanity.

Notes

CHAPTER I

Images and Reality of America's Widowed

1. T. Eliot. (1930). "Bereavement as a Problem for Family Research and Technique," *The Family* 11(June): 114–16.
2. C. Sanders. (1980–81). "Comparison of Younger and Older Spouses in Bereavement Outcome," *OMEGA: The Journal of Death and Dying* 11(3): 217–222.
3. F. M. Berardo. (1968). "Widowhood Status in the United States: Perspectives on a Neglected Aspect of the Family Life Cycle." *Family Coordinator* 17: 191–203. R. Williams. (1961). "Changing Status, Roles, and Relationships," in Clark Tibbitts (ed.), *Handbook of Social Gerontology* (Chicago: University of Chicago Press), 475.
4. G. Owen, R. Fulton, and E. Markusen. (1982–83). "Death at a Distance: A Study of Family Survivors," *OMEGA: The Journal of Death and Dying* 13(3): 191–225.
5. E. Lindemann. (1944). "Symptomatology and Management of Acute Grief," *American Journal of Psychiatry*, 101, 141–148. E. Lindemann. (1979). *Beyond Grief: Studies in Crisis Intervention.* NY: Jason Aronson, 59–60.
6. L. Cargan and M. Melko. (1982). *Singles: Myths and Realities.* Beverly Hills, CA: SAGE, 218.
7. T. Holmes and R. Rahe. (1967). "The Social Readjustment Rating Scale," *Journal of Psychosomatic Research* 11: 213–18.
8. A. Kraus and A. Lilienfeld. (1959). "Some Epidemiologic Aspects of the High Mortality Rate in the Young Widowed Group," *Journal of Chronic Disease* 10: 207–17. K. Helsing, M. Szklo, and G. Com-

stock. (1981). "Factors Associated with Mortality after Widowhood," *American Journal of Public Health* 71(8): 802–9. J. Kaprio, M. Koskenvuo, and H. Rita. (1987). "Mortality after Bereavement: A Prospective Study of 95,647 Widowed Persons," *American Journal of Public Health* 77(3): 283–87. D. C. Maddison and A. Viola. (1968). "The Health of Widows in the Year Following Bereavement," *Journal of Psychosomatic Research* 12: 292–306. C. M. Parkes and R. Brown. (1972). "Health After Bereavement: A Controlled Study of Young Boston Widows and Widowers," *Psychosomatic Medicine* 34(5): 449–61. J. Smith, J. Mercy, and J. Conn. (1988). "Marital Status and the Risk of Suicide," *American Journal of Public Health* 78(1): 78–80.

9. Kaprio, Koskenvuo, and Rita.
10. C. Balkwell. (1981). "Transition to Widowhood: A Review of the Literature," *Family Relations* 30: 117–27. Smith, Mercy, and Conn.
11. G. Haas-Hawkings. (1978). "Intimacy as a Moderating Influence on the Stress of Loneliness in Widowhood," *Essence* 2(4): 249–58. H. Lopata. (1973). "Self-Identity in Marriage and Widowhood," *Sociological Quarterly* 14(3): 407–18.
12. Berardo. C. Pihlblad, D. Adams, and H. Rosencranz. (1973). "Socioeconomic Adjustment to Widowhood," *OMEGA: The Journal of Death and Dying* 3: 323–30.
13. C. Blanchard, E. Blanchard, and J. Becker. (1976). "The Young Widow: Depressive Symptomatology Throughout the Grief Process," *Psychiatry* 39(4): 394–99. R. Carey. (1979–80). "Weathering Widowhood: Problems and Adjustment of the Widowed During the First Year," *OMEGA: The Journal of Death and Dying* 10(2): 163–74. W. Gove. (1972). "The Relationship Between Sex Roles, Marital Status, and Mental Illness," *Social Forces* 51: 34–44.
14. E. Bock and I. Webber. (1972). "Suicide Among the Elderly: Isolating Widowhood and Mitigating Alternatives," *Journal of Marriage and the Family* 34: 24–31. H. Resnick and J. Cantor. (1970). "Suicide and Aging," *Journal of the American Geriatric Society* 18: 152–58. F. Wenz. (1976). "Suicide and Marital Status: A Case of High Suicide Rate Among the Widowed," *Crisis Intervention* 7(4): 149–61. Smith, Mercy, and Conn.
15. G. Gorer. (1965). "The Pornography of Death," in G. Gorer (ed.), *Death, Grief and Mourning*. Garden City, NY: Doubleday, 192–199.
16. D. Kent. (1965). *Aging–Fact and Fancy*. U.S. Department of Health, Education, and Welfare, OA No. 224, (U.S. Government Printing Office, Washington, D.C.), 14.
17. T. Des Pres. (1976). *The Survivor*. NY: Oxford University Press.
18. K. Vonnegut. (1973). *Cat's Cradle* (New York: Dell). 64–65.

19. M. Collins. (1987). "Next Season, It'll Be a Man's Game," *USA Today,* May 19, p. 3D.
20. United States Bureau of the Census. (March, 1984). *Detailed Population Characteristics: 1980 Census of the Population, Part I: United States Summary* Vol. 1, Ch. D., Washington, D.C.: U.S. Government Printing Office, 1-67, 1-68.
21. United States Bureau of the Census. (1980). "Marital Status and Living Arrangements: March 1979." *Current Population Reports; Population Characteristics* (Series P-20, No. 349, February).
22. U.S. Bureau of the Census, 1980. U.S. Bureau of the Census, 1984.
23. B. Neugarten. (1968). "Adult Personality: Toward a Psychology of the Life Cycle." In B. L. Neugarten (Ed.) *Middle Age and Aging.* Chicago: University of Chicago, 86.
24. J. Peterson and M. Briley. (1977). *Widows and Widowhood.* (Chicago: Follett), ix.
25. United States Bureau of the Census. (1987). *Statistical Abstract of the United States: 1987—107th Edition* (Washington, D.C.: U.S. Government Printing Office), 497.
26. American Council of Life Insurance. (1985). *1985 Life Insurance Fact Book Update* (Washington, D.C.: Author), 5–46.
27. Carey.

CHAPTER 2
Experiencing Bereavement

1. P. Rosenblatt, R. Walsh, and D. Jackson. (1976). *Grief and Mourning in Cross-cultural Perspective* (New Haven, Conn. HRAF Press), 15.
2. T. Holmes and R. Rahe. (1967). "The Social Readjustment Rating Scale" *Journal of Psychosomatic Research* 11: 213–18.
3. M. Friedman, quoted in R. Bailey. (1987). "Traumas Produce Similar Effects." *The Valley News* (Lebanon, N.H.), May 21, 1987, p. 2.
4. M. Brodsky, D. Sato, L. Iseri, L. Wolff, and B. Allen. (1987). "Ventricular Tachyarrhythmia Associated with Psychological Stress: The Role of the Sympathetic Nervous System," *Journal of the American Medical Association* 257(15), 2064–67. M. Brodsky, quoted in "A 'Broken Heart' Can . . . Kill You." (1987). *The Valley News* (Lebanon, N.H.), April 18, 1987, p. 14.
5. R. Bartrop, L. Lazarus, E. Luckhurst, L. Kiloh, and R. Penny. (1977). "Depressed Lymphocyte Function After Bereavement," *Lancet* 1(April 16): 834–36.
6. M. Hofer, C. Wolff, S. Friedman, and J. Mason. (1977). "Psychoendocrine Study of Bereavement." *Psychosomatic Medicine* 39: 481–504.

7. G. Engel, M. Frader, C. Barry, and D. Schalch. (1971). "Changes During Experimentally Induced Sadness," *Psychosomatic Medicine* 33: 471.
8. S. Schleifer, S. Keller, M. Camerino, J. Thornton, and M. Stein. (1983). "Suppression of Lymphocyte Stimulation Following Bereavement," *Journal of the American Medical Association* 250(3): 131–40.
9. W. Farr. (1858). "Influence of Marriage on the Mortality of the French People," *Transactions of the National Association for the Promotion of Social Science:* 504–12.
10. K. Helsing, M. Szklo, and G. Comstock. (1981). "Factors Associated with Mortality after Widowhood." *American Journal of Public Health* 71(8): 802–9.
11. E. Bock and I. Webber. (1972). "Suicide Among the Elderly: Isolating Widowhood and Mitigating Alternatives." *Journal of Marriage and the Family* 34: 24–31. G. Haas-Hawkings. (1978). "Intimacy as a Moderating Influence on the Stress of Loneliness in Widowhood," *Essence* 2(4): 249–58. A. Kraus and A. Lilienfeld. (1959). "Some Epidemiologic Aspects of the High Mortality Rate in the Young Widowed Group," *Journal of Chronic Disease* 10: 207–17. H. Resnick and J. Cantor. (1970). "Suicide and Aging," *Journal of the American Geriatric Society* 18: 152–58. J. Smith, J. Mercy, and J. Conn. (1988). "Marital Status and the Risk of Suicide," *American Journal of Public Health* 78(1): 78–80.
12. M. Szklo, quoted in "A Shorter Future for Widowed Men." (1981). *New York Times* (August 2), p. E22.
13. C. Balkwell. (1981). "Transition to Widowhood: A Review of the Literature," *Family Relations* 30: 117–27.
14. W. Gove. (1972). "The Relationship Between Sex Roles, Marital Status, and Mental Illness," *Social Forces* 51: 34–44. C. M. Parkes and R. Brown. (1972). "Health After Bereavement: A Controlled Study of Young Boston Widows and Widowers," *Psychosomatic Medicine* 34(5): 449–61.
15. J. Miller. (1976). *Toward a New Psychology of Women* (Boston: Beacon), 87–88.
16. L. Bugen. (1977). "Human Grief: A Model for Prediction and Intervention," *American Journal of Orthopsychiatry* 47(2): 196–206.
17. R. Lifton. (1973). *Home From the War* (New York: Simon & Schuster). R. Lifton. (1976). *History and Human Survival* (New York: Vantage).
18. T. Mann. (1927). *The Magic Mountain* (New York: Alfred Knopf), 849.

19. R. Blood, Jr., and D. Wolfe. (1960). *Husbands and Wives: The Dynamics of Married Living.* N.Y.: The Free Press. E. Luckey. (1961). "Perceptual Congruence of Self and Family Concepts as Related to Marital Interaction," *Sociometry*, 24, 234–250. J. Veroff and S. Feld. (1970). *Marriage and Work in America: A Study of Motives and Roles.* N.Y.: Van Nostrand Reinhold.
20. H. Lopata. (1973). "Self-Identity in Marriage and Widowhood," *Sociological Quarterly*, 14(3), 407–418.
21. R. DiGiulio. (1984). "Identity Loss and Reformulation in Young, Middle-Aged and Older Widowed Women," *Dissertation Abstracts International*, 42(04), 1217A (University Microfilms No. DA8416087). L. Thomas, R. DiGiulio, and N. Sheehan. (1988). "Identity Loss and Psychological Crisis in Widowhood: A Re-Evaluation," *International Journal of Aging and Human Development*, 26(3), 225–239.

CHAPTER 3
Identity Loss and Reformulation

1. E. Erikson. (1963). *Childhood and Society*, 2d ed. (New York: Norton), 262.
2. Erikson, *Childhood and Society*, 261.
3. R. Gould and R. Gould. (1976). "Personal Growth and Marital Consequences" (Paper presented at the 84th Annual Convention of the American Psychological Association, Miami, Florida, May 1976).
4. W. Kilpatrick. (1975). *Identity and Intimacy* (New York: Delacorte), 30.
5. E. Erikson. (1980). "The Freud-Jung Correspondence," in E. Smelser and E. Erikson (eds.), *Themes of Work and Love in Adulthood* (Cambridge, Mass.: Harvard University Press), 48.
6. R. Bellah, R. Madsen, W. Sullivan, A. Swidler, and S. Tipton. (1986). *Habits of the Heart: Individualism and Commitment in American Life* (New York: Harper & Row), 93.
7. H. Lopata. (1979). *Women as Widows.* New York: Elsevier, 201.
8. J. Miller. (1983). "Why the Fathers Cannot Solve the Problems: Some Possible Clues," in M. McGavran Murray (ed.), *Face to Face: Fathers, Mothers, Masters, Monsters—Essays for a Nonsexist Future* (Westport, Conn.: Greenwood), 134.
9. C. Gilligan. (1982). *In a Different Voice* (Cambridge, Mass.: Harvard University Press), 156.
10. C. Gilligan. (1979). "Women's Place in Man's Life Cycle," *Harvard Educational Review* 49: 431–46.

11. N. Chodorow. (1974). "Family Structure and Feminine Personality," in M. Zimbalist Rosaldo and L. Lamphere (eds.), *Woman, Culture, and Society* (Stanford, Calif.: Stanford University), 50.
12. J. Kaprio, M. Koskenvuo, and H. Rita. (1987). "Mortality After Bereavement: A Prospective Study of 95,647 Widowed Persons," *American Journal of Public Health* 77(3): 283–87. B. McMahon and T. Pugh. (1965). "Suicide in the Widowed," *American Journal of Epidemiology* 81: 23–31. J. Smith, J. Mercy, and J. Conn. (1988). "Marital Status and the Risk of Suicide," *American Journal of Public Health* 78(1): 78–80. S. Stack. (1980). "The Effects of Marital Dissolution on Suicide," *Journal of Marriage and the Family* 42:83–91.
13. J. Miller. (1976). *Toward a New Psychology of Women* (Boston: Beacon), 86.
14. E. Stanky, quoted in " 'Homesick' Stanky Resigns." (1977). *New York Times* (June 24), pp. A17, A20.
15. D. Levinson. (1978). *The Seasons of a Man's Life* (New York: Ballantine), 62.
16. R. Peck and H. Berkowitz. (1964). "Personality and Adjustment in Middle Age," in B. Neugarten *et al.* (eds.), *Personality in Middle and Late Life* (New York: Atherton), 15–43. L. Rubin. (1984). *Intimate Strangers: Men and Women Together* (New York: Harper & Row), 131–32. L. Troll. (1975). *Early and Middle Adulthood.* Monterey, Calif.: Brooks/Cole), 64–65.
17. S. Freud. (1908). "Civilized" Sexual Morality and Modern Nervousness, in *Collected Papers,* vol. 2 (London: Hogarth, 1948), 76–99.
18. E. Erikson. (1979). *Identity and the Life Cycle* (New York: Norton), 42.
19. R. DiGiulio. (1984). "Identity Loss and Reformulation in Young, Middle-Aged and Older Widowed Women." *Dissertation Abstracts International,* 42(04), 1217A. (University Microfilms No. DA8416087). L. Thomas, R. DiGiulio, and N. Sheehan. (1988). "Identity Loss and Psychological Crisis in Widowhood" *International Journal of Aging and Human Development,* 26(3), 225–239.
20. Kilpatrick.
21. L. Pincus. (1976). *Death and the Family: The Importance of Mourning* (New York: Vintage), 203.
22. Y. Lennon. (1981). "In Gratitude" *New York Times* (January 18, Letter), p. E24.
23. I. Podobnikar, quoted in D. Gelman. (1983). "A Great Emptiness," *Newsweek* (November 7, 1983), 120–26.
24. P. Linville. (1987). "Self-Complexity as a Cognitive Buffer Against

Stress-Related Illness and Depression," *Journal of Personality and Social Psychology* 52(4): 663–76.

25. M. Komarovsky. (1967). *Blue-Collar Marriage* (New York: Random House). H. Lopata. (1979). *Women as Widows*. N.Y.: Elsevier. L. Rainwater, R. Coleman, and G. Handel. (1959). *Workingman's Wife* (New York: Oceana Publications). A. S. Rossi. (1965). "Barriers to the Career Choice of Engineering, Medicine or Science Among American Women," in J. Mattfelt and C. Van Aken (eds.), *Women and the Scientific Professions* (Cambridge, Mass.: MIT Press).
26. H. Lopata. (1975). "Widowhood: Societal Factors in Life Span Disruptions and Alternatives," in N. Datan and L. Ginsberg (eds.), *Life-Span Developmental Psychology* (New York: Academic Press), 230.
27. E. Schlaffer and C. Bernard. (1978). "The Survivors: Some Hypotheses on the Significance for Older Women of the Loss of Spouse (English summary)," *Zeitschrift für Gerontologie* 11(1): 90–97.
28. T. Holmes and R. Rahe. (1967). "The Social Readjustment Rating Scale," *Journal of Psychosomatic Research* 11: 213–18. D. Gallagher, L. Thompson, and J. Peterson. (1982). "Psychosocial Factors Affecting Adaptation to Bereavement in the Elderly," *International Journal of Aging & Human Development* 14(2): 79–95.

CHAPTER 4
Growing Through Widowhood

1. American Psychiatric Association. (1980). *Diagnostic and Statistical Manual of Mental Disorders* (3d ed.) (Washington, D.C.: Author), 333.
2. W. Delong and E. Robins. (1961). "The Communication of Suicidal Intent Prior to Psychiatric Hospitalization: A Study of 87 Patients," *American Journal of Psychiatry* 117: 695–705. G. Murphy. (1975). "The Physician's Responsibility for Suicide," *Annals of Internal Medicine* 82: 301–9. A. Nicholi, Jr., ed. (1978). *The Harvard Guide to Modern Psychiatry*. (Cambridge, Mass.: Harvard University Press), 594.
3. C. Parkes. (1975). "Determinants of Outcome Following Bereavement," *OMEGA: Journal of Death and Dying* 6(4): 303–23. Parkes, C. (1979). *Bereavement: Studies of Grief in Adult Life* (New York: International Universities Press), 89–90.
4. M. Goin, R. Burgoyne, and J. Goin. (1979). "Timeless Attachement to a Dead Relative," *American Journal of Psychiatry* 136(7): 988–89.
5. T. Yamamoto, K. Okonogi, T. Iwasaki, and S. Yoshimura. (1969). "Mourning in Japan," *American Journal of Psychiatry* 12(5): 74.

6. C. Hobson. (1964). "Widows of Blackton," *New Society* (September): 13.
7. P. Marris. (1958). *Widows and Their Families* (London: Routledge and Kegan Paul).
8. C. Parkes. (1970). " 'Seeking' and 'Finding' a Lost Object: Evidence from Recent Studies of the Reaction to Bereavement," *Social Science and Medicine* 4(2): 187–201.
9. L. Judd, quoted in E. Ubell. (1988). "You Can Fight Depression" *Parade* (May 8), 16–17.
10. E. Palmore, ed. (1970). *Normal Aging: Reports from the Duke Longitudinal Study, 1955–1969* (Durham, N.C.: Duke University Press), 86.
11. W. Worden (1982). *Grief Counseling and Grief Therapy,* (New York: Springer), 29.
12. J. Bowlby. (1980). *Attachment and Loss, Volume Three: Loss, Sadness and Depression* (New York: Basic), 87.
13. E. Durkheim. (1951). *Suicide: A Study in Sociology* (Glencoe, Ill.: Free Press), 259.
14. F. M. Berardo. (1968). "Widowhood Status in the United States: Perspectives on a Neglected Aspect of the Family Life Cycle," *Family Coordinator* 17: 191–203. E. Bock and I. Webber. (1972). "Suicide Among the Elderly: Isolating Widowhood and Mitigating Alternatives," *Journal of Marriage and the Family* 34: 24–31. J. Kaprio, M. Koskenvuo, and H. Rita. (1987). "Mortality after Bereavement: A Prospective Study of 95,647 Widowed Persons," *American Journal of Public Health* 77(3): 283–87. B. McMahon and T. Pugh. (1965). "Suicide in the Widowed," *American Journal of Epidemiology* 81: 23–31. H. Resnick and J. Cantor. (1970). "Suicide and Aging," *Journal of the American Geriatric Society* 18: 152–58. J. Smith, J. Mercy, and J. Conn. (1988). "Marital Status and the Risk of Suicide," *American Journal of Public Health* 78(1): 78–80. S. Stack. (1980). "The Effects of Marital Dissolution on Suicide," *Journal of Marriage and the Family* 42: 83–91.
15. E. Shneidman. (1987). "At the Point of No Return," *Psychology Today* (March): 54–58.
16. B. Raphael. (1983). *The Anatomy of Bereavement* (New York: Basic), 198. R. Weiss, ed. (1974). *Loneliness: The Experience of Emotional and Social Isolation* (Cambridge, Mass.: MIT Press).
17. H. Lopata. (1973). "Self-identity in Marriage and Widowhood," *Sociological Quarterly* 14(3): 407–418. H. Lopata. (1981). "Widowhood and Husband Sanctification," *Journal of Marriage and the Family* (May): 439–50.

18. M. Hunt. (1966). *The World of the Formerly Married* (New York: McGraw-Hill), 103–104.
19. United States Bureau of the Census. (1977). "Household and Families by Type: March 1977," *Current Population Reports; Population Characteristics.* (Series P-20, No. 313, September).
20. R. Loewinsohn. (1979). *Survival Handbook for Widows* (Chicago: Follett), 115–18. M. Nye. (1978). *But I Never Thought He'd Die: Practical Help for Widows* (Philadelphia: Westminster), 140. I. Taves. (1981). *The Widow's Guide* (New York: Schocken), 28–29.

CHAPTER 5
Growing Beyond Widowhood

1. E. Roosevelt. (1958). *On My Own* (New York: Harper & Brothers), 1.
2. Roosevelt, ibid.
3. J. Sadat. (1987). *A Woman of Egypt* (New York: Simon & Schuster), 456.
4. D. Maddison and W. Walker. (1967). "Factors Affecting the Outcome of Conjugal Bereavement," *British Journal of Psychiatry* 113(2): 1057–67.
5. J. Bowlby. (1980). *Attachment and Loss, Volume Three: Loss, Sadness and Depression* (New York: Basic), 93.
6. C. Lewis. (1961). *A Grief Observed* (London: Faber), 59.
7. A. Paton. (1969). *For You Departed* (New York: Scribner), 156.
8. L. Pincus. (1976). *Death and the Family: The Importance of Mourning* (New York: Vintage), 203–4.
9. M. Gordon, quoted in I. Taves. (1981). *The Widow's Guide* (New York: Schocken), 185.
10. R. Tagore. (1961). "Fireflies," in A. Chakravarty, Ed., *A Tagore Reader* (New York: Macmillan), 339–40.
11. Roosevelt, *On My Own,* 2.
12. Roosevelt, ibid.
13. J. Smith, quoted in "Samantha Smith's Vision an Inspiration to Mother." (1986). *New York Times,* (December 14), p. 68.
14. J. Smith, quoted in "Samantha Smith Memorial Unveiled." (1986). *Record-Journal* (Meriden, Conn.), (December 23), p. 26.
15. Personal communication, June 1987.
16. J. Smith, quoted in "Samantha Smith's Vision an Inspiration to Mother."
17. C. King. (1969). *My Life With Martin Luther King, Jr.* (New York: Holt, Rinehart and Winston), 329.

18. King, ibid.
19. B. White, quoted in L. Katz. (1987). "Inquiry: I'm Having a Great Time Doing the Work I Love," *USA Today* (June 11), p. 11A.
20. B. White. (1987). *Betty White In Person* (New York: Doubleday), 180–85.
21. B. White, quoted in L. Katz, ibid.
22. B. White, ibid.
23. B. White, quoted in L. Katz, ibid.

CHAPTER 6
The Value of Personal Relationships

1. G. Haas-Hawkings. (1978). "Intimacy as a Moderating Influence on the Stress of Loneliness in Widowhood," *Essence* 2(4): 249–58. H. Harlow and R. Zimmerman. (1959). "Affectional Responses in the Infant Monkey," *Science* 130: 412–32. M. Lowenthal and L. Weiss. (1976). "Intimacy and Crises in Adulthood," *The Counseling Psychologist* 6(1): 10–15. R. Spitz and K. Wolf. (1946). "Anaclitic Depression," *Psychoanalytic Study of the Child* 2: 313–42. L. Thomas. (1982). "Sexuality and Aging: Essential Vitamin or Popcorn?" *The Gerontologist* 22(3): 240–43.
2. E. Bankoff. (1983). "Social Support and Adaptation to Widowhood," *Journal of Marriage and the Family* 45(4): 827–39.
3. G. Arling. (1976). "The Elderly Widow and Her Family, Neighbors, and Friends," *Journal of Marriage and the Family* 38: 757–68. C. Barrett. (1974). "The Development and Evaluation of Three Therapeutic Group Interventions for Widows" (Unpublished Ph.D. dissertation, University of Southern California). F. Berardo. (1970). "Survivorship and Social Isolation: The Case of the Aged Widower," *Family Coordinator* 19: 11–25. E. Bock and I. Webber. (1972). "Suicide Among the Elderly: Isolating Widowhood and Mitigating Alternatives," *Journal of Marriage and the Family* 34: 24–31. H. Lopata. (1969). "Loneliness: Forms and Components," *Social Problems* 17(2): 248–62. D. Maddison and W. Walker. (1967). "Factors Affecting the Outcome of Conjugal Bereavement," *British Journal of Psychiatry* 113(2): 1057–67. C. Parkes and R. Brown. (1972). "Health After Bereavement: A Controlled Study of Young Boston Widows and Widowers," *Psychosomatic Medicine* 34(5): 449–61. R. Weiss, ed. (1973). *Loneliness: The Experience of Emotional and Social Isolation* (Cambridge, Mass.: MIT Press).
4. B. Raphael. (1983). *The Anatomy of Bereavement* (New York: Basic), 181.
5. Raphael, ibid.

6. T. Des Pres. (1976). *The Survivor.* New York: Oxford University Press.
7. R. Carey. (1979–80). "Weathering Widowhood: Problems and Adjustment of the Widowed During the First Year," *Omega: Journal of Death and Dying* 10(2): 163–74. J. Hilgard, M. Newman, and F. Fisk. (1960). "Strength of Adult Ego Following Childhood Bereavement," *American Journal of Orthopsychiatry* 30: 788–98. H. McCubbin, C. Joy, A. Cauble, J. Comeau, J. Patterson, and R. Needle. (1980). "Family Stress and Coping: A Decade Review," *Journal of Marriage and the Family* 42(4): 855–71.
8. J. Ablon. (1971). "Bereavement in a Samoan Community," *British Journal of Medical Psychology* 44: 329–37.
9. E. Lindemann. (1944). "Symptomatology and Management of Acute Grief," *American Journal of Psychiatry* 101: 141–48.
10. Ablon, ibid.
11. E. Volkart and S. Michael. (1957). "Bereavement and Mental Health," in A. Leighton *et al.* (eds.), *Explorations in Social Psychiatry* (New York: Basic), 300.
12. Parkes and Brown.
13. E. Hetherington. (1972). "Effects of Father Absence on Personality Development of Adolescent Daughters," *Developmental Psychology* 7: 313–26.
14. B. Adams. (1968). "The Middle-Class Adult and his Widowed or Still-Married Mother," *Social Problems* 16: 50–59. C. Balkwell. (1981). "Transition to Widowhood: A Review of the Literature," *Family Relations* 30: 117–27. H. Lopata. (1979). *Women as Widows* (New York: Elsevier North Holland), 194–200.
15. D. Manning. (1985). *Comforting Those Who Grieve* (San Francisco: Harper & Row), 53.
16. K. Walker, A. McBride, and M. Vachon. (1977). "Social Support Networks and the Crisis of Bereavement," *Social Science and Medicine* 2: 35–41.
17. E. Bankoff, ibid. P. Silverman. (1972). "Widowhood and Preventative Intervention," *Family Life Coordinator* 21: 95–104. Walker, McBride, and Vachon.
18. G. Engel. (1967). "The Concept of Psychosomatic Disorder," *Psychosomatic Research* 11: 3–9. H. Friedman and S. Booth-Kewley. (1987). "The 'Disease-Prone' Personality," *American Psychologist* 42(6): 539–55. A. Schmale. (1958). "Relationship of Separation and Depression to Disease," *Psychosomatic Medicine* 20: 259–77.
19. M. Lowenthal and C. Haven. (1968). "Interaction and Adaptation:

Intimacy as a Critical Variable," *American Sociological Review* 33: 20–30.

20. B. Shaw. (1946). "Man and Superman," in *Nine Plays*. New York: Dodd, Mead and Co., 551–552.
21. H. Bahr and C. Harvey. (1980). "Correlates of Morale Among the Newly Widowed," *Journal of Social Psychology* 110(2): 219–33. G. Dooghe, L. Vanderleyden, and F. Van-Loon. (1980). "Social Adjustment of the Elderly Residing in Institutional Homes: A Multivariate Analysis," *International Journal of Aging & Human Development* 11(2): 163–76. M. Vachon, A. Sheldon, W. Lance, W. Lyall, J. Rogers, and S. Freeman. (1982). "A Controlled Study of Self-Help Intervention for Widows," *Psychological Medicine* 12: 1380–84.
22. L. Morgan. (1976). "A Re-examination of Widowhood and Morale," *Journal of Gerontology* 31(6): 687–95.
23. Berardo. Lowenthal and Haven. Lowenthal and Weiss.
24. Lowenthal and Weiss.
25. B. Allan, quoted in D. Gelman. (1983). "A Great Emptiness," *Newsweek* (November 7): 120–26.
26. Parkes & Brown.
27. D. Green and D. Nemzer. (1973). "Changes in Cigarette Smoking by Women: An Analysis, 1966 and 1970," *Health Services Reports* 88(7): 631–36.
28. J. Smith, J. Mercy, and J. Conn. (1988). "Marital Status and the Risk of Suicide," *American Journal of Public Health* 78(1): 78–80.

CHAPTER 7
Remarriage

1. A. Cherlin. (1981). *Marriage, Divorce, Remarriage* (Cambridge: Harvard University Press), 29–30. W. Cleveland and D. Gianturco. (1976). "Remarriage Probability After Widowhood: A Retrospective Method," *Journal of Gerontology* 31(1): 99–103. National Center for Health Statistics. (1984). *Advance Report of Final Marriage Statistics, 1981. Monthly Vital Statistics Report,* vol. 32, no. 9, supplement (Washington, D.C.: U.S. Government Printing Office), 9. U.S. Bureau of the Census. (1977). *Population Characteristics. Marriage, Divorce, Widowhood, and Remarriage by Family Characteristics: June, 1975,* series P-20, no. 312 (Washington, D.C.: U.S. Government Printing Office), 13–15. U.S. Bureau of the Census. (1980). *Population Characteristics. Marital Status and Living Arrangements, March 1979,* series P-20, no. 349 (Washington, D.C.: U.S. Government Printing Office), 5, 7. U.S. Bureau of the Census. (1984). *Detailed Population Characteristics, 1980 Census of Population, Part 1: United*

States Summary, vol. 1, ch. D (Washington, D.C.: U.S. Government Printing Office), 1–67, 1–68.

2. U.S. Bureau of the Census, March, 1984, ibid.
3. W. Gove. (1973). "Sex, Marital Status, and Mortality," *American Journal of Sociology* 79, 45–67. G. Gurin, J. Veroff, and S. Feld. (1980). *Americans View Their Mental Health* (New York: Basic). R. Larson. (1978). "Thirty Years of Research on the Subjective Well-Being of Older Americans," *Journal of Gerontology* 33: 109–29.
4. J. Stryckman. (1981). "The Decision to Remarry: The Choice and Its Outcome," (Paper presented at the joint meetings of the Gerontological Society of America and the Canadian Association of Gerontology, Toronto, November 8–12).
5. "Widowed Canadians Who Remarry Have Higher Morale and Better Self-Image." (1982). *Ageing International* 9(3): 19.
6. L. White. (1979). "Sex Differentials in the Effect of Remarriage on Global Happiness," *Journal of Marriage and the Family* 41: 869–76.
7. R. Jacob and B. Vinick. (1979). *Re-engagement in Later Life: Re-employment and Remarriage* (Stamford, Conn.: Greylock). W. McKain. (1969). *Retirement Marriage* (Storrs, Conn.: Storrs Agricultural Experiment Station, Monograph 3). B. Schlesinger. (1968). "Remarriage—An Inventory of Findings," *The Family Coordinator* 17: 248–51. B. Schlesinger. (1971). "The Widow and Widower and Remarriage: Selected Findings," *Omega* 2: 10–18.
8. H. Lopata. (1979). *Women as Widows* (New York: Elsevier North Holland), 169.
9. A. Cherlin. (1978). "Remarriage as an Incomplete Institution," *American Journal of Sociology* 84(3): 634–50. L. Kizirian. (1977). "Remarriage: A Study of the Factors Leading to Success or Failure," *Dissertation Abstracts International* 38(12A), 146. T. Monahan. (1956). "The Changing Nature and Instability of Remarriage," *Marriage and Family Living* 21: 134–38. M. Nye. (1978). *But I Never Thought He'd Die* (Philadelphia: Westminster).
10. A. Swidler. (1980). "Love and Adulthood in American Culture," in N. Smelser and E. Erikson (eds.), *Themes of Love and Work in Adulthood* (Cambridge, Mass.: Harvard University Press), 121.
11. J. Miller. (1976). *Toward a New Psychology of Women* (Boston: Beacon), 84–85.
12. B. Maddox. (1975). *The Halfparent* (London: Andre Deutsch), 3.
13. McKain.
14. J. Peterson. (1980). *On Being Alone* (Washington, D.C.: National Retired Teachers Association/AARP), 5.

15. "Widowed Canadians."
16. McKain.
17. L. Pincus. (1976). *Death and the Family: The Importance of Mourning* (New York: Vintage), 124.
18. M. Moss and S. Moss. (1979). "Remarriage: A Triadic Relationship" (Paper presented at the 37th conference of the American Association of Marriage and Family Therapy, Washington, D.C., October 5). M. Moss and S. Moss. (1980). "The Image of the Deceased Spouse in Remarriage of Elderly Widow(er)s," *Journal of Gerontological Social Work* 3(2): 59–70.
19. Moss and Moss, 1980, ibid.
20. M. Davenport, quoted in D. Gelman. (1983). "A Great Emptiness," *Newsweek:* (November 7): 120–26.

CHAPTER 8
Mutual Support Groups

1. B. Rush. (1835). *Medical Inquiries and Observations Upon the Diseases of the Mind* (Philadelphia: Grigg & Elliott).
2. D. Eden, A. Shirom, J. Kellermann, J. Aronson, and J. French. (1977). "Stress, Anxiety and Coronary Risk in a Supportive Society," in C. D. Spielberger and I. G. Sarason (eds.), *Stress and Anxiety,* vol. 4 (New York: John Wiley).
3. National Institute of Mental Health. (1981). *Plain Talk About Mutual Help Groups: People Who Know Just How You Feel* (Washington, D.C.: U.S. Government Printing Office, DHHS Publication No. ADM 81-1138.
4. P. Silverman. (1974). "Background to the Development of the Widow-to-Widow Program," in P. R. Silverman, D. MacKenzie, M. Pettipas, and E. Wilson (eds.), *Helping Each Other in Widowhood* (New York: Health Services), 4.
5. C. Barrett. (1978). "The Effectiveness of Widows' Groups in Facilitating Change," *Journal of Consulting and Clinical Psychology* 46(1): 20–31. W. McCourt, R. Barnett, J. Bremner, and A. Becker. (1976). "We Help Each Other: Primary Prevention for the Widowed," *American Journal of Psychiatry* 133: 98–100. P. Silverman. (1981). *Helping Women Cope with Grief* (Beverly Hills, Calif.: Sage), 106. M. Vachon, W. Lyall, J. Rogers, K. Freedman-Letofsky, and S. Freeman. (1980). "A Controlled Study of Self-Help Intervention for Widows," *American Journal of Psychiatry* 137: 1380–84.
6. D. Maddison and A. Viola. (1968). "The Health of Widows in the Year Following Bereavement," *Journal of Psychosomatic Research,* 12: 292–306.

7. Barrett. S. Sandsberg. (1981). Veiledning Av Etterlatte. Noen Erfaringer Fra et Aksjonsforskningsprosjekt. (Counseling the Bereaved: Experiences from an Action-Oriented Research Project) *Tidsskrift For Norsk Psykologforening,* Suppl. 1: 78–88. P. Silverman and A. Cooperband. (1975). "On Widowhood: Mutual Help and the Elderly Widow," *Journal of Geriatric Psychiatry* 8(1): 9–27. Vachon et al.
8. M. Leibermann and L. Borman. (1981). "Researchers Study THEOS," *THEOS* (September), 3–6.
9. Winnipeg YWCA. (1977). "The Widows' Consultation Centre: Establishment and Development as a Pilot Project" (Winnipeg, Manitoba: YWCA, June, mimeo).
10. Personal communication, October 1982.

CHAPTER 9
Growing Together

1. J. Goldstein, A. Freud, and A. Solnit. (1980). *Before the Best Interests of the Child* (New York: Free Press), 7. J. Goldstein, A. Freud, and A. Solnit. (1984). *Beyond the Best Interests of the Child* (New York: Free Press), 16.
2. J. Goldstein, A. Freud, and A. Solnit. (1984), ibid, 19.
3. E. Ford and S. Englund. (1978). *For the Love of Children: A Reality Therapy Approach to Raising Your Child* (New York: Anchor), 42–43.
4. R. Fulton. (1967). "On the Dying of Death," in E. Grollman (ed.), *Explaining Death to Children* (Boston: Beacon), 46–47.
5. E. Grollman. (1967). "Prologue," in E. Grollman (ed.), *Explaining Death to Children* (Boston: Beacon), 21.
6. Grollman, ibid.
7. A. Cain and J. Fast. (1966). "Children's Disturbed Reactions to Parent Suicide," *American Journal of Orthopsychiatry* 36: 873–80.
8. R. Meryman, interviewed by B. Stein. (1981). "A Widower Advises Wearing Out One's Grief like a Suit of Clothes," *People,* April 20, 97–98.

Suggested Readings

Moving Through Widowhood

Bereavement: A Magazine of Hope and Healing is an informative, supportive, and even entertaining magazine for those who are bereaved, and for those who wish to understand and help the grief-stricken. Available from Bereavement Publishing, 350 Gradle Road, Carmel, Ind. 46032

BERNSTEIN, JOANNE E. *Loss and How to Cope With It*. New York: Houghton Mifflin/Clarion, 1977.

A brief but sensitive treatment focusing on feelings and questions involved in losing a loved one.

BRYANT, BETTY. *Leaning Into the Wind: The Wilderness of Widowhood*. Philadelphia: Fortress, 1975.

A thought-provoking journal by a woman whose husband committed suicide.

COLGROVE, MELBA; BLOOMFIELD, HAROLD; AND MCWILLIAMS, PETER. *How to Survive the Loss of a Love*. Allen Park, Mich.: Leo Press, 1976.

An easily readable and supportive book on loss of love in general, especially helpful in the early days of widowhood.

GROLLMAN, EARL A. *Living When a Loved One Has Died*. Boston: Beacon, 1977.

An excellent general text for adjusting to life following the loss of a loved one.

———. *Time Remembered: A Journal for Survivors*. Boston: Beacon, 1987.

Dr. Grollman has constructed a unique work: a combined self-help book-plus-diary that has spaces for the widow to keep a journal, accompanied by supportive text.

KUSHNER, HAROLD S. *When Bad Things Happen to Good People.* New York: Avon, 1983.

Thoroughly human, Dr. Kushner writes from his heart following the death of his young son. Much of his insight and wisdom in addressing the "why me?" questions apply to widowed people.

MERYMAN, RICHARD. *Hope—A Loss Survived.* Boston: Little, Brown, 1984.

A sensitive account of a man who lived through the illness and death of his wife.

PETERSON, JAMES A. *On Being Alone.* Washington, D.C.: 1980.

This widely distributed pamphlet is available at no charge from the Widowed Persons Service, Box 199, Long Beach, California 90801. It contains practical advice especially helpful for those recently widowed.

SCHOEN, ELIN. *Widower: A Daughter's Compelling Account of How a Man Overcame Grief and Loneliness.* New York: William Morrow, 1984.

The daughter of a widowed man writes of her father's experiences following thirty-seven years of marriage, and of his hasty attempt to remarry.

SEIGEL, BERNIE S. *Love, Medicine and Miracles.* New York: Harper & Row, 1988.

The crucial importance of mind, attitude, and spirit in healing after a loss or illness. Chapter Three—"Disease and the Mind"—is especially informative for widowed persons.

THEOS Foundation, Inc. *Survivors' Outreach Series.* Pittsburgh, Pa.: THEOS, no date.

A superb set of eight glossy magazine issues, each addresses a variety of concerns and is written especially for the newly widowed person. Available from THEOS's national headquarters.

Moving Beyond Widowhood

ALBEE, LOU. *Over Forty—Out of Work?* Englewood Cliffs, N.J.: Prentice-Hall, 1970.

A collection of good ideas for the middle-aged and older person about reentering the work force.

BOLLES, RICHARD N. *What Color is Your Parachute? A Practical Manual for Job-Hunters and Career-Changers.* Berkeley, Calif.: Ten Speed, revised annually.

"Parachute" can help even those in the job market to identify occupational interests and strengths. It is simply the best vocational guidance book on the market today.

CAINE, LYNN. *Lifelines.* Garden City, N.Y.: Doubleday and Co., 1978.

Insightful thoughts by the author of *Widow* on overcoming loneliness and stress, facing life as a single parent, and contemplating new romantic relationships.

HOFFMAN, RAY. *Extra Dollars: Easy Moneymaking Ideas for Retired People.* New York: Stein & Day, 1977.

For the person without great amounts of cash who wishes to start a modest business.

KUSHNER, HAROLD S. *When All You've Ever Wanted Isn't Enough.* New York: Summit, 1986.

Indispensable help in redefining what we thought we wanted in life.

LESHAN, EDA. *Oh, To Be 50 Again! On Being Too Old for a Midlife Crisis.* New York: Times, 1986.

An honest, tender, and at times gripping book written by a sensitive and perceptive family counselor who ponders what it means to have reached age sixty. I especially recommend chapter 3: "The Never-Ending Search for Oneself."

LEVINSON, DANIEL J. *The Seasons of a Man's Life.* New York: Ballantine, 1978.

While it does not specifically address the effects of death of a spouse or widowhood (few men's books do), "Seasons" is a fascinating outline of the predictable crises faced by men as they move through adulthood, occupation, and marriage.

NEWMAN, MILDRED, AND BERKOWITZ, BERNARD. *How to be Your Own Best Friend.* New York: Ballantine, 1971.

A classic self-help book from the "self-improvement era," this thin paperback can help widowed people challenge their feelings of having been victimized, understanding the control they still retain over their personal happiness.

PETERSON, JAMES A., AND BRILEY, MICHAEL P. *Widows and Widowhood: A Creative Approach to Being Alone.* New York: Association, 1977.

A guidebook approach for widowed people that is quite comprehensive and practically oriented.

POWELL, JOHN. *Fully Human, Fully Alive.* Niles, Ill.: Argus, 1976.

A gem of a book that helps us realize how our vision of our life actually shapes that life we ultimately live.

SESKIN, JANE. *Young Widow.* New York: Ace, 1975.

A fine description of a widow's transformation into a self-sufficient woman following the illness and death of her husband.

ZIMMETH, MARY. *The Woman's Guide to Re-Entry Employment.* Mankato, Minn.: Gabriel, 1979.

A readable and very practical guide for women covering all aspects of returning to work from interviewing to career planning.

Widowed People and Their Families

D'Arcy, Paula. *Song for Sarah: A Young Mother's Journey Through Grief and Beyond.* Wheaton, Ill.: Harold Shaw, 1980.

A touching story based on a diary kept by an expectant mother who experiences the sudden death of her husband and young daughter.

Grollman, Earl A. (ed.) *Explaining Death to Children.* Boston: Beacon, 1967.

Grollman, Earl A. *Talking About Death: A Dialogue Between Parent and Child.* Boston: Beacon, 1976.

Both of Dr. Grollman's books are superb for the widow with children: They are well-written, thorough, and thoughtful in addressing the "pornography of death" our society holds so strongly.

Pincus, Lily. *Death and the Family.* New York: Vintage, 1976.

A series of case studies on family mourning in Britain by a therapist and social worker. Especially interesting is her description of the type of mourning widowed persons experience as a result of the previous marriage relationship.

Start, Clarissa. *On Becoming a Widow.* St. Louis, Missouri: Concordia, 1973.

An honest and frank book about the author's changed life as a widowed women needing to meet responsibilities toward parents and children. She has a "can-do" optimism.

Taves, Isabella. *The Widow's Guide: Practical Advice on How to Deal with Grief, Stress, Health, Children & Family, Money, Work & Finally, Getting Back Into the World.* New York: Schocken, 1981.

Just what the title says: A practical guide especially for such "nitty-gritty" matters as dealing with finances and occupation.

Temes, Roberta. *Living With an Empty Chair* (expanded edition). New York: Irvington Publishers, 1984.

Warmly illustrated and gently written book on helping the family deal with grief and adjusting to the realities of life as a single person.

Helping Widowed People

AARP. *Widowed Persons Service Organization Manual.* Washington, D.C.: AARP.

Available to groups organizing an AARP Widowed Persons Service Program (See "Sources of Organized Support" below).

Decker, Bea. *After the Flowers Have Gone.* Grand Rapids, Mich.: Zondervan, 1973.

One of the first personal accounts of widowhood by the founder of THEOS (They Help Each Other Spiritually) self-help groups.

Hill, Karen. *Helping You Helps Me: A Guide Book for Self-Help Groups.* Ottawa, Ontario: Canadian Council on Social Development, 1985.

An excellent, free resource to guide the beginning and continuation of a self-help group.

Hiltz, Starr R. *Creating Community Services for the Widowed.* Port Washington, N.Y.: Kennikat Press, 1976.

Another guide to setting up support services for widowed people based on a consultant service for widows in New York.

Kübler-Ross, Elisabeth. *On Death and Dying.* New York: Macmillan, 1969.

Kübler-Ross, Elisabeth. *Questions and Answers on Death and Dying.* New York: Macmillan, 1974.

Although her books are of optimal help for the terminally ill and their families, both books have worth for widowed people attempting to understand the stages of dying and death, and for those helping others move through loss, whether anticipated or actual.

Lopata, Helena Z. *Women as Widows: Support Systems.* New York: Elsevier, 1979.

The report on her comprehensive study of Chicago widows, including old-age beneficiaries, widowed mothers of eligible children, and remarried widows. Lopata describes the value of family and support groups on their adjustment in widowhood.

Lopata, Helena Z. *Widowhood in an American City.* Cambridge, Mass.: Schenkman, 1973.

A thorough analysis of the social world of urban American widows 50–64 years of age and those older than age 65. Lopata is a foremost scholar on the subject.

Lynch, James J. *The Broken Heart: The Medical Consequences of Loneliness.* New York: Basic, 1977.

An early and definitive text on the connection between loneliness and illness, it stresses the importance of human companionship for emotional and physical health.

Manning, Doug. *Comforting Those Who Grieve: A Guide for Helping Others.* New York: Harper & Row, 1985.

A practical and spiritually oriented guide from an insightful person who has ministered for over thirty years.

Silverman, Phyllis. *Helping Women Cope With Grief.* Beverly Hills, Calif.: Sage, 1981.

An excellent resource on helping to ease the grief of birthmothers, battered women, and widows.

Silverman, Phyllis. *Mutual Help Groups: Organization and Development* (Sage Human Services Guides: Vol. 16). Beverly Hills, Calif.: Sage, 1980.

Silverman, Phyllis. *Widow-to-Widow*. New York: Springer, 1986.

Silverman, Phyllis, and Campbell, Scott. *Widower*. Englewood Cliffs, N.J.: Prentice-Hall, 1987.

Three fine resources. Silverman is a pioneer of the "widow-to-widow" support concept.

Worden, William J. *Grief Counseling & Grief Therapy: A Handbook for the Mental Health Practitioner*. New York: Springer, 1982.

An excellent resource for those counseling the bereaved. Particularly illuminating of particular types of losses like suicide and sudden deaths.

Sources of Organized Support

Sources of Organized Support: United States

The following listings are national or regional in scope; a few are international. All offer support, self-help services, general or specialized information, or literature concerned with helping the widowed grow through widowhood and beyond. Groups and organizations listed below are often able to direct you to local chapters near your home.

American Association of State Colleges and Universities
1 Dupont Circle
Suite 700
Washington, DC 20036

Publishes *Alternatives for Later Life and Learning: Some Programs Designed for Older Persons at State Colleges and Universities,* which is of value to widowed men and women who seek higher-education programs specially designed for older persons.

American National Red Cross
Office of Community Volunteer Services
National Headquarters
Washington, DC 20006

Along with its well-known role in disaster relief, the Red Cross also has many programs specifically for widowed people, delivered through local chapters.

Barr-Harris Center for the Study of Separation and Loss During Childhood
180 North Michigan Avenue
Chicago, IL 60601

This Center provides direct services to families with children nine years of age and younger who have lost a parent through death. They also have a community education and consultation service.

Center for Loss and Life Transitions
3735 Broken Bow Road
Fort Collins, CO 80526

This organization offers comprehensive services to those who have experienced loss, including clinical care, education, and training for those who help the bereaved.

Chrysalis Center
P.O. Box 26367
St. Louis, MO 63136

A bereavement resource center for funeral directors.

Compassionate Friends, Inc.
P.O. Box 3696
Oak Brook, IL 60522-3696

With almost five hundred chapters across the United States, Compassionate Friends provides help for bereaved parents.

Commission on Pastoral Bereavement Counseling
10 East 73d Street
New York, NY 10021

Serving newly bereaved persons in the New York metropolitan area, the CPBC is an organized communal network for extended spiritual and emotional counseling.

Concerns of Police Survivors, Inc.
16921 Croom Road
Brandywine, MD 20613

CPS provides outreach programs to newly widowed persons, consisting of group discussions, educational programs, and seminars.

Contact Teleministries U.S.A., Inc.
Pouch A
Harrisburg, PA 17109

This unique organization has 105 help-line centers in the United States, with 47 providing reassurance calls to the homebound, and 40 providing telecommunications services for the deaf.

Displaced Homemakers Network, Inc.
1411 K Street N.W., Suite 930
Washington, DC 20005

This is a relatively little-known organization that can be tremendously helpful to widowed women who may have spent little time in the work force. The Displaced Homemakers Network gives preemployment help and preparation to adults who have spent years caring for a family but have few labor-market experiences. Send a large self-addressed stamped envelope to them for more information.

Elderhostel
100 Boylston Street
Boston, MA 02116

Begun in 1975, the Elderhostel program allows persons over sixty years of age to spend time on a college campus, often combined with sightseeing and other activities including college courses, seminars, and workshops.

Emotions Anonymous
P.O. Box 4245
St. Paul, MN 55104

This support group for those with emotional problems was begun by adapting the "twelve-step program" of Alcoholics Anonymous to their needs.

Empire State College
P.O. Box 88
Saratoga Springs, NY 12866

For adults who already possess an undergraduate degree, Empire State College offers a guide to nontraditional *graduate* programs offered at 112 colleges. Request the *Innovative Graduate Programs Directory*.

Families of Suicide Victims/Families of Homicide Victims
Enrichment Groups
Child and Family Services
1680 Albany Avenue
Hartford, CT 06105

Connecticut's Division of Child and Family Services holds support groups at irregular intervals under the direction of trained professionals including social workers. They have groups for Spanish-speaking bereaved people, as well as mutual support and self-help groups for families who have lost a member through suicide or murder.

Family Service Association of America
11700 W. Lake Park Drive
Milwaukee, WI 53224

Oriented toward helping families cope with stress.

Foreign Policy Association
205 Lexington Avenue
New York, NY 10016

An exciting yet little-known discussion group called the "great decisions" program of the Foreign Policy Association gives Americans the chance to form a discussion group (or join an existing group) that discusses eight major foreign policy issues each year. Results of group and individual opinions are tabulated and sent to political figures and the media. Write the Foreign Policy Association for a free brochure describing the program.

Forty-Plus Clubs
c/o Forty-Plus
1718 P Street, N.W.
Washington, DC 20036

These clubs are nonprofit associations located in many major cities that help businessmen and -women reenter the work force.

Foster Grandparent Program
ACTION
806 Connecticut Avenue, N.W.
Washington, DC 20525

Both the Foster Grandparent Program and the Senior Companion Program offer job opportunities to low-income men and women who are sixty years of age or older. Write ACTION for more information, or check your telephone directory's "white pages."

Foundation of Thanatology
630 West 168th Street
New York, NY 10032

Organization concerned with issues of death and bereavement for professionals and scholars. They sponsor symposia and publish texts on all death-related issues.

Grief Education Institute
1780 S. Bellaire Street, Suite 132
Denver, CO 80222

This institute offers seminars, public education programs, and workshops for helping professionals, as well as support groups or individual counseling for bereaved people.

Help for Families of Homicide Victims
Victim Services Agency
2 Lafayette Street
New York, NY 10007

Provides counseling programs and crisis support as well as specialized services and assistance in obtaining financial aid.

Institute of Lifetime Learning
1909 K Street, N.W.
Washington, DC 20049

Along with the Widowed Persons Service, the Institute of Lifetime Learning is probably one of the most valuable resources available to help widowed adults move beyond widowhood. The institute promotes opportunities for older persons to pursue educational interests, prepare for new careers, and become involved in media and new technologies. It will also provide a list of over 800 institutions of higher education that extend free or reduced tuition benefits to older widowed men and women.

Although the institute is a joint service of the National Retired Teachers Association and the AARP, one does not have to belong to either to benefit from their many programs and services.

In fact, they will provide career education programs that can be "tailored" to each group's interests and needs. Write to American Association of Retired Persons at the office that serves your state (below) or contact the main office in Washington, DC.

Area I: Connecticut, Maine, Massachusetts, New Hampshire, Vermont, Rhode Island:

823 Park Square Building
Boston, MA 02116

Area II: Delaware, New Jersey, New York, Pennsylvania:

919 Third Avenue, 28th Floor
New York, NY 10022

Area III: Kentucky, Maryland, North Carolina, Virginia, District of Columbia, West Virginia:

1680 Duke Street
2nd Floor
Alexandria, VA 22314

Area IV: Alabama, Florida, Georgia, Mississippi, South Carolina, Tennessee:

Cambridge Building
2965 Flowers Road South, Suite 233
Atlanta, GA 30341

Area V: Illinois, Indiana, Michigan, Ohio, Wisconsin:

2720 Des Plaines Avenue
Suite 113
Des Plaines, IL 60018

Area VI: Iowa, Kansas, Minnesota, Missouri, Nebraska, North Dakota, South Dakota:

1125 Grand Avenue
Suite 1401
Kansas City, MO 64106

Area VII: Arkansas, Louisiana, New Mexico, Oklahoma, Texas:

700 University Tower
6440 North Central Expressway
Dallas, TX 75206

Area VIII: Colorado, Idaho, Montana, Utah, Wyoming:

709 Kearns Building
136 South Main Street
Salt Lake City, UT 84101

Area IX: Alaska, Arizona, California, Hawaii, Nevada, Oregon, Washington:

Suite 422
4201 Long Beach Boulevard
Long Beach, CA 90807

Make Today Count
101½ South Union Street
Alexandria, VA 22314-3348

This is an international organization that has local chapters for people with life-threatening illnesses.

Mature Temps
1114 Avenue of the Americas
New York, NY 10036

A private employment agency, Mature Temps will test the older worker for skills related to office jobs. They have offices outside New York City, but write to the above address for more information.

NAIM, U.S. Catholic Conference
Family Life Division
721 North LaSalle Drive
Chicago, IL 60610

Called "NAIM" after a biblical widow's village, this organization is for Catholic widowed persons; most chapters are in Illinois and the central United States.

National Action Forum for Midlife and Older Women
Health Sciences Center
State University of New York
Stony Brook, NY 11794

The forum is designed to be an advocacy center for all issues of concern to middle-aged and older women. They publish a newsletter called "Hot Flash."

National Mental Health Association
1021 Prince Street
Alexandria, VA 22314-2971

Provides information about grief and bereavement and other matters of concern to the bereaved.

National Association of Military Widows
4023 25th Road North
Arlington, VA 22207

An association that sponsors support groups, social events, and a referral service for the newly widowed, NAMW has also lobbied for laws to benefit the survivors of military action.

National Center for Death Education
656 Beacon Street
Boston, MA 02215

A library and resource center containing books, films, and other materials on the subjects of death, dying, and bereavement. Workshops and continuing education programs are offered.

National Coalition on Older Women's Issues
2401 Virginia Avenue, N.W.
Washington, DC 20037

Emphasizing employment, retirement income and health, this Coalition of organizations and individuals works for research and public policies that benefit middle-aged and older women.

National Council on Family Relations (NCFR)
1910 West County Road B
Suite 147
St. Paul, MN 55113

NCFR is the oldest multidisciplinary organization of family professionals in the United States. Of great potential help to professionals who work with the widowed, NCFR offers information about family life, encourages research on families, promotes family life education, and draws together professionals such as psychologists, counselors, educators, physicians, nurses, lawyers, and researchers—all of whom share an abiding interest in the family.

National Hospice Organization
1901 North Moore Street, #901
Arlington, VA 22209

National Hospice Organization can provide information about local hospice programs for the terminally ill and their families, and bereavement counseling.

National Self-Help Clearinghouse
Graduate School and University Center
City University of New York
33 West 42d Street
New York, NY 10036

An umbrella of support and information for national self-help groups, with local chapters in many states.

Older Women's League
730 11th Street, N.W., Suite 300
Washington, DC 20001

This organization serves as an advocate for all issues concerning older women.

Parents Without Partners
8807 Colesville Road
Silver Spring, MD 20910

National organization with over one thousand local chapters for all single parents, including widowed single parents. Local chapters typically have activities and support groups for parents, children, and adolescents.

The Peace Corps
ACTION
806 Connecticut Avenue, N.W.
Washington, DC 20525

The Peace Corps offers Americans the chance to share their expertise with others in underdeveloped countries. And there is no age limitation, nor is being married required.

Public Affairs Committee
381 Park Avenue South
New York, NY 10016

Their publication *New Paths to Learning: College Education for Adults* outlines nontraditional ways of pursuing higher education, including credit for life experience and credit through television and weekend courses.

Ray of Hope, Inc.
P.O. Box 2323
Iowa City, IA 52244

For survivors of suicide, Ray of Hope provides telephone counseling and support services. They also have available presentations, printed matter, and videotapes.

Seasons: Suicide Bereavement
4777 Naniloa Drive
Salt Lake City, UT 84117

A national organization with local chapters on the subject of the bereavement of survivors of suicide.

Senior Community Service Employment Program
Office of National Programs for Older Workers,
Employment Training Administration
Department of Labor
Room 6122
601 D Street, N.W.
Washington, DC 20213

SCSEP offers skills training and part-time employment to older persons with relatively low incomes.

Society of Military Widows, Inc.
5535 Hempstead Way
Springfield, VA 22151-4094

The SMW has been established for surviving spouses of deceased career military personnel, including those killed during active duty.

Suicide Survivors Grief Groups
5124 Grove Street
Minneapolis, MN 55436

This organization has various publications and presentations for families and friends of suicide victims.

Survivors of Suicide-National Office
Suicide Prevention Center, Inc.
P.O. Box 1393
Dayton, OH 45401

SOS has group discussions, newsletters, telephone referrals, and educational group programs and presentations all aimed to help friends and families of suicide victims.

THEOS Foundation
1301 Clark Building
717 Liberty Avenue
Pittsburgh, PA 15222

THEOS, both an acronym for They Help Each Other Spiritually and the Greek word for *God,* enables and promotes mutual self-help specifically for the widowed in the United States and Canada. Since 1962, THEOS has formed and maintained local groups, linked individuals for one-to-one support, conducted regional conferences and workshops, published material on grief and widowhood, and educated the public on supportive sympathizing with the widowed.

Veterans Employment Assistance Program
NCOA Headquarters
P.O. Box 33616
San Antonio, TX 72833

Not only veterans but widowed spouses of deceased veterans are eligible for free services in finding employment. They can help prepare a résumé, and will send that completed résumé to hundreds of hiring companies.

Volunteers in Service to America (VISTA)
806 Connecticut Avenue, N.W.
Room 10100
Washington, DC 20525

VISTA provides volunteers to assist groups serving low-income Americans, including senior citizens.

Widowed Persons Service
Program Department, AARP
1909 K Street, N.W.
Washington, DC 20049

Along with THEOS, WPS is a most comprehensive source of available help specifically for the widowed American. It offers outreach volunteers to visit the newly bereaved, a telephone referral service the widowed person can call for referral information and assistance, group sessions, training materials (including the publication *Insights*), and help with financial assistance for those desiring to launch a local support group for the widowed. They will provide an organizer to act as a consultant, planning and launching the first meeting and providing materials and other expertise.

In fact, WPS offers the widest range of services for widowed people in the United States. For full information about starting a local chapter or information about existing services, contact the program specialist in social outreach and support at the Widowed Persons Service.

Sources of Organized Support: Canada

National

Canadian Council on Social Development
P.O. Box 3505
Ottawa, Ontario K1Y 4G1

Provides free information on creating and maintaining self-help groups.

Local Sources of Organized Support: Canada

(For specific location and telephone numbers of each THEOS chapter, call THEOS National Headquarters at area code 412-471-7779.)

ALBERTA

LOSS—Loving Outreach for Survivors of Sudden Death
13308 91st Street
Edmonton, Alberta T5E 3P8

BRITISH COLUMBIA

Community Contacts for the Bereaved
Community Services
45845 Wellington Avenue
Chilliwack, British Columbia

An active and well-established support program, Community Contacts seeks to get in touch with the widowed through letters, telephone calls and, ultimately, personal contact, in which the widow meets a volunteer who has moved through widowhood. Listening, discussion, sharing, and networking with other community resources are benefits of Community Contacts.

LIFE (Living Is For Everyone)
101–395 West Broadway
Vancouver, British Columbia V5Y 1A7

MANITOBA

Widow's Consultation Centre
YWCA

447 Webb Place
Winnipeg, Manitoba R3B 2P2

Another highly active organization for the widowed, they pioneered Widow-to-Widow Volunteer Aide outreach programs in Canada; and the Women's Resource Centre (at the same address) has made available *The New Practical Guide for Widows,* an information kit designed to give guidance to the newly widowed and those who assist them.

NOVA SCOTIA

Community Contact for
the Widowed
1725 Garden Street
Halifax, Nova Scotia B3H 3R5

ONTARIO

Bereavement Resources
Canadian Mental Health
Association
Windsor Essex County Branch
880 Ouellette Avenue, Suite 901
Windsor, Ontario N9A 1C7

Widow-to-Widow
75 McNab Street, South
Hamilton, Ontario L8P 3C1

THEOS Chapters in:
Toronto (West)
Mississauga
Willowdale
Whitby
St. Catharine
Scarborough

QUEBEC

Widow-to-Widow Services
5500 Westbury Avenue
Montreal, Quebec H3W 2W8

SASKATCHEWAN

Saskatoon Community Contact
for the Widowed
1254 Crescent Boulevard
Saskatoon, Saskatchewan S7M
3W6

Sources of Organized Support: England & Europe

Cruse, the Organization for Widows and their Children
The Charter House
6 Lion Gate Gardens
Richmond, Surrey, England

As the most comprehensive service for the widowed in Britain, Cruse utilizes "cells," or small support groups of six to twelve widows, who meet for mutual support and company. They also maintain a number of Cruse Clubs, which offer social events and activities and professional counseling through involvement of clergy, doctors, and social workers.

Cruse is also highly focused on the welfare of the children of widowed parents and offers services accordingly.

International Federation of Widows and Widowers
Organizations (FIAV)

Cremerstraat 3
6665 CZ Driel
The Netherlands

An international organization of organizations and advocacy groups that serve the widowed, the International Federation publishes informational pamphlets and acts on behalf of all issues of concern to the widowed.

The Samaritans
Church of St. Stephen's Walbrook
London EC4, England

Begun in 1953, the Samaritans is an organization for those in despair or contemplating suicide. They have a telephone service staffed through the day and night for those in trouble, and they offer a "befriending service" whereby the bereaved can obtain a "one-to-one" nonprofessional volunteer friend.

The Society of Compassionate Friends
27a St. Columba's Close
Coventry, Warwickshire, England

Originally founded as a mutual support group for bereaved parents, both in the United States and Great Britain the Compassionate Friends carry out their mission well. I especially recommend the "friends" to those widowed who may also have lost a child at the same time they lost their spouse and thus need much support and compassion.

Local Sources of Organized Support: U.S.A.

(For specific location and telephone numbers of each THEOS chapter, call THEOS National Headquarters at area code 412-471-7779.)

ALABAMA

Widowed Persons Service
3215 Sterling Road
Birmingham, AL 35213

Decatur Area Widowed Persons Service
2947 Lynnwood Avenue, S.W.
Decatur, AL 35601

Huntsville Widowed Persons Service
1915 Stevens Drive, N.E.
Huntsville, AL 35801

Widowed Persons Service, Montgomery
3014 Norman Bridge Road
Montgomery, AL 36105

WPS of Tuscaloosa
Route 1, Box 5
Tuscaloosa, AL 35405

ALASKA

WPS of Anchorage
8449 Jupiter
Anchorage, AK 99507

Widowed Persons Service
1305 21st Avenue
Fairbanks, AK 99701

Widowed Persons Service
230 South Franklin Street, #810
Juneau, AK 99801

ARIZONA

Sun Cities Area WPS
P.O. Box 1145
Sun City, AZ 85372

Priority One Ministries
3201 South Terrace
Tempe, AZ 85282

Widowed-to-Widowed Services
312 South Third Avenue
Tucson, AZ 85718

ARKANSAS

Widowed Persons Service
East Arkansas Area Agency on Aging,
311 South Main
Jonesboro, AR 72403

WPS of North Little Rock
Central Arkansas Area Agency on Aging,
706 West 4th Street
North Little Rock, AR 72114

THEOS chapters in:
Bella Vista
Benton
Hot Springs Village
Little Rock

CALIFORNIA

Martin Luther Hospital Medical Center
1830 West Romneya Drive
Anaheim, CA 92805

Bereavement Support Group
6256 Barbara Lane
Auburn, CA 95603

Widows and Widowers Unlimited
404 River Oaks Drive
Bakersfield, CA 93309

Grief-to-Growth Bereavement Group
9350 Civic Center Drive
Beverly Hills, CA 90101

Brea Widowed Persons Service
500 South Siewers
Brea, CA 92621

Hospice of the Monterey Peninsula
P.O. Box 223139
Carmel, CA 93923

Creative Widowhood Program
Hall Vanhook Funeral Chapel
341 West Third Street
P.O. Box 893
Chico, CA 95926

Christian Widowed Fellowship
P.O. Box 27881
Concord, CA 94527

Widowed Persons Service of Del Norte
P.O. Box 1476
Crescent City, CA 95531

Workshops for Widowed Persons
10 Macomber Way
Danville, CA 94526

WPS of Downey, California
11500 Brookshire Avenue
Downey, CA 90241

Eel Valley WPS
P.O. Box 431
Fortuna, CA 95540

Widowed Program
Granada Hills Community Hospital
10445 Balboa Boulevard
Granada Hills, CA 91344

The Widow-to-Widow Outreach Program
338 Pier Avenue
Hermosa Beach, CA 90254

Widows' Network
3483 Golden Gate Way, Suite 2
Lafayette, CA 94549

New Directions
1720 Termino Avenue
Long Beach, CA 90801

Center for the Widowed
10345 West Pico Boulevard
Los Angeles, CA 90064

Grief-to-Growth Bereavement Group
Stephen S. Wise Temple
15500 Stephen Wise Drive
Los Angeles, CA 90077

Project Via
1700 McHenry Village Way #4
Modesto, CA 95350

Widowed Persons Service
1021 Douglas Avenue
Modesto, CA 95350

Mid-Peninsula Widows and Widowers Association
P.O. Box 4043
Mountain View, CA 94040

WPS of Placentia, CA
401 East Chapman Avenue
Placentia, CA 92670

The Widow-to-Widow Support Group
Rancho Palos Verdes Department of Leisure Services
30940 Hawthorne Boulevard
Rancho Palos Verdes, CA 90274

Wilson and Kratzer Mortuaries
Civic Center Chapel
24th Street at Barrett
Richmond, CA 94804

WPS of Ridgecrest
529 Kevin Court
Ridgecrest, CA 93555

WPS of Roseville
P.O. Box 178
Roseville, CA 95678

Bereavement Network Resources of Sacramento, Inc.
P.O. Box 660365
Sacramento, CA 95813

Bereavement Outreach Program
5370 Elvas Avenue, Suite B
Sacramento, CA 95819

Widowed Persons Association of California
2628 El Camino Ave., Suite D-18
Sacramento, CA 95821

Marin County Grief Counseling Program
P.O. Box 792
San Anselmo, CA 94960

Widowed Persons Service of San Bernardino County
3700 Mountain Avenue, #3A
San Bernardino, CA 92404

Widows' Group, Senior Service Team
3851 Rosecrans
San Diego, CA 92110–3190

G.R.O.W. (Gaining Recovery of Widowhood)
218 Santa Anita Street
San Gabriel, CA 91776

The Widow-to-Widow Support Group
San Pedro Peninsula Hospital Home Care
1386 West 7th Street
San Pedro, CA 90732

The Centre for Living with Dying
305 Montague Expressway
Santa Clara, CA 95054

The Widow-to-Widow Support Group
Emeritus College
1900 West Pico Boulevard
Santa Monica, CA 90405

Hospice of the Conejo
191 Wilbur Road
Thousand Oaks, CA 91360

Widowed Persons Service
P.O. Box 0141
Twenty-Nine Palms, CA 92277

Widows Helping Other Widows
2025 Sonoma Boulevard
Vallejo, CA 94590

The Widow-to-Widow Support Group
1211 Preston Way
Venice, CA 90291

WPS of Ventura
Ted Mayr Funeral Home
3150 Loma Vista Road
Ventura, CA 93003

Widowed Persons Service
2100 Belford Drive
Walnut Creek, CA 94598

Anew Widowed Group
P.O. Box 141
Woodland Hills, CA 91365

THEOS chapters in:
Arcadia
Oroville

COLORADO

Widowed Persons Service
3197 Sunrise Circle
Canon City, CO 81212

Colorado Springs Widowed Persons Service
2525 Hwy. 115 South
Colorado Springs, CO 80903

Widowed Persons Service
1565 Clarkson Street
Denver, CO 80218

Widowed Persons Service
c/o Colorado Mountain Community College
1402 Blake Avenue
Glenwood Springs, CO 81601

Widows-Widowers Service of Mesa County
1170 Colorado Avenue
Grand Junction, CO 81501

THEOS chapter in:
Boulder

CONNECTICUT

Coping with Widowhood Program
Family Life Office of the Diocese of Bridgeport
238 Jewett Avenue
Bridgeport, CT 06606

Death of a Spouse Family Life Enrichment Group
Child and Family Services
1680 Albany Avenue
Hartford, CT 06105

Widow-to-Widow Phone Line
Hartford Region YMCA
135 Broad Street
Hartford, CT 06105

Widowed Persons Service
Manchester Health Department
41 Centre Street
Manchester, CT 06040

Tri-Towns WPS
Community Mental Health Affiliates, Inc.
36 Russell Street
New Britain, CT 06052

Connecticut Mutual Self-Help Support Network
19 Howe Street
New Haven, CT 06511

WPS of New London County
4 Flanders Road
Niantic, CT 06357

Ecumenical Widows/Widowers Support Group
450 Race Brook Road
Orange, CT 06477

COPES (Community of People Extending Support)
c/o Bouton & Reynolds Funeral Home
545 Bedford Street
Stamford, CT 06904

THEOS chapters in:
Bridgeport
New Britain
Norwalk

DISTRICT OF COLUMBIA

SE/NE WPS of Washington, D.C.
622 Nicholson St., N.W.
Washington, DC 20011

Widowed Persons Outreach—Iona House
4200 Butterworth Place, N.W.
Washington, DC 20016

FLORIDA

Widowed Persons Service
Christ Lutheran Church
2911 Del Prado Blvd.
Cape Coral, FL 33904

Widowed Persons Service of Broward County
2312 South Andrews Avenue
Fort Lauderdale, FL 33316

Widowed Persons Service of Alachua County, Inc.
Catholic Charities Office
1717 N.E. 9th
Gainesville, FL 32604

Widowed Persons Program
Florida Community College at Jacksonville
Department of Continuing Education,
Women's Center
101 West State Street
Jacksonville, FL 32202

Community Widowed Persons Service
3611 Luther Lane
Kissimmee, FL 32741

Widowed Persons Service
P.O. Box 952
Lehigh Acres, FL 33936

North Dade Catholic Widow and Widowers Club
Visitation Church
100 NE 191st Street
Miami, FL 33169

WPS of Naples, Florida
850 6th Avenue, North
Naples, FL 33940

Widowed Persons Service of
Marion County
Central Florida Community
College
P.O. Box 1388
Ocala, FL 32678

WPS of Orange County, Fl., Inc.
1794 Curry Ford Road
Orlando, FL 32806

Widowed Persons Service
5950 Old Spanish Trail
Unit #14
Pensacola, FL 32504

WPS Port St. Lucie
402 S. E. Whitmore Drive
Port St. Lucie, FL 33452

Widowed Persons Service Pinellas
County
3803 Haines Road, North
St. Petersburg, FL 33703

Widow-to-Widow and Widows
and Friends
405 Indian River Avenue, Apt. 506
Titusville, FL 32796

Widow-to-Widow
Brevard Community College
1111 North Washington
Titusville, FL 32780

WPS of Lake County
Route 2, Box 123
Umatilla, FL 32784

Widowed Persons Service of South
Saratoga County
930 Tamiami Trail South
Venice, FL 34285

Palm Beach County Widowed
Persons Service
P.O. Box 2265
West Palm Beach, FL 33402

THEOS chapters in:
North Bay (Clearwater area)
Orlando

GEORGIA

Atlanta WPS/QLS
4487 Greenleaf Circle, S.W.
Atlanta, GA 30331

Grief Care
4550 Peachtree Road
Atlanta, GA 30319

Widowed Persons Service
Life Enrichment Services
3715 Lavista Road
Decatur, GA 30033

Widowed Persons Service
1085 Holly Drive, N.W., #4
Gainesville, GA 30501

Widowed Persons Service
First United Methodist Church
Route 1, Box 755
Newnan, GA 30263

IDAHO

Living Again
1055 North Curtis Road
Boise, ID 83705

Widowed Persons Service
1755 Pocatello County Road
Pocatello, ID 83201

THEOS chapter in:
Twin Falls

ILLINOIS

Widowed Persons Service
241 West Park Avenue
Aurora, IL 60506

Belleville Area Widowed Persons
Service
201 North Church Street
Belleville, IL 62221

Widowed Persons Service of Jackson County
209 South Mark Court
Carbondale, IL 62901

Widow/Widower Outreach Program
Consultation & Education Dept.
Ravenswood Community Mental Health Center
4545 North Damen Avenue
Chicago, IL 60625

Salvation Army
"Why Me, Lord?"
229 West Main Street
Decatur, IL 62523

Family Counseling Service of Illinois
1114 Church Street
Evanston, IL 60202

Williamson County Programs on Aging, Inc.
212 East Walnut Street
Herrin, IL 62948

Widowed Persons Service
21 Spinning Wheel Road, Apt. 7K
Hinsdale, IL 60521

Widowed Outreach Network
c/o Condell Memorial Hospital
900 South Garfield
Libertyville, IL 60048

THEOS chapters in:
- Bloomington
- Champaign-Urbana
- Charleston
- Dupage (Wheaton)
- Elmhurst
- Mattoon
- Springfield
- Taylorville
- Winnetka

INDIANA

Project Comfort
Parkview Memorial Hospital
2200 Randallia Drive
Fort Wayne, IN 46805

Widowed Persons Outreach
Mental Health Association of Lake County
2450 169th Street
Hammond, IN 46323

WPS of Jeffersonville, Ind.
503 Hopkins Lane
Jeffersonville, IN 47130

WPS of Delaware County
203 N. College Avenue
Muncie, IN 47306

Parenting Guidance Center
1625 West Main Street
Richmond, IN 47374

Widowed Persons Service of Wayne County
306 South 10th Street
Richmond, IN 47347

Widowed-to-Widowed
1007 East Washington Street
South Bend, IN 46617

Greater Speedway Area WPS
5065 W. 16th Street
Speedway, IN 46224

THEOS chapters in:
- Northeast Indianapolis
- Indianapolis (two chapters)
- Indianapolis (Greenwood)
- Jeffersonville

IOWA

Des Moines Widowed Persons Service
RR 1, Box 87
Adel, IA 50003

Burlington Medical Center
602 North Third Street
Burlington, IA 52601

Riverview Rehabilitation Center
624 North Fourth Street
Burlington, IA 52601

Widowed Persons Service—Clinton
202 Ankeny Building
Clinton, IA 52732

Quad City Widowed Persons Service Information, Referral and Assistance, Inc.
311 Ripley Street
Davenport, IA 52801

Widowed Persons Service
1419 Gaines
Davenport, IA 52801

La Dos (Life After Death of Spouse)
Des Moines Area Religious Council
3816 36th Street
Des Moines, IA 50310

WPS of Worth County
Route 1
Kensett, IA 50448

Rock River Widowed Persons Service
311 South Marshall
Rock Rapids, IA 51246

THEOS chapters in:
Ottumwa
Cedar Rapids
Sioux City

KANSAS

Widowed Persons Service of Abilene
Area Hospice Memorial Hospital
511 N.E. Tenth Street
Abilene, KS 67410

WPS of Kansas City, Kansas
1236 Grandview
Kansas City, KS 66102

WPS of Johnson Co., Kansas
P.O. Box 14633
Lenexa, KS 66215

Widowed To Widowed
2001 Claflin
Manhattan, KS 66502

Widowed Persons Service
521 N. Delrose
Wichita, KS 67208

THEOS chapters in:
Great Bend
Kansas City
Olathe (Kansas City area)
Overland Park (Kansas City area)

KENTUCKY

WPS of Central City, Ky.
508 Broad Street
Central City, KY 42330

Widowed Persons Service of Christian, Trigg, and Todd Counties
735 North Drive
Hopkinsville, KY 42240

Widowed Persons Service of London Laurel County
Sue Bennett College
London, KY 40741

Accord, Inc.
Counseling and Referral Service
P.O. Box 5208
Louisville, KY 40205

Louisville Widowed Persons Service
P.O. Box 6593
Louisville, KY 40206

Widowed Persons Service
727 Park Avenue Court
Madisonville, KY 42345

WPS of Owensboro
P.O. Box 2421
Owensboro, KY 43201

Widowed Persons Service
257 Seminole Drive
Paducah, KY 42001

Widowed Persons Service of Caldwell, Lyon, and Crittenden Counties
115 McGoodwin Street
Princeton, KY 42445

THEOS chapter in:
Mayfield

LOUISIANA

Widowed Persons Service
1304 Bertrand Drive, Suite E-4
Lafayette, LA 70506

WPS of Monroe
Rt. 2, Box 593
Marion, LA 71260

Comfort Ministry
301 Camp Street
New Orleans, LA 70130

THEOS chapters in:
Baton Rouge
New Orleans

MAINE

Widowed Persons Service of Greater Bangor, Inc.
c/o Eastern Area Agency on Aging
P.O. Box 70
Brewer, ME 04412

Widowed Persons Service of Waterville
c/o YMCA
Box 233
Waterville, ME 04901

MARYLAND

Hospice Services of Howard County
Bethany United Methodist Church
2875 Bethany Lane
Ellicott City, MD 21043

Widowed Persons Service of Calvert County
Route 2, Box 358
Huntington, MD 20639

Patuxent Widowed Persons Service
P.O. Box 1087
Seabrook, MD 20706

WPS of Montgomery County
14201 Notley Road
Silver Spring, MD 20904

Widowed Persons Service of Worcester County
MAC Multiservice Center
P.O. Box 159
Snowhill, MD 21863

MASSACHUSETTS

WPS of Acton, Mass.
67 Drummer Road
Acton, MA 01720

Young Widows and Widowers, Ltd.
4 Whiffletree Circle
Andover, MA 01810

Widowed To Widowed Program
Arlington Council on Aging
27 Maple Street
Arlington, MA 02174

Bereavement Support of Franklin County
P.O. Box 121
Greenfield, MA 01302

Widow-to-Widow
Widowed Life Line Program
69 Summer Street
Haverhill, MA 01830

Omega: Emotional Support Services for the Ill and Bereaved
270 Washington Street
Somerville, MA 02143

WPS of Greater Springfield, MA
109 Wayne Street
Springfield, MA 01118

Westport Widow/Widowers Support Group
816 Main Road
Westport, MA 02790

Bridge to Other Widowed
15 Ripley Street
Worcester, MA 01610

MICHIGAN

Widow-to-Widow Support Network
P.O. Box 220, Antrim County Building
Bellaire, MI 49615

Widowed Persons Service of Central Berrien County
P.O. Box 252
Berrien Springs, MI 49103

Cranbrook Hospice Care
1669 West Maple Road
Birmingham, MI 48009

Mature Minglers Senior Center
7273 Wing Lake Road
Birmingham, MI 48010

Welcome to the Widowed
St. Columban
1775 Melton
Birmingham, MI 48008

New Beginnings
775 South Main (Central Office)
Chelsea, MI 48118

W.O.W., Inc.
Northwest Chapter
18235 Faust Street
Detroit, MI 48219

"HOPE" Bereavement Group
13130 Woodward
Highland Park, MI 48203

WPS of Holland, MI
561 E. End Drive
Holland, MI 49423

St. Josepth Hospital Bereavement Group
302 Kensington
Flint, MI 48502

WINGS., Widows in New Growth
P.O. Box 151
Flushing, MI 48433

WISER (Widowed In Service)
Schoolcraft College/Santeiu Funeral Home
1139 Inkster Road
Garden City, MI 48135

Widowed Persons Service—
G.R.A.C.E.
38 Fulton West
Grand Rapids, MI 49503

Widow/Widower Reassurance
Program
Jackson County Department on
Aging
134 West Cortland Street
Jackson, MI 49201

Grief Recovery Group
Lapeer Area Hospice
Lapeer County General Hospital
1375 North Main Street
Lapeer, MI 48446

WISER (Widowed In Service)
Livonia
Schoolcraft College/Women's
Resource Center
18600 Haggerty Road
Livonia, MI 48152

Mt. Morris Widow to Widow
1194 East Mt. Morris Road
Mt. Morris, MI 48458

Widowed Persons Service of
Lawton, Michigan
37011 County Road 374
Paw Paw, MI 49079

Widowed Support Groups
St. Clair County Council on Aging
821 7th Street
Port Huron, MI 48060

Horizons
339 Walnut, Box 128
Rochester, MI 48063

You Are Not Alone
Pixley Memorial Chapel
322 West University Drive
Rochester, MI 48063

Community Human Services, Inc.
332 South Main Street
Romeo, MI 48065

Shrine Widowed
2123 Roseland
Royal Oak, MI 48073

Widows Together
c/o Kaul Funeral Home
28433 Jefferson Avenue
St. Clair Shores, MI 48081

Bereavement Resource Center
2506 Niles Avenue
St. Joseph, MI 49085

Space, Room to Grow
National Council of Jewish
Women
30233 Southfield Road, #100
Southfield, MI 48076

PAL (Personal Approach to Loss)
c/o A.J. Desmond & Sons Funeral
Directors
2600 Crooks Road
Troy, MI 48084

"HOPE"
Elton Black & Son Funeral
Home
1233 Union Lake Road
Union Lake, MI 48085

Widowed Coping Together
6455 Harper
Waterford, MI 48095

MINNESOTA

Widowed Persons Service
519 Minnesota Avenue
Bemidji, MN 56601

Widowed Persons Service of Itasca Co.
Rural Route 1, Box 196
Bovey, MN 55709

Widowed Persons Service
c/o Community Action
1415 Mary
Brainerd, MN 56401

Widowed Persons Service
Serving Wilkin and Richland Counties
501 Oak Street
Breckenridge, MN 56520

Grief Center
14050 Nicollet Avenue, Suite 312
Burnsville, MN 55447

Grief Support Volunteer Program
Wright County Human Services Courthouse
Buffalo, MN 55313

St. Mary's Grief Support Center
St. Mary's Medical Center
407 East Third Street
Duluth, MN 55805

Widowed Persons Service of Douglas and Stevens Counties
c/o RSVP
P.O. Box 3026
Elbow Lake, MN 56531

Fulda-Slayton Widowed Persons Service
404 Third Street, N.E.
Fulda, MN 56131

Widowed Persons Service of International Falls Area
411 8th Street
International Falls, MN 56649

Grief Therapy Groups
Minneapolis Age & Opportunity Center
1801 Nicollet Avenue
Minneapolis, MN 55403

WPS of Park Rapids, Minn.
Menagho/Sebeka & Akeley/Nevis
600 Pleasant Avenue
Park Rapids, MN 56470

WPS, Rochester, Minn.
Box 733
Rochester, MN 55903

WPS of Chicago Co., Minn. (North Branch)
Rt. 2, Box 188
Rush City, MN 55069

Widowed Persons Service
c/o Caritas Family Services
305 7th Avenue North, Suite 100
St. Cloud, MN 56301

Northern St. Louis County Social Services
P.O. Box 1148
307 First Street South
Virginia, MN 55792

Widowed Persons Service
Community Education
611 West Fifth Street
P.O. Box 787
Willmar, MN 56201

Widowed Persons Service
RR 1, Box 185
Winona, MN 55987

Widowed Persons Service
Worthington Area Community Education
Senior Citizens Program
1450 Collegeway
Worthington, MN 56187

THEOS chapters in:
Columbia Heights (Minneapolis)
Coon Rapids
Mankato
Owatoona
Sauk Centre

MISSISSIPPI

Widowed Persons Service of Hattiesburg
Rt. 6, Box 1674
1714 First Terrace
Hattiesburg, MS 39401

MISSOURI

WPS of Eastern Jackson County
1522 S. 9th Street
Blue Springs, MO 64015

WPS of Brookfield
216 E. Clark Street
Brookfield, MO 64628

Widowed Persons Service
Livingston County Courthouse
Box 445, S.W. Corner, 1st Floor
Chillicothe, MO 64601

WPS of Columbia, Mo.
Boone Co. Council on Aging
123 S. 9th Street
Columbia, MO 65201

Widowed Persons Service of Branson
P.O. Box 303
Forsyth, MO 65653

S.O.S. (Survivors Of Sorrow)
10901 Winner Road
Independence, MO 64050

Widowed Persons Service
Family and Children's Services
3217 Broadway #500
Kansas City, MO 64111

Widowed Persons Service of Lebanon
1027 Springfield
Lebanon, MO 65536

Widowed Persons Service of Lee's Summit, Mo.
308 North Murray Road
Lee's Summit, MO 64063

Widowed Persons Service of Maryville, Mo.
216 West 7th
Maryville, MO 64468

Widowed Persons Service of Kimberling City
Route 4, Box 2520
Reeds Spring, MO 65737

Widowed Persons Service
605 West Price
Savannah, MO 64485

Widowed Persons Service of Springfield
1649 Catalina
Springfield, MO 65804

LIFT (Living Information For Today)
4228 South Kings Highway
St. Louis, MO 63109

St. Louis Widowed Persons Service
5000 Cedar Plaza Parkway, Room 104
St. Louis, MO 63128

Wife-Widow-Woman Project of National Council of Jewish Women
8420 Delmar Boulevard, Suite 203
St. Louis, MO 63124

THEOS chapters in:
Arnold (St. Louis)
Bethany (St. Louis)
Des Peres (West St. Louis)
Kirkwood (St. Louis)
Lemay–Jefferson Barracks
Poplar Bluff
Southwest City (St. Louis)
Spanish Lake–Florissant

MONTANA

Widowed Persons Service
2049 Phoebe Drive
Billings, MT 59102

WPS of Great Falls
Box 7241
Great Falls, MT 59406

WPS of Hamilton, Mont.
1201 South Second Street
Hamilton, MT 59840

Widowed Persons Service of Missoula
1706 Sherwood Street
Missoula, MT 59802

Widowed Persons Service of Lake County
Western Montana Area Agency on Aging
802 Main, Box 4027
Polson, MT 59860

NEBRASKA

Widowed Persons Service
P.O. Box 87
Aurora, NE 68818

Widowed Persons Service
129 N. 10th Street, Room 230
Lincoln, NE 68508

Widowed Persons Service of Saline County
Box 236
Wilber, NE 68465

THEOS chapters in:
Grand Island
Holdrege
Kearney
Lincoln (Northeast)
Omaha
Lexington
Bellevue (Omaha)
Northwest Omaha

NEVADA

THEOS chapter in:
Las Vegas

NEW JERSEY

HOPE, Inc. (Helping Other People Evolve)
Camden County Office on Aging
120 White Horse Pike
Haddon Heights, NJ 08059

Christian One Partner Organization (COPO)
198 Old Bergen Road
Jersey City, NJ 07305

Widowed Persons Service of Morris County
62 Elm Street
Morristown, NJ 07960

THEOS chapter in:
Montclair
Willingboro

NEW MEXICO

WPS of Albuquerque
1747 Altez, N.E.
Albuquerque, NM 87112

WPS of Deming
2100 South Slate Street
Deming, NM 88030

Widowed Persons Service of Chavez County
129 West Walnut
Rosewell, NM 88201

Widowed Persons Service of Santa Fe, Inc.
3353 La Avendia de San Marcos
Santa Fe, NM 87501

WPS of Silver City/Grant County, N.M.
P.O. Box 771
Silver City, NM 88062

THEOS chapter in:
Albuquerque

NEW YORK

Emerging Butterfly
c/o Unitarian Universalist Church
405 Washington Avenue
Albany, NY 12206

Widowed Persons Service of The Capital District, Inc.
930 Madison Avenue
Albany, NY 12208

St. Mary's Wellness Institute
427 Guy Park Avenue
Amsterdam, NY 12010

Widowed Persons Service
Cayuga Community College
Franklin Street
Auburn, NY 13021

Widow/Widowers Club of the Southern Tier
Lourdes Hospital
169 Riverside Drive
Binghamton, NY 13905

Widowed Outreach Service
Trinity Lutheran Church
P.O. Box 12
Brewster, NY 13905

Calvary Hospital Bereavement Services
1740 Eastchester Road
Bronx, NY 10461

Bay Ridge Widows Support Group
Union Center for Women
8101 Ridge Boulevard
Brooklyn, NY 11209

Metropolitan WPS
c/o South Beach Psychiatric Center
532 Neptune Avenue, 2nd Floor
Brooklyn, NY 11224

The "We Can Make It" Club
130 St. Edwards Street, #3D
Brooklyn, NY 11201

Widow/Widowers Support Group
137 Field Street
Corning, NY 14830

Delaware County Widowed Persons Group
Office for the Aging
Court Street
Delhi, NY 13753

Widows and Widowers of Queens
244-17 61st Avenue
Douglaston, NY 11362

Widow/Widower Support Group
St. Joseph's Hospital
Elmira, NY 14901

Widowed Persons Service of Nassau and Queens
Littaner Bldg. 6, Room 207
75-59 263rd Street
Glen Oaks, NY 11004

WPS of Greater Glens Falls Area
8 Notre Dame Street
Glens Falls, NY 12801

Widows & Widowers of Orange County
Orange County Department of Mental Health
Division C & E, Drawer 471
Harriman Drive
Goshen, NY 10924

Young Widows and Widowers of Westchester
Westchester Jewish Community Services
141 North Central Avenue
Hartsdale, NY 10530

The Bereavement Center of Family Service Association of Nassau
129 Jackson Street
Hempstead, NY 11550

Bereavement & Loss Center
170 East 83rd Street
New York, NY 10028

Services to the Widowed
Jewish Board of Family and Children's Services
33 West 60th Street
New York, NY 10023

New Images for the Widowed
310 Lexington Avenue
New York, NY 10016

Social Networks for the Widowed
c/o New Images for Widows, #96
310 Lexington Avenue
New York, NY 10016

Vassar Brothers Hospital Support Services for Widows & Widowers
Reade Place
Poughkeepsie, NY 12601

Diocese of Rockville Centre
Office of Family Ministry
50 North Park Avenue
Rockville Centre, NY 11570

Haven of Schenectady, Inc.
1101 Parkwood Boulevard
Schenectady, NY 12308

St. Monica's Group for Widowed Men & Women
P.O. Box 301
Syosset, NY 11791

Hope for Bereaved
Family Life Education
1342 Lancaster Avenue
Syracuse, NY 13210

Widowed Unlimited, Inc.
26 Jasmine Lane
Valley Stream, NY 11581

Good Samaritan Hospital
1000 Montauk Highway
West Islip, NY 11795

Family Service of Westchester
470 Mamaroneck Avenue
White Plains, NY 10605

Peninsula Counseling Center
124 Franklin Place
Woodmere, NY 11598

NORTH CAROLINA

WPS of Asheville, N.C.
P.O. Box 516
Arden, NC 28704

W.O.W. (Widows On the Way)
7507 Watercrest Road
Charlotte, NC 28211

THEOS chapters in:
Raleigh
New Bern

NORTH DAKOTA

THEOS chapters in:
Fargo
Grand Forks

OHIO

Widowed to Widowed of Summit County
Cuyahoga Valley Counseling Center
839 East Market Street
Akron, OH 44305

Widowed Persons Service of Athens
Factory Road
Albany, OH 45710

WPS—Grief, Support & Education Ctr.
415 South Main Street
Canton, OH 44720

Widowed Persons Service of Hamilton County, Inc.
3330 Erie Avenue
Cincinnati, OH 45208

Going Onward After Loss (GOAL)
10225 Greenview
Columbia Station, OH 44028

Center for New Directions
Focus on Widowhood Program
51 Jefferson Avenue
Columbus, OH 43215

Franklin County WPS
1180 Shanley Drive
Columbus, OH 43224

Widows and Widowers
(with School-age Children)
467 Brevoort Road
Columbus, OH 43124

WPS of Preble County
201 East Main Street
Eaton, OH 45320

Widowed Persons Service of Darke County, Inc.
132 Ridgeview Drive
Greenville, OH 45331

Widowed Persons Service of Hamilton/Fairfield, Inc.
9 Maple Court
Hamilton, OH 45013

Widows and Widowers Fellowship of the Greater Miami Valley Area, Inc.
651 East Drive
Kettering, OH 45429

Forum for Death Education and Counseling
Central Office
2211 Arthur Ave.
Lakewood, OH 44107

Maria Stein Center
Young Widowed Support Group
2365 St. John's Road
Maria Stein, OH 45860

Widowed Persons Service of Washington County
Central Christian Church
807 Colgate Drive
Marietta, OH 45750

"One is a Whole Number"
Support Group
4575 East Lake Road
Sheffield Lake, OH 44054

WPS of Richland County
82 Marvin Avenue
Shelby, OH 44875

Widowed Persons Service of
Seneca County
Box 621
Tiffin, OH 44883

Catholic Service League
5385 Market St.
Youngstown, OH 44512

Widowed Persons Service of
Youngstown
2801 Market Street
Youngstown, OH 44507

THEOS chapters in:
Chagrin Falls
Elmore-Genoa
Fremont
Kenwood-Madiere (Cincinnati)
Medina
Wadsworth
Mansfield
Zanesville

OKLAHOMA

Grief Workshops
1301 South Boston Avenue
Tulsa, OK 74119

Widowed Persons Service of Tulsa
240 E. Apache
Tulsa, OK 74106

OREGON

Widowed Persons Service
877 South 4th Street
Coos Bay, OR 97420

WPS of Corvallis
760 NW 21st Street
Corvallis, OR 97330

Widowed Persons Service of
Cottage Grove
P.O. Box 585
Cottage Grove, OR 97424

Widowed Persons Service of
Eugene and Springfield, OR
2650 Baker Boulevard
Eugene, OR 97403

WPS of Portland, Ore.
1848 NE 19th Avenue
Portland, OR 97212

WPS of Roseburg
Douglas County Health Center
Roseburg, OR 97470

PENNSYLVANIA

Visiting Nurse Association of
Lehigh County
315 Linden Street
Allentown, PA 18101

Widowed Persons Service
542 South Fourth Street
Hamburg, PA 19526

New Beginnings
Good Samaritan Hospital Hospice
Program
Lebanon, PA 17042

Living a New Life
R.D. 9, Box 237
Mountaintop, PA 18707

Widow and Widower Counseling
and Referral Service
8033 Old York Road (Main office)
Philadelphia, PA 19117

Widow and Widower Counseling and Referral Service
8001 Roosevelt Boulevard
Philadelphia, PA 19152

Widowed Persons Service—Pittsburgh East
121 Race Street
Pittsburgh, PA 15218

Widowed of Reading, Allentown, Pottsville (W.R.A.P.)
St. Francis Center
900 West Market Street
Orwigsburg, PA 17961

Living for a New Life (L.N.L.) Group for the Widowed
Office for Family Life
300 Wyoming Avenue
Scranton, PA 18503-1279

Widowed Persons Service of Shenango Valley
603-B West Ridge Avenue
Sharpsville, PA 16150

To Live Again (TLA)
P.O. Box 73
Wynnewood, PA 19096

Widowed Persons Service of Youngwood
Westmoreland County Community College
Youngwood, PA 15697

THEOS chapters in:
Butler
Canonsburg
Elizabeth Twp–Greenock
Erie
Greensburg
Greentree
Grove City
Harrisburg
Meadville
Murrysville
New Kensington
Baldwin (Pittsburgh)
Bellevue (Pittsburgh)
East End (Pittsburgh)
Oakmont-Verona
Penn Hills
Greater Susquehanna (Selingsgrove)
Titusville
Uniontown
West Chester
York
Williamsport

RHODE ISLAND

Tiverton Widows & Widowers
207 Canonicus Street
Tiverton, RI 02878

THEOS chapter in:
Providence

SOUTH CAROLINA

Widowed Persons Service
217 Lakeside Drive
Aiken, SC 29801

THEOS chapter in:
Anderson

SOUTH DAKOTA

Widowed Persons Service
1820 Wisconsin, S.W.
Huron, SD 57350

Widowed Persons Service of McCook County and Salem
Ransey Baptist Church
Montrose, SD 57048

Siouxland WPS
2212 S. Sherman Avenue
Sioux Falls, SD 57105

Widowed Persons Service
701 2nd Avenue, N.E.
Watertown, SD 57201

THEOS chapters in:
Brookings
Rapid City
Sioux Falls

TENNESSEE

FORWARD
St. Paul's Episcopal Church
305 West 7th Street
Chattanooga, TN 37402

O'Conner Senior Center
611 Winona Street
Knoxville, TN 37917

ALIVE Hospice
2313 Hillsboro Road
Nashville, TN 37212

THEOS chapters in:
Tri-City (Elizabethton)
Nashville

TEXAS

Austin Widowed Persons Service
11729 Running Fox Trail
Austin, TX 78759

For the Love of Christi
One Cielo Center
1250 Capital of Texas Highway South
Austin, TX 78746

Widowed Persons Service
2100 Highway Drive
Copperas Cove, TX 76522

WPS of Corpus Christi
P.O. Box 3046
Corpus Christi, TX 78404

WPS Serving Dallas
6130 Preston Haven
Dallas, TX 75230

Denton Widowed Persons Service
2609 Jamestown
Denton, TX 76201

WPS of El Paso
1233 Southwestern
El Paso, TX 79912

WPS of Tarrant County
3550 S.W. Loop 820
Fort Worth, TX 76133

LIFELINE
12711 Pebblebrook
Houston, TX 77024

WPS of Hockley County
105 Cypress
Levelland, TX 79336

Widowed Persons Service
c/o Paris Junior College
2400 Clarksville Street
Paris, TX 75460

WPS of San Antonio
P.O. Box 18091
San Antonio, TX 78218

WPS of Bell County
710 W. Park
Temple, TX 76503

Arkansas-Texas Widowed Persons Service
c/o East Texas State University
P.O. Box 5518
Texarkana, TX 75505

Smith County WPS
2809 S. Robertson
Tyler, TX 75701

WPS of Victoria, TX
RSVP of Craig House
207 N. Navarro Street
Victoria, TX 77901

WPS of Tyler Co.
P.O. Box 987
Woodville, TX 75979

THEOS chapters in:
Amarillo
Cranfills Gap
Lubbock
Texarkana

UTAH

WPS of Ogden, Utah
740 Ben Lomand Drive
Ogden, UT 84403

Widowed Persons Service
P.O. Box 521102
Salt Lake City, UT 84152

VIRGINIA

Haven of Northern Virginia, Inc.
4606 Ravensworth Road
Annandale, VA 22003

Northern Virginia Hotline
P.O. Box 187
Arlington, VA 22210

HOPE (Helping Other People with Empathy) Support Group for Widowed Persons
c/o Reid Funeral Home
P.O. Box 930
Ashland, VA 23005

LOFT (Living Objectives For Today)
201 First Street, North
Charlottesville, VA 22901

Harrisonburg-Rockingham WPS
1371 Devon Lane
Harrisonburg, VA 22801

LIFT (Living In Faith Together)
c/o J. T. Morriss & Son Funeral Home
P.O. Box 12
Hopewell, VA 23860

Peninsula WPS
235 Harpersville Rd.
Newport News, VA 23601

WPS of Loudoun County
709 Riverview Court
Sterling, VA 22170

Widowed Persons Service of Northern Virginia
10711 Hunter Station Road
Vienna, VA 22180

WPS of Tidewater, VA
748 Largo Drive
Virginia Beach, VA 23464

WPS of Waynesboro, Virginia
749 Maple Avenue
Waynesboro, VA 22939

Widowed Persons Service Serving Lancaster and Northumberland County
Route 1, Box 1101
Weems, VA 22576

WPS of Winchester, Clarke and Frederick
Frederick Co. Extension Service
Frederick Co. Court House
2nd Floor
Winchester, VA 22601

THEOS chapter in:
Fredericksburg

WASHINGTON

WICS Widowed Information and Consultation Services
2122 112th Avenue, NE
Bellevue, WA 98004

Bellingham Widowed Lifeline Series
322 Holly
Bellingham, WA 98225

W.I.C.S.
883 Highway 20
Coupeville, WA 98239

W.I.C.S.
P.O. Box 5546
Everett, WA 98201

"Let's Talk"
c/o Senior Services
P.O. Box 951
Friday Harbor, WA 98250

WPS of Grand Coulee Dam Area
Box 525
Grand Coulee, WA 99133

Bereavement Services, Tri-Cities Chaplaincy
7514 West Yellowstone
Kennewick, WA 99337

Widow-Widower Support Group of Thurston County
3913 Southglen, SE
Olympia, WA 98501

Widow-Widower Support
United Methodist Church
1224 East Legion Way
Olympia, WA 98501

WICS
3028 South Lorne Street
Olympia, WA 98501

VA Medical Center
1660 South Columbian Way
Seattle, WA 98108

Widows and Widowers
11212 21st Street, SW
Seattle, WA 98146

WICS
7601 Aurora Avenue, North
Seattle, WA 98103

WICS (Main Office)
15407 First Avenue South
Suite D
Seattle, WA 98148

WICS (Northend Branch)
17962 Midvale North
Seattle, WA 98133

WICS
Family Services of King County
107 Cherry Street
Seattle, WA 98104

Widowed Persons Service of Clallam County
446 Hooker Road
Sequim, WA 98362

Widowed Persons Service of Greater Spokane
East 3707 21st Avenue
Spokane, WA 99223

Acquainted with Grief
1002 South Yakima Avenue
Tacoma, WA 98405

WICS
223 North Yakima Avenue
Tacoma, WA 98403

Widow to Widow Support Group
364 Catherine, B-9
Walla Walla, WA 99362

WICS
c/o YMCA
212 First Street
Wenatchee, WA 98801

WEST VIRGINIA

East River Regional WPS
P.O. Box 122
Bluefield, WV 24701

WISCONSIN

New Horizons
c/o Walworth County Department of Aging
Route 3, Box 287
Elkhorn, WI 53121

Widowed Person's Club
Lake Geneva, WI 53147

KAYRA
4201 Beverly Road
Madison, WI 53711

Alpha-Omega Venture
1113 Elizabeth Avenue
Marinette, WI 54143

NAIM Conference
Adult Family Ministry
Nazareth Hall
3501 South Lake Drive
Milwaukee, WI 53201

WPS of Oshkosh
1408 E. Nevada Avenue
Oshkosh, WI 54901

WPS of Watertown
North 1010 Highway EM
Watertown, WI 53094

THEOS chapter in:
Darlington

WYOMING

WPS of Rock Springs
210 Agret
Rock Springs, WY 82901

Index